INCREDIBLE
SURVIVAL
STORIES

T0105313

INCREDIBLE SURVIVAL STORIES

TALES OF DEATH-DEFYING TREKS ACROSS THE GLOBE

EDITED BY JAY CASSELL

Foreword by Veronica Alvarado

Skyhorse Publishing

Skyhorse Publishing books may be purchased in bulk at special discounts for sales promotion, corporate gifts, fund-raising, or educational purposes. Special editions can also be created to specifications. For details, contact the Special Sales Department, Skyhorse Publishing, 307 West 36th Street, 11th Floor, New York, New York 10018 or info@skyhorsepublishing.com

Skyhorse® and Sky horse Publishing® are registered trademarks of Skyhorse Publishing Inc.®, a Delaware Corporation

www.skyhorsepublishing.com 10 9 8 7 6 5 4 3 2 1

Library of Congress Cataloging-in-Publication Data is available on file.

Cover design by Tom Lau
Cover photo credit: "First Ascent of the Matterhorn" by Gustave Doré

Print ISBN: 978-1-5107-1377-2
Ebook ISBN: 978-1-5107-1382-6

Printed in China

TABLE OF CONTENTS

FOREWORD

When we are young, we often dream of undertaking great feats: To climb Mount Everest. To skydive. To travel to the Arctic. To trek across the deserts. To enter the heat of battle. To tame the savage beast. And while some of us will never journey much farther than our own backyards, others of us will venture to the farthest corners of the Earth in true tests of the body, mind, and soul.

A thirst for adventure seems to be an innate part of the human spirit. From scaling the planet's highest peaks to descending to its greatest depths, from engaging with the most ferocious of creatures to entering into the deadliest frays of combat, men and women constantly, and consciously, place themselves directly in the path of peril. And although some lose their lives when facing risks, many more live to tell the tales of dangerous adventures and death-defying encounters. So while it is an indelible part of human nature to seek adventure, it is equally a part of our spirit to survive that peril. This book, *Incredible Survival Stories*, features twenty-one unforgettable tales, from across time and spanning the globe, of the unconquerable human spirit.

Organized into three distinct parts, this book is a spirited collection of daring, and in some cases unbelievable, tales of survival. The first grouping of stories—"Surviving Adventure"—tells of nine encounters of danger, discovery, and defeats of the unknown. Episodes from the great explorer of the ancient Orient Marco Polo, the infamous medieval circumnavigator Sir Francis Drake, and the Scandinavian geographer Sven Hedin are all here, in the midst of scorching heat, raging waters, and unfathomable to dangers, all in the quest to push the boundaries of human ingenuity and endurance.

At times we also must test our capacity for survival against one another in the most deadly arenas of war. The second grouping of stories pays homage to the ferocity of armed combat. From disputes over territories, to civil wars, to global conflicts, these stories demonstrate that sometimes the utmost peril that we must survive comes from our fellow human beings.

And yet, on other occasions, our greatest obstacle to survival is the elements. The third section of this book features stories that take place in exotic locales, demonstrating the true depth of perilous possibilities that our Mother Earth has to throw at us. The savage beasts and deadly climate in "Amazonia Extremis," the endless, breath-sucking sandstorms in "The Sands of the Gobi," and the bitter cold of "88 Degrees South," as well as five other tales, show just a handful of the dangers that man has found a way to endure and conquer.

So while each of these tales is unique in its telling, they all prove that survival is truly of the fittest, be that physically or intellectually.

—Veronica Alvarado
Fall 2016

SECTION ONE

SURVIVING ADVENTURES

CHAPTER 1

DRAKE'S CIRCUMNAVIGATION

By Richard Hakluyt

Sir Francis Drake at Bucklands Abbey by
Marcus Gheerants, circa 1590.

Editor's Note: Traditional sixteenth century spelling, grammar, and punctuation
have been retained.

The famous voyage of Sir Francis Drake into the South sea, and therehence about the whole Globe of the earth, begun in the yeere of our Lord 1577.

THE 15 day of November, in the yeere of our Lord 1577. M. Francis
Drake, with a fleete of five ships and barkers, and to the number of 164
men, gentlemen and sailers, departed from Plimmouth, giving out his pretended voyage for Alexandria: but the wind falling contrary, hee was forced

the next morning to put into Falmouth haven in Cornewall, where such and so terrible a tempest tooke us, as few men have seene the like, and was in deed so vehement, that all our ships were like to have gone to wracke: but it pleased God to preserve us from that extermitie, and to afflict us onely for that present with these two particulars: The mast of our Admirall which was the Pellican, was cut over boord for the safegard of the ship, and the Marigold was driven ashore, and somewhat bruised for the repairing of which damages wee returned agains in Plimmouth, and having recovered those harmes, and brought the ships againe to good state, we set forth the second time from Plimmouth, and set saile the 13 day of December following.

Drake's vessel, the *Golden Hind*.

The 25 day of the same moneth we fell with the Cape Cantin, upon the coast of Barbarie, and coasting along, the 27 day we found an Island called Mogador, lying one mile distant from the maine, betweene which Island and the maine, we found a very good and safe harbour for our ships to the in, as also very good entrance, and voyde of any danger.

On this Island our Generall erected a pinnesse, whereof he brought out of England with him foure already framed, while these things were in doing, there came to the waters side some of the inhabitants of the countrey, shewing foorth their flags of truce, which being seene of our Generall, hee sent his ships boate to the shore, to know what they would: they being willing to come aboord, our men left there one man of our company for a pledge, and brought two of theirs aboord our ship, which by signes shewed our Generall, that the next day they would bring some provision, as sheepe, capons and hennes, and such like: whereupon our Generall bestowed amongst them some linnen cloth and shooes, and a javeling, which they very joyfully received, and departed for that time.

The next morning they failed not to come againe to the waters side, and our Generall againe setting out our boate, one of our men leaping over rashly ashore, and offering friendly to imbrace them, they set violent hands on him, offering a dagger to his throte if hee had made any resistance, and so laying him on a horse, caried him away: so that a man cannot be too circumspect and warie of himselfe among such miscreants.

Our pinnesse being finished, wee departed from this place the 31 and last day of December, and coasting along the shore, wee did descrie, not contrary to our expectation, certaine Canters which were Spanish fishermen, to whom we gave chase and tooke three of them, and proceeding further we met with 3 Caravels and tooke them also.

The 17 day of January we arrived at Cape Blanco, where we found a ship riding at anchor, within the Cape, and but two simple Mariners in her, which ship we tooke and caried her further into the harbour, where we remained 4 dayes, and in that space our General mustered, and trayned his men on land in warlike maner, to make them fit for all occasions.

In this place we tooke of the Fishermen such necessaries as wee wanted, and they could yeeld us, and leaving heere one of our litle barkes called the Benedict, wee tooke with us one of theirs which they called Canters, being of the burden of 40 tunnes or thereabouts.

All these things being finished, wee departed this harbour the 22 of Januarie, carying along with us one of the Portugall Caravels which was bound to the Island of Cape Verde for salt, where of good store is made in one of those Islands.

The master or Pilot of that Caravel did advertise our Generall that upon one of those Islands called Mayo, there was great store of dryed Cabritos, which a few inhabitants there dwelling did yeerely make ready for such of the kings Ships as did there touch being bound for his countery of Brasile or elsewhere. Wee fell with this Island the 27 of January, but the Inhabitants would in no case traffique with us, being thereof forbidden by the kings Edict: yet the next day our Generall sent to view the Island, and the likelihoods that might be there of provision of victuals, about threescore and two men under the conduct and government of Master Winter and Master Doughtiue, and marching towards the chiefe place of habitation in this Island (as by the Portugall wee were informed) having travailed to the mountains the space of three miles, and arriving there somewhat before the day breake, we arrested our selves to see day before us, which appearing, we found the inhabitants to be fled: but the place, by reason that it was manured, wee found to be more fruitfull then the other part, especially the valleys among the hils.

Here we gave our selves a little refreshing, as by very ripe and sweete grapes, which the fruitfulnesse of the earth at that season of the yeere yielded us: and that season being with us the depth of Winter, it may seeme strange that those fruites were then there growing: but the reason thereof is this, because they being betweene the Tropike and the Equinoctiall, the Sunne passeth twise in the yeere through their Zenith over their heads, by meanes whereof they have two Summers, & being so neere the heate of the line they never lose the heate of the Sunne so much, but the fruites have their increase and continuance in the midst of Winter. The Island is wonderfully stored with goates and wilde hennes, and it hath salt also without labour, save onely that the people gather it into heapes, which continually in great quantitie is increased upon the sands by the flowing of the sea, and the receiving heate of the sunns kerning the same, so that of the increase thereof they keeps a continuall traffique with their neighbours.

Amongst other things we found here a kind of fruit called Cocos, which because it is not commonly knowen with us to England, I thought good to make some description of it.

The tree beareth no leaves nor branches, but at the very top the fruit growth in clusters, hard at the top of the branch of the tree, as big every severall fruite as a mans head: but kerning taken off the uttermost barke, which you shall find to bee very full of strings or sinowes, as I may terme them, you shall come to a hard shell which may holde of quantitie in liquor a pint commonly, or some a quart, and some lesse: within that shell of the thickness of halfe an inch good, you shall have a kinde of hard substance and very white, no lesse good and sweete then almonds: within that againe a certaine cleare liquor, which being drunke, you shall not onely finde it very delicate and sweete, but most comfortable and cordiall.

After wee had satisfied our selves with some of these fruites, wee marched further into the Island, and saw great store of Cabritos alive, which were so chased by the inhabitants, that wee could doe no good towards our provision, but they had layde cout as it were to stoppe our mouths withal, certaine olde dryed Cabritos, which being but ill, and small and few, wee made no account of it.

Being returned to our ships, our General departed hence the 31 of this moneth, and sayled by the Island of S. Iago, but farre enough from the danger of the inhabitants, who shot and discharged at us three peeces, but thy all fell short of us, and did us no harme. The Island is fayre and large, and as it seemeth, rich and fruitfull, and inhabited by the portugals, but the mountains and high places of the Island are sayd to be possessed by the Moores, who having bin slaves to the Portugals, to ease themselves, made escape to the desert places of the Island, where they abide with great strength.

Being before this Island, we espied two ships under sayle, to the one of which wee gave chase, and in the end boorded her with a ship-boat without resistance, which we found to be a good prize, and she yielded unto us good store of wine: which prize our General committed to the custodie of Master Doughtie, and retaining the Pilot, sent the rest away with his Pinnesse, giving them a Butte of wine and some victuals, and their wearing clothes, and so they departed.

The same night wee came with the Island called by the Portugals, IIha del fogo, that is, the burning Island: in the Northside whereof is a consuming fire, the matter is sayde to be of Sulphure, but notwithstanding it is like to bee a commodious Island, because the Portugals have built, and doe inhabite there.

Upon the south side thereof lyeth a most pleasant and sweete Island, the trees whereof are always greene and faire to looke upon, in respect whereof they cakk it Ilha Brava, that is, the brave Island. From the bankes thereof into the sea doe run in many places reasonable streames of fresh waters easie to be come by, but there was no convenient roade for our ships: for such was the depth, that no ground could bee had for anchoring, and it is reported, that ground was never found in that place, so that the tops of Fogo burne not so high in the ayre, but the rootes of Brava are quenched as low in the sea.

Being departed from these Islands, we drew towards the line, where wee were becalmed the space of 3 weekes, but yet subject to divers great stormes, terrible lightnings and much thunder: but with this miserie we had the com- moditie of great store of fish, as Dolphins, Bonitos, and flying fishes, whereof some fell into our shippes, wherehence they could not rise againe for want of moisture, for when their wings are drie, they cannot flie.

From the first day of our departure from the Islands of Cape Verde, wee sayled 54 days without sight of land, and the first land that we fell with was the coast of Brasil, which we saw the fift of April in ye height at 33 degrees towards the pole Antarctike, and being discovered at sea by the inhabitants of the countrey, they made upon the coast great from for a sacrifice (as we learned) to the devils, about which they use conjurations, making heapes of sande and other ceremonies, that when any ship shall goe about to stay upon their coast, not onely sands may be gathered together in shoals in every place but also the stormes and tempests may arise, to the casting away of ships and men, whereof (as it is reported) there have bene divers experiments.

The seventh day in a mightie great storme both of lightning, rayne and thunder, wee lost the Canter which we called the Christopher: but the eleventh day after, by our Generale great care inn dispersing his ships, we found her againe, and the place where we met, our Generall calle the Cape of Joy, where every ship tooke in some water. Here we found a good temperature and sweet ayre, a very faire and pleasant countrey with an exceeding fruitfull soyle, where were great store of large and mightie Deere, but we came not to the sight of any people: but traveiling further into the countrey, we perceived the footing of the people in the clay-ground, shewing that they were men of great stature. Being returned to our ships, we wayed anchor, and ranne somewhat further, and harboured our selves betweene a rocke and the maine, where by meanes of the rocke that brake the force of the sea, we rid very safe, and upon this rocke we killed for our provision certaine sea-wolves, commonly called with us Seales.

From hence we went our course to 36 degrees, and entred the great river of Plate, and ranne into 54 and 55 fadomes, and a halfe of fresh water, where wee filled our water by the ships side: but our Generall finding here no good harborough, as he thought he should, bare out againe to sea the 27 of April, and in bearing out we lost sight of our Flieboate wherein master Doughtie was, but we saying along, found a fayre and reasonable good Bay wherein were many, and the same profitable Islands, one whereof had so many Seales, as would at the least have laden all our shippes, and the rest of the islands are as it were laden with foules which is wonderfull to see, and they of divers sortes. It is a place very plentifull of victuals, and hath in it no wants of fresh water.

Our Generall after certaine dayes of his abode in this place, being on shore in an Island, the people of the countrey shewed themselves unto him, leaping and dauncing, and entred into traffique with him, but they would not received anything at any mans hands, but the same must bee cast upon the ground. They are so cleane, comely, and strong bodies, swift on foote, and seeme to be very active.

The eighteenth day of May our Generall thought it needful to have a care of such Ships as were absent ant therefore indeavouring to seeke the Fleinboate wherein master Doughtie was, we espied here againe the next day: and whereas certaine of our ships were sent to discovere the coast and to search an harbour, the Marygold and the Canter being imployed in that businesse, came unto us and gave us understanding of a safe harbour that they had found, wherewith all our ships bare, and entred it, where we watered and made new provisions of victuals, as by Seales, whereof we slew to the number of 200. or 300. in the space of an houre.

Here our Generall in the Admiral rid close aboord the Flieboate, and tooke out of her all the provisions of victuals and what els was in her, and hailing her to the Lande, set fire to her, and so burnt her to save the iron worke: which being a doing, there came downe of the countrey certaine of the people naked, saving only about their waste the skinne of some beast with the furre or haire on, and something also wreathed on their heads: their faces were painted with divers colours, and some of them had on their heads the similitude of hornes every man his bow which was an ell in length, and a couple of arrows. They were very agill people and quicke to deliver, and seemed not to be ignorant in the feates of warres, as by their order of ranging a few men, might appeare. These people would not of a long time receive any thing at our handes; yet at length our Generall being ashore, and they dancing after their accustomed maner about him, and hee once turning his backe towards them, one leapt suddenly to him, and tooke his cap with his golde band off his head, and ran a little distance from him and shared it with his fellow, the cap to the one, and the band to the other.

Having dispatched all our businesse in this place, wee departed and set sayle, and immediately upon our setting foorth we lost our Canter which was absent three or foure dayes but when our General had her againe, he tooke out the necessaries, and so gave her over neere to the Cape of Good Hope.

The next day after being the twentieth of June, wee harboured our selves againe in a very good harborough, called by Magellan Port S. Julian, where we found a gibbet standing upon the maine, which we supposed to be the place where Magellan did execution upon some of his disobedient and rebellious company.

The two and twentieth day our Generall went ashore to the maine, and in his companie, John Thomas, and Robert Winterhie, Oliver the Master gunner, John Brewer, Thomas Hood, and Thomas Drake, and entering on land, they presently met with the two or three of the countrey people, and Robert Winterhie having in his hands a bowe and arrows, went about to make a shoote of pleasure, and in his draught his bowstring brake, which the rude Savages taking as a token of warre, began to bend the force of their bowes against our company, and drove them to their shifts very narrowly.

In this Port our Generall began to enquire diligently of the actions of M. Thomas Doughtie, and found them not to be such as he looked for, but tending rather to contention or mutinie, or some other disorder, whereby (without redresse) the successe of the voyage might greatly have been hazarded: whereupon the company was called together and made acquainted with the particulars of the cause, which were found partly by master Doughties owne confession, and partly by the evidence of the fact, to be true: which when our Generall saw, although his private affection to M. Doughtie (as hee then in the presence of us all sacredly protested) was great, yet the care he had of the state of the voyage, of the expectation of her Majestie, and of the honour of his countrey did more touch him, (as indeede it ought) then the private respect of one man: so that the cause being thoroughly heard, and all things done in good order as neere as might be the course of our lawes in England, it was concluded that M. Doughtie should receive punishment according to the qualitie of the offence: and he seeing no remedie but patience for himselfe, desired before his death to receive the Communion, which he did at the hands of M. Fletcher our Minister, and our Generall himselfe accompanied him in that holy action: which being done, and the place of execution made ready, hee having embraced our Generall and taken his leave of all the companie, with prayer for the Queenes majestie and our realme, in quiet sort laid his head to the blocke, where he ended his life. This being done, our Generall made divers speeches to the whole company, perswading us to unitie, obedience, love, and regard of our voyage; and for the better confirmation thereof, willed every man the next Sunday following to prepare himself to receive the Communion, as Christian brethren and friends ought to doe, which was done in very reverent sort, and so with good contentement every man went about his businesee.

The 17 day of August we departed the port of S. Julian, & the 20 day we fell with the straight or freat of Magellan going into the south sea, at the Cape or headland whereof we found the bodie of a dead man, whose flesh was cleane consumed.

The 21 day we entered The Straight, which we found to have many turnings, and as it were shuttings up, as if there were no passage at all, by

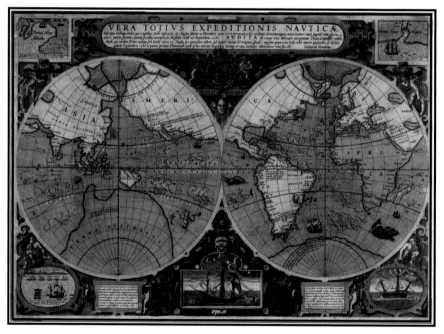

Engraved map showing Drake's circumnavigation around the globe, date unknown.

meanes whereof we had the wind often against us, so that some of the fleete recovering a Cape or point of land, others should be forced to turne backe againe, and come to an anchor where they could.

In this straight there be many faire harbors, with store of fresh water, but they lacke their best commoditie: for the water is there of such depth, that no man shal find ground to anchor in, except it bee in some narrow river or corner, or betweene some rocks, so that if any extreme blasts or contrary winds do come (whereunto the place is much subject) it careith with it no small danger.

The land on both sides is very huge & mountainous, the lower mountains whereof, although they be monstrous and wonderfull to looke upon for their height, yet there are others which in height exceede them in a straight maner, reaching themselves above their fellows so high, that betweene them did appeare three regions of cloudes.

These mountains are covered with snow: at both the southerly and Easterly of the straight there are Islands, among which the sea hath his indraught into the streights, even as it bath in the maine entrance of the freat.

This straight is extreme cold, with frost and snow continually; the trees seeme to stoope with the burden of the weather, and yet are greene continually, and many good and sweete herbes doe very plentifully grow and increase under them.

The bredth of the straight is in some place a league, in some other places 2 leagues, and three leagues, and in some other 4. leagues, but the narrowest place hath a league over.

The 24 of August we arrived at an Island in the streights, where we found great store of foule which could not flie, of the bignesse of geese, whereof we killed in lesse then one day 3000 and victualled our selves thoroughly therewith.

The 6 day of September we entred the South sea at the Cape or head shore.

The seventh day wee were driven by a great storme from the entering into the South sea two hundred leagues and odde in longitude, and one degree to the Southward of the Streight: in which height, and so many leagues to the Westward, the fifteenth day of September fell out the Eclipse of the Moone at the houre of sixe of the clocke at night: but neither did the Eclipticall conflict of the Moone impayre our state, nor her clearing againe amend us a whit, but the accoustomed Eclipse of the Sea continued in his force, wee being darkened more then the Moone seven fold.

From the Bay (which we called The Bay of Severing of Friends) wee were driven backe to the Southward of the streights in 57 degrees and a terce: in which height we came to an anker among the Islands, having there fresh and very good water, with herbes of singular virtue. Not farre from hence we entred another Bay, where wee found people both men and women in their Canoas, naked, and ranging from one Island to another to seeke their meat, who entered traffique with us for such things as they had.

We returning hence Northward againe, found the 3 of October three Islands, in one of which was such plenty of birdes as is scant credible to report.

The 8 day of October we lost sight of one of our Consorts wherein M. Winter was, who as then we supposed was put by a storme into the streights againe, which at our returne home wee round to be true, and he not perished, as some of our company feared.

Thus being come into the height of The Streights againe, we ran, supposing the coast of Chili to lie as the generall Maps have described it, namely Northwest, which we found to lie and trend to the Northeast and Eastwards, whereby it appeareth that this part of Chili hath not bene truly hitherto discovered, or at the least not truly reported for the space of 12 degrees at the least, being set downe either of purpose to deceive, or of ignorant conjecture.

We continuing our course, fell the 29 of November with an Island called la Mocha, were we cast anchor, and our Generall hoysing out our boate, went with ten of our company to shore, where wee found people, whom the cruell and extreme dealings of the Spaniards have forced for their owne safetie and libertie to flee from the maine, and to fortifie themselves in this Island. We being on land, the people came downe to us to the water side with shew of great courtesie, bringing to us potatoes, rootes, and two very fat sheepe, which our Generall received and gave them other things for them, and had promised to have water there: but the next day repayring againe to the shore, and sending two men aland with barrels to fill water, the people taking them for Spaniards (to whom they use to shew no favour if they take them) layde violent hands on them, and as we thinke, slew them.

Out Generall seeing this, stayed here no longer, but wayed anchor, and set sayle towards the coast of Chili, and drawing towards it, we mette neere to the shore an Indian in a Canoa, who thinking us to have bene Spaniards, came to us and tolde us, that at a place called S. Iago, there was a great Spanish ship laden from the kingdome of Peru: for which good newes our Generall gave him divers trifles, wherof he was glad, and went along with us and brought us to the place, which is called the port of Valparizo.

When we came thither, we found indeede the ship riding at anker, having in her eight Spaniards and three Negros, who thinking us to have bene Spaniards and their friends, welcomed us with a drumme, and made ready a Bottija of wine of Chili to drinke to us: but as soone as we were entred, one of our company called Thomas Moone began to lay about him, and stroke one of the Spanyards, and sayd unto him, Abaxo Perro, that is in English, Goe downe dogge. One of these Spaniards seeing persons of that quality in those seas, all to crossed, and blessed himselfe: but to be short, were stowed them under hatches all save one Spaniard, who suddenly and desperately leapt over boord into the sea, and swamme ashore to the towne of S. Iago, to give them warning of our arrivall.

They of the towne being not above 9. households, presently fled away and abandoned the towne. Our generall manned his boate, and the Spanish-ships boate, and went to the Towne, and being come to it, we rifled it, and came to a small chappell which wee entred, and found therein a silver chalice, two cruets, and one altar-cloth, the spoyle whereof our Generall gave to M. Fletcher his minister.

We found also in this towne a warehouse stored with wine of Chili, and many boords of Cedar-wood, all which wine we brought away with us, and certaine of the boords to burne for fire-wood: and so being come aboord, wee departed the Haven, having first set all the Spaniards on land, saving one John Griego a Greeke borne whom our Generall carried with him for his Pilot to bring him into the haven of Lima.

When we were at sea, our Generall rifled the ship, and found in her good store of the wine of Chili, and 25000 pezoes of very pure and fine gold of Baldivia, amounting in value to 37000 ducats of Spanish money, and above. So going on our course, wee arrived next at a place called Coquimbo, where our Generall sent 14 of his men on land to fetch water: but they were espied by the Spaniards, who came with 300 horsemen and 200 footemen, and slewe one of our men with a piece, the rest came aboord in safetie, and the Spaniards departed: wee went on shore againe, and buried our man, and the Spaniards came downe againe with a flag of truce, but we set sayle and would not trust them.

From hence we went to a certaine port called Tarapaza, where being landed, we found by the Sea side a Spaniard lying asleepe, who had lying by him 13 barres of silver, which weighed 4000 ducats Spanish; we tooke the silver, and left the man.

Not farre from hence going on land for fresh water, we met with a Spaniard and an Indian boy driving 8 Llamas or sheepe of Peru which are as big as asses; every of which sheepe had on his backe 2 bags of leather, each bagge conteining 50 li weight of fine silver: so that bringing both the sheepe and their burthen to the ships, we found in all the bags 800 pound weight of silver.

Here hence we sailed to a place called Arica, and being entred the port, we found there three small barkes which we rifled, and found in one of them 57 wedges of silver, each of them weighing about 20 pound weight, and every of these wedges were of the fashion and bignesse of a brickbat. In all these 3 barkes we found not one person: for they mistrusting no strangers, were all gone aland to the Towne, which consisteth of about twentie houses, which we would have ransacked if our company had bene better and more in number. But our Generall contented with the spoyle of the ships, left the Towne and put off againe to sea and set sayle for Lima, and by the way met with a small barke, which he boorded, and found in her good store of linen cloth, whereof taking some quantitie, he let her goe.

To Lima we came the 13 day of February, and being entred the haven, we found there about twelve sayle of ships lying fast moored at an anker, having all their sayles carried on shore; for the masters and marchants were here most secure, having never bene assaulted by enemies, and at this time feared the approach of none such as we were. Our generall rifled these ships, and found in one of them a chest full of royals of plate, and good store of silkes and linen cloth, and tooke the chest into his owne ship, and good store of the silkes and linen. In which ship hee had newes of another ship called the Cacafuego which was gone toward Paita, and that the same shippe was laden with treasure: whereupon we staied no longer here, but cutting all the cables of the shippes in the haven, we let them drive whither they would, either to sea or to the shore, and with all speede we followed the Cacafuego toward Paita, thinking there to have found her: but before wee arrived there, she was gone from thence towards Panama, whom our Generall still pursued, and by the way met with a barke laden with ropes and tackle for ships, which hee boorded and searched, and found in her 80 li. weight of golde, and a crucifixe of gold with goodly great Emerauds set in it which he tooke, and some of the cordage also for his owne ship.

From hence we departed, still following the Cacafuego, and our Generall promised our company, that whosoever could first descrie her, should have his chaine of gold for his good newes. It fortuned that John Drake going up into the top, descried her about three of the clocke, and about six of the clocke we came to her and boorded her, and shotte at her three peeces of ordinance, and strake downe her Misen, and being entered, we found in her great riches, as jewels and precious stones, thirteene chests full of royals of plate, foure score pound weight of golde, and sixe and twentie tunne of silver. The place where we tooke this prize was called Cape de San Francisco, about 150 leagues from Panama.

The Pilots name of this Shipp was Francisco, and amongst other plate that our Generall found in this ship, he found two very faire guilt bowles of silver, which were the Pilots: to whom our Generall sayd: Senior Pilot, you have here two silver cups, but I must needes have one of them: which the

Pilot because hee could not otherwise chuse, yielded unto, and gave the other to the steward of our General ships.

When this Pilot departed from us, his boy sayde thus unto our Generall: Captaine, our ship shall be called no more the Cacafuego, but the Cacaplata, and your shippe shall bee called the Cacafuego: which pretie speech of the Pilots boy ministred matter of laughter to us, both then and long after.

When our Generall had done what hee would with this Cacafuego hee cast her off, and wee went on our course still towards the West, and not long after met with a ship laden with linen and cloth and fine Chin-dishes of white earth, and great store of China-silks, of all which things wee tooke as we listed.

The owner himselfe of this shipe was in her, who was a Spanish Gentleman, from whom our Generall tooke a Fawlcon of golde, with a great Emeraud in the breast thereof, and the Pilot of the ship he tooke also with him, and so cast the ship off.

This Pilot brought us to the haven of Guatulco, the towne whereof, as he told us, had but 17 Spaniards in it. Assoone as we were entered this haven, wee landed, and went presently to the towne, and to the Towne-house, where we found a Judge sitting in judgement, being associate with three other officers, upon three Negros that had conspired the burning of the Towne: both which Judges & prisoners we tooke and brought them a shipboard, and caused the chiefe Judge to write his letter to the Towne, to command all the Townesmen to avoid, that we might safely water there. Which being done, and they departed, we ransacked the Towne, and in one house we found a pot of the quantitie of a bushel, full of reals of plate, which we brought to our ship.

And here one Thomas Moone one of our company, tooke a Spanish Gentleman as hee was flying out of the towne, and searching him, he found a chaine of golde about him, and other jewels, which he tooke, and so let him goe.

At this place our General among other Spaniards, set ashore his Portugall Pilote, which hee tooke at the Islands of Cape Verde, out of a ship of S. Mary port of Portugall: and having set them ashore, we departed hence, and sailed to the island of Canno, where our Generall landed, and brought to shore his owne ship, and discharged her, mended, and graved her, and furnished our ship with water and wood sufficiently.

And while wee were here, we espied a shippe, and set saile after her, and tooke her, and found in her two Pilots, and a Spanish Governour, going for the Islands of the Philippinas: we searched the shippe, and tooke someof her merchandizes, and so let her goe. Our Generall at this place and time, thinking himselfe both in respect of his private injuries received from the Spaniards, as also of their contempts and indignities offered to our countrey and Prince in generall, sufficiently satisfied, and revenged: and supposing that her Majestie at his returne would rest contented with this service, purposed to continue no longer upon the Spanish coasts, but began to consider and to consult of the best way for his Countrey.

He thought it not good to returne by the Streights, for two speciall causes: the one, lest the Spaniards should there waite, and attend for him in great number and strength, whose hands, hee being left but one ship, could not possibly escape. The other cause was the dangerous situation of the mouth of the streights in the South sea, where continuall stormes reigning and blustering, as he found by experience, besides the shoalds and sands upon the coast, he thought it not a good course to adventure that way: he resolved therefore to avoyde these hazards, to goe forward to the Islandes of the Malucos, and therehence to saile the course of Portugals by the Cape of Buena Esperanza.

Upon this resolution, hee beganne to thinke of his best way to the Malucos, and finding himselfe where he now was becalmed, he saw that necessitie hee must be forced to take a Spanish course, namely to sayle somewhat Northerly to get a winde. Wee therefore set saile, and sayled 600 leagues at the least for a good winde, and thus much we sailed from the 16 of April, till the 3 of June.

The 5 day of June, being in 43 degrees towards the pole Arctike, we found the ayre so colde, that our men being grievously pinched with the same complained of the extremitie thereof, and the further we went, the more the colde increased upon us. Whereupon we thought it best for that time to seeke the land, and did so, finding it not mountainous, but low plaine land, till wee came within 38 degrees towards the line. In which height it pleased God to send us into a faire and good Baye, with a good winde to enter the same.

In this Baye we anchored, and the people of the Countrey having their houses close by the waters side, shewed themselves unto us, and sent a present to our Generall.

When they came unto us, they greatly wondred at the things that wee brought, but our Generall (according to his naturall and accustomed human-itie) courteously intreated them, and liberally bestowed on them necessary things to cover their nakednesse, whereupon they supposed us to be gods, and would not be perswaded to the contrary: the presents which they sent to our Generall, were feathers, and calles of net-worke.

Their houses are digged round about with earth, and have from the uttermost brimmes of the circle, clifts of wood set upon them, joining close together at the toppe like a spire steeple, which by reason of that closenesse are very warme.

Their beds is the ground with rushes strowed on it, and lying about the house, have the fire in the midst. The men go naked, the women take bul-rushes, and kembe them after the manner of hempe, and thereof make their loose garments, which being knit about their middles, hang down about their hippes, having also about their shoulders a skinne of Deere, with the haire upon it. These women are very obedient and serviceable to their husbands.

After they were departed from us, they came and visited us the second time and brought with them feathers and bags of Tabacco for presents: And when they came to the top of the hill (at the bottome whereof we had pitched our tents) they staied themselves: where one appointed for speaker wearied himselfe with making a long oration, which done, they left their bowes upon the hill, and came downe with their presents.

In the meane time the women remaining on the hill, tormented them-selves lamentably, tearing their flesh from their cheeks, whereby we perceived that they were about a sacrifice. In the meane time our Generall with his company went to prayer, and to reading of the Scriptures, at which exercise they were attentive, & seemed greatly to be affected with it: but when they were come unto us, they restored againe unto us those things which before we bestowed upon them.

The newes of our being there being spread through the Countrey, the people that inhabited round about came downe, and amongst them the King himselfe, a man of a goodly stature, & comely personage, with many other tall and warlike men: before whose comming were sent two Ambassadors to our Generall, to signifie that their King was comming, in doing of which message, their speach was continued about halfe an houre. This ended, they by signes requested our Generall to send some thing by their hand to their king, as a token that his comming might be in peace: wherein our Generall having satisfied them, they returned with glad tidings to their King, who marched to us with a princely majestie, the people crying continually after their manner, and as they drew neere unto us, so did they strive to behave themselves in their action with comelinesse.

In the fore-front was a man of a goodly personage, who bare the scepter or mace before the King, whereupon hanged two crownes, a lesse and a bigger, with three chaines of a marveilous length: the crownes were made of knit worke wrought artificially with fethers of divers colours: the chaines were made of a bonie substance, and few be the persons among them that are admitted to weare them: and of that number also the persons are stinted, as some ten, some 12 &c. Next unto him which bare the scepter, was the King himselfe, with his Guard about his person, clad with Conie skins, & other skins: after them followed the naked common sort of people, every one having his face painted, some with white, some with blacke, and other colours, & having in their hands one thing or another for a present, not so much as their children, but they also brought their presents.

In the meane time our Generall gathered his men together, and marched within his fenced place, making against their approching a very warre-like shew. They being trooped together in their order, and a generall salutation being made, there was presently a generall silence. Then he that bare the scepter before the King, being informed by another, whom they assigned to that office, with a manly and loftie voyce proclaymed that which the other spake to him in secrete, continuing halfe an houre: which ended, and a generall as it were given, the King with the whole number of men and women (the children excepted) came downe without any weapon, who descending to the foote of the hill, set themselves in order.

In comming towards our bulwarks and tents, the scepter bearer began a song, observing his measures in a daunce, and that with a stately countenance, whom the King with his Guarde, and every degree of persons following, did in like maner sing and daunce, saving onely the women, which daunced & kept silence. The General permitted them to enter within our bulwarke, where they continued their song and daunce a reasonable time. When they had satisfied themselves, they made signes to our General to sit downe, to whom the King, and divers others made several orations, or rather supplications, that hee would take their province and kingdome into his hand, and become their King, making signes that they would resigne unto him their right and little of the whole land, and become his subjects. In which, to perswade us the better, the King and the rest, with one consent, and with great reverence, joyfully singing a song, did set the crowne upon his head, inriched his necke with all their chaines, and offred unto him many other things, honouring him by the name of Hioh, adding thereunto as it seemed, a signe of triumph: which thing our Generall thought not meete to reject, because he knew not what honour and profit it might be to our Countrey. Wherefore in the name, and to the use of her Majestie he tooke the scepter, crowne, and dignitie of the said Countrey into his hands, wishing that the riches & treasure thereof might so conveniently be transported to the inriching of her kingdom at home, as it aboundeth in ye same.

The common sorte of people leaving the King and his Guarde with our Generall, scattered themselves together with their sacrifices among our peo-ple, taking a diligent views of every person: and such as pleased their fancie, (which were the yongest) they inclosing them about offred their sacrifices unto them with lamentable weeping, scratching, and tearing the flesh from their faces with their nailes, whereof issued abundance of blood. But wee used signes to them of disliking this, and stayed their hands from force, and directed them upwards to the living God, whom onely they ought to worship. They shewed unto us their wounds, and craved helpe of them at our hands, whereupon we gave them lotions, plaisters, and oyntments, agreeing to the state of their griefes, beseeching God, to cure their diseases. Every third day they brought their sacrifices unto us, until they understood our meaning, that we had no pleasure in them: yet they could not be long absent from us, but dayly frequented our company to the houre of our departure, which departure seemed so grievous unto them, that their joy was turned into so-row. They intreated us, that being absent we would remember them, and by stealth provided a sacrifice, which we misliked.

Our necessarie businesse being ended, our Generall with his company travailed up into the Countrey to their villages, where we found herdes of Deere by 1000. in a company, being most large, and fat of body.

We found the whole Countrey to bee a warren of a strange kinde of Connies, their bodies in bignesse as be the Barbary Connies, their heads as the heads of ours, the feete of a Want, and the taile of a Rat being of great length: under her chinne is on either side a bag, into the which she gathereth her me-ate, when she hath filled her bellie abroad. The people eate their bodies, and make great accompt of their skinnes, for their Kings coate was made of them.

Our Generall called this Countrey Nova Albion, and that for two causes: the one in respect of the white bankes and cliffs, which lie towards the sea: and the other, because it might have some affinitie with our Countrey in name, which sometime was so called.

There is no part of earth heere to bee taken up, wherein there is not some probable shew of gold or silver.

At our departure hence our General set up a monument of our being there, as also of her Majesties right and title to the same, namely a plate, nailed upon a faire great poste, where-upon was ingraven her Majesties name, the day and yeere of our arrival there, with the free giving up of the province and people into her Majesties hands, together with her highnesse picture and armes, in a peece of six pence of current English money under the plate, whereunder was also written the name of our Generall.

It seemeth that the Spaniards hitherto had never bene in this part of the Countrey, neither did ever discover the land by many degrees, to the Southwards of this place.

After we had set saile from hence, wee continued without sight of land till the 13 day of October following, which day in the morning wee fell with certaine Islands 8 degrees to the Northward of the line, from which Islands came a great number of Canoas, having in some of them 4 in some 6 and in some also 14 men, bringing with them cocos, and other fruites. Their Canoas were hollow within, and cut with great arte and cunning, being very smooth within and without, and bearing a glasse as if it were a horne daintily burnished, having a prowe, and a sterne of one sort, yielding inward circle-wise, being of a great height, and full of certaine white shels for a braverie, and on each side of them lie out two peeces of timber about a yard and a halfe long, more or lesse, according to the smalnesse, or bignesse of the boate.

This people have the nether part of their eares cut into a round circle, hanging downe very lowe upon their cheeks, whereon they hang things of a reasonable weight. The nailes of their hands are an ynche long, their teeth are as blacke as pitch, and they renew them often, by eating of an herbe with a kinde of powder, which they always carrie about them in a cane for the same purpose.

Leaving this Island the night after we fell with it, the 18 of October, we lighted upon divers others, some whereof made a great shew of Inhabitants.

Wee continued our course by the Islands of Tagulada, Zelon, and Zewarra, being friends to the Portugals, the first whereof hath growing in it great store of Cinnamom.

The 14 of November we fell with the Islands of Malcuo, which day at night (having directed our course to runne with Tydore) in coasting along the Island of Mutyr, belonging to the King of Ternate, his Deputie or Vice-king seeing us at sea, came with his Canoa to us without all feare, and came aboord, and after some conference with our Generall, willed him in any wise to rune in with Ternate, and not with Tydore, assuring him that the King would bee glad of his comming, and would be ready to doe what he would require, for which purpose he himselfe would that night be with the King, and tell him the newes, with whom if he once dealt, hee should finde that as he was a King, so his word should stand: adding further, that if he went to Tydore before he Ternate, the King would have nothing to doe with us, because hee held the Portugall as his enemie: whereupon our General resolved to runne with Ternate, where the next morning early we came to anchor, at which time our Generall sent a messenger to the king with a velvet cloke for a present, and token of his comming to be in peace, and that he required nothing but traffique and exchange of marchandize, whereof he had good store, in such things as he wanted.

In the meane time the Vice-king had bene with the king according to his promise, signifying unto him what good things he might receive from us by traffique: whereby the King was mooved with great liking towards us, and sent to our Generall with speciall message, that hee should have what things he needed, and would require with peace and friendship, and moreover that hee would yeeld himselfe, and the right of his Island to bee at the pleasure and commandement of so famous a Prince as we served. In token whereof he sent of our Generall a signet, and within short time after came in his owne person, with boates, and Canoas to our ship, to bring her into a better and safer roade then she was in at present.

In the meane time, our Generals messenger beeing come to the Court, was met by certaine noble personages with great solemnitie, and brought to the King, at whose hands hee was most friendly and graciously intertained.

The King purposing to come to our ship, sent before 4. great and large Canoas, in every one whereof were certaine of his greatest states that were about him, attired in white lawne of cloth of Calicut, having over their heads from the one ende of the Canoa to the other, a covering of thinne perfumed mats, borne up with a frame made of reedes for the same use, under which every one did sit in his order according to his dignitie, to keepe him from the heate of the Sunne, divers of whom beeing of good age and gravitie, did make an ancient and fatherly shew. There were also divers yong and comely men attired in white, as were the others: the rest were souldiers, which stood in comely order round about on both sides, without whom sate the rowers in certaine galleries, which being three on a side all along the Canoas, did lie from the side thereof three or foure yardes, one being orderly builded lower then another, in every of which galleries were the number of 4 score rowers.

These Canoas were furnished with warlike munition, every man for the most part having his sword and target, with his dagger, beside other weapons, as launces, calivers, darts, bowes and arrowes: also every Canoa had a small cast base mounted at the least one full yarde upon a stocke set upright.

Thus comming neere our shippe, in order they rowed about us, one after another, and passing by, did their homage with great solemnitie, the great personages beginning with great gravitie and fatherly countenances, signifying that ye king had sent them to conduct our ship into a better roade.

Soone after the King himselfe repaired, accompanied with 6 grave and ancient persons, who did their obeisance with marveilous humilitie. The king was a man of tall stature, and seemed to be much delighted with the sound of our musicke, to whom as also to his nobilitie, our Generall gave presents, wherewith they were passing well contented.

At length the King craved leave of our Generall to depart, promising the next day to come aboord, and in the meane time to send us such victuals, as were necessarie for our provision: so that the same night we received of them meale, which they call Sagu, made of the tops of certaine trees, tasting in the mouth like sowre curds, but melteth like sugar, whereof they make certaine cakes, which may be kept the space of ten yeeres, and yet then good to be eaten. We had of them store of rice, hennes, unperfect and liquid sugar, sugar canes, and a fruite which they call Figo, with store of cloves.

The King having promised to come aboord, brake his promise, but sent his brother to make his excuse, and to intreate our Generall to come on shoare, offring himself pawne aboord for his safe returne. Whereunto our Generall consented not, upon mislike conceived of the breach of his promise, the whole company also utterly refusing it. But to satisfie him, our General sent certaine of his Gentlemen to the Court, to accompany the King's brother, reserving the Vice-king for their safe returne. They were received of another brother of the kings, and other states, and were conducted with great honour to the Castle. The place that they were brought unto, was a large and faire house, where were at the least 1000 persons assembled.

The King being yet absent, there sate in their places 60 grave personages, all which were said to be of the kings Counsel. There were besides 4 grave persons, apparelled all in red, downe to the ground, and attired on their heads like the Turkes, and these were said to be Romanes, and Ligiers there to keepe continual traffike with the people of Ternate. There were also 2 Turks Ligiers in this place, and one Italian. The king at last came in guarded with 12 launces covered over with a rich canopy, with embossed gold. Our men accompanied with one of their Captaines called Moro, rising to meete him, he graciously did welcome, and intertaine them. He was attired after the manner of the Countrey, but more sumptuously then the rest. From his waste downe to the ground, was all cloth of golde, and the same very rich: his legges were bare, but on his feete were a paire of Shooes, made of Cordovan skinne. In the attire of his head were finely wreathed hooped rings of gold, and about his necke he had a chaine of perfect golde, the linkes whereof were great, and one folde double. On his fingers hee had six very faire jewels, and sitting in his chaire of estate, at his right hand stood a page with a fanne in his hand, breathing and gathering the ayre to the King. The fanne was in length two foote, and in bredth one foote, set with 8 saphyres, richly imbrodered, and knit to a staffe 3. foote in length, by the which the Page did hold, and moove it. Our Gentlemen having delivered their message, and received order accordingly, were licensed to depart, being safely conducted backe againe by one of the kings Counsell.

This Island is the chiefest of all the Islands of Maluco, and the King hereof is King of 70 Islands besides. The king with his people are Moores in religion, observing certaine new Moones, with fastings: during which fasts, they neither eat nor drinke in the day, but in the night.

After that our Gentlemen were returned, and that we had heere by the favour of the king received all necessary things that the place could yeeld us: our General considering the great distance, and how farre he was yet off from his Countrey, thought it not best here to linger the time any longer, but waying his anchors, set out of the Island, and sayled to a certaine little Island to the Southwards of Celebes, where we graved our ship, and continued there in that and other businesses 26 dayes. This Island is throughly growen with wood of a large and high growth, very straight and without boughes, save onely in the head or top, whose leaves are not much differing from our broome in England. Amongst these trees night by night, through the whole land, did shew themselves and infinite swarme of fiery wormes flying in the ayre, whose bodies beeing no bigger then our common English flies, make such a shew and light, as if every twigge or tree had bene a burning candle. In this place breedeth also wonderfull store of Bats, as bigge as large hennes: of Crayfishes also heere wanted no plentie, and they of exceeding bignesse, one whereof was sufficient for 4 hungry stomacks at a dinner, beeing also very good, and restoring meate, whereof we had experience: and they digge themselves holes in the earth like Conies.

When wee had ended our businesse here, we waied, and set saile to runne for the Malucos: but having at that time a bad winde, and being amongst the Islands, with much difficultie wee recovered to the Northward of the Island of Celebes, where by reason of contrary winds not able to continue our course to runne Westwards, we were inforced to alter the same to the Southward againe, finding that course also to be very hard and dangerous for us, by reason of infinite shoalds which lie off, and among the Islands: whereof wee had too much triall to the hazard and danger of our shippe and lives. For of all other dayes upon the 9 of Januarie, in the yeere 1579 wee ranne suddenly upon a rocke, where we stucke fast from 8 of the clocke at night, til 4 of the clocke in the afternoone the next day being indeede out of all hope to escape the danger: but our Generall as hee had alwayes hitherto shewed himselfe couragious, and of a good confidence in the mercie and protection of God: so now he continued in the same, and lest he should seeme to perish wilfully, both he, and we did our best indevour to save our selves, which it pleased God so to blesse, that in the ende we cleared our selves most happily of the danger.

We lighted our ship upon the rockes of 3 tunne of cloves, 8 peeces of ordinance, and certaine meale and beanes: and then the winde (as it were in a moment by the speciall grace of God) changing from the starreboord to the larboord of the ship, we hoised our sailes, and the happy gale drove our ship off the rocke into the sea againe, to the no litle comfort of all our hearts, for which we gave God such prayse and thanks, as so great a benefite required.

The 8. of Februarie following, wee fell with the fruitfull Island of Barateve, having in the meane time suffered many dangers by windes and shoalds. The people of this Islands are comely in body and stature, and of a civil behaviour, just in dealing, and courteous to strangers, whereof we had the experience sundry wayes, they being most glad of our presence, and very ready to releeve our wants in those things which their Countrey did yeelde. The men goe naked, saving their heads and privities, every man having something or other hanging at their eares. Their women are covered from the middle downe to the foote, wearing a great number of bracelets upon their armes, for some had 8 upon each arme, being made some of bone, some of horne, and some of brasse, the lightest whereof by our estimation waied two ounces apeece.

With this people linnen-cloth is good marchandize, and of good request, whereof they make rols for their heads, and girdles to weare about them.

Their Island is both rich and fruitfull: rich in golde, silver, copper, and sulphur, wherein they seeme skilfull and expert, not onely to trie the same, but in working it also artificially into any forme and fashion that pleaseth them.

Their fruits be divers and plentiful, as nutmegs, ginger, long pepper, lemmons, cucumbers, cocos, figu, sagu, with divers other sorts: and among all the rest, wee had one fruite, in bignesse, forme, and huske, like a Bay berry, hard of substance, and pleasant of taste, which being sodden, becommeth soft, and is a most good and wholsome victuall, whereof we tooke reasonable store, as we did also of the other fruits and spices: so that to confesse a trueth, since the time that we first set out of our owne Countrey of England, we happened upon no place (Ternate onely excepted) wherein we found more comforts and better meanes of refreshing.

At our departure from Barateve, we set our course for Java major, where arriving, we found great courtesie, and honourable entertainment. This Island is governed by 5 Kings, whom they call Rajah: as Rajah Donaw, and Rajah Mang Bange, and Rajah Cabuccapollo, which live as having one spirite, and one minde.

Of these five we had foure a shipboord at once, and two or three often. They are wonderfully delighted in coloured clothes, as red and greene: their upper parts of their bodies are naked, save their heads, whereupon they weare a Turkish roll, as do the Maluccians: from the middle downward they weare a pintado silke, trailing upon the ground, in colour as they best like.

The Maluccians hate that their women should be seene of strangers: but these offer them of high courtesie, yea the kings themselves.

The people are of goodly stature, and warlike, well provided of swords and targets, with daggers, all being of their owne worke, and most artificially done, both in tempering their mettall, as also in the forme, whereof we bought reasonable store.

They have an house in every village for their common assembly: every day they meete twise, men, women, and children, bringing with them such victuals as they thinke good, some fruites, some rice boiled, some hennes roasted, some sagu, having a table made 3 foote from the ground, whereon they set their meate, that every person sitting at the table may eate, one rejoycing in the company of another.

They boile their rice in an earthen pot, made in forme of a sugar loafe, being ful of holes, as our pots which we water our gardens withall, and it is open at the great ende, wherein they put their rice dried, without any moisture. In the meane time they have ready another great earthen pot, set fast in a fornace, boiling full of water, whereinto they put their pot with rice, by such measure, that they swelling become soft at the first, and by their swelling stopping the holes of the pot, admit no more water to enter, but the more they are boiled, the harder and more firme substance they become, so that in the end they are a firme & good bread, of the which with oyle, butter, sugar, and other spices, they make divers sorts of meates very pleasant of taste, and nourishing to nature.

The French pocks is here very common to all, and they helpe themselves, sitting naked from ten to two in the Sunne, whereby the venomous humour is drawen out. Not long before our departure, they tolde us, that not farre off there were such great Ships as ours, wishing us to beware: upon this our Captaine would stay no longer.

From Java Major we sailed for the cape of Good Hope, which was the first land we fell withall: neither did we touch with it, or any other land, untill we came to Sierra Leona, upon the coats of Guinea: notwithstanding we ranne hard aboord the Cape, finding the report of the Portugals to be most false, who affirme, that it is the most dangerous Cape of the world, never without intolerable stormes and present danger to travelers, which come neere the same.

This Cape is a most stately thing, and the fairest Cape we saw in the whole circumference of the earth, and we passed by it the 18 of June.

From thence we continued our course to Sierra Leona, on the coast of Guinea, where we arrived the 22 of July, and found necessarie Provisions, great store of Elephants, Oisters upon trees of one kind, spawning and increasing infinitely, the Oister suffering no budde to grow. We departed thence the 24 day.

We arrived in England the third of November 1580. being the third yeere of our departure.

CHAPTER 2

FLORENCE NIGHTINGALE IN EGYPT

By Florence Nightingale

You are DEAR GOOD PEOPLE. I have found here no end of letters from you. All good news.

We arrived here on Saturday morning, 16th, and Mr. B. said we would send into Cairo for the letters, and we would go up the Pyramids, because then, if anything had happened, we should at all events have secured them. This though said in joke, I believe pretty much expressed the feelings of all, viz., that it was a very good thing to have the Pyramids to occupy our attention while waiting for the letters. However, a greater than Mr. B. de-cided—the khamsin—and it made its decision with so loud a voice, that to the Pyramids we could not go. So Mr B. and I mounted our asses and rode into Cairo for the letters, which we found after a world of trouble, and after frequently hearing there were none. Many and thick and happy ones, thank God; you are very good people. Nothing, however, decisive as to whether it is possible for us to go to Greece; so we came back again for and wandered about old Cairo in the afternoon.

Sunday we went in to church upon our asses; and meeting the Murrays, just landed, went in to luncheon, and then to call upon the I—You have no idea how strange it is to come back again into the world of life, and civilised wants and customs, after having been for three months and a half in the land of graves—amidst death and a world of spirits. But the spirits of the old Egyptians are such good company, and preach such nice cheerful sermons upon death and a hereafter.

I never shall forget the strange feeling, as we sailed up to Cairo on Satur-day, of hearing a band of military music in the distance—we who have heard nothing but the music of the stars, or the still small voice of the dead, for a whole winter.

This morning we set finally and resolutely out for the Pyramids; but we had not reached the shore before it became invisible for the sand clouds; the wind covered us with water—it was hopeless. We said to the asses, wait—a welcome word to the Egyptian, who will wait for twenty four hours without moving, if you tell him—and came back, and at this moment I can hardly write, and cannot even see Roda. We are keeping on the boat, till we have accomplished these unaccomplishable Pyramids, and are lying off Gizeh, as it is too far to go from Cairo.

And now for Memphis—beautiful, poetic, melancholy Memphis. No one had prepared us for its beauty. We thought of it as a thing to be done; tiresome after Thebes. We had three fair days of sailing from Minich, and had not been ashore. The last night a storm arose, and we were obliged to anchor; but rain—three drops!—fell, and the wind was so terrified that it fainted away. By dint of tacking we got on the next day to Bedreshayn, but took the little boat to get there. Paolo went up to the village for asses, we starving and shivering meanwhile in the boat; and shortly we saw Gad return, driving before him a troop of asses, about thirty or forty (Gad, if I mistake not, means "a troop"). After some delay we mounted (no ass having a bridle), and rode along a causeway till we came to the most beautiful spot you can imagine. I have seen nothing like it except in my dreams, certainly not in Egypt; a palm forest, the old palms springing out of the freshest grass; the ground covered with a little pink flower (of which I have tried in vain to preserve a plant for you) and the most delicate little lilac dwarf iris. Here and there a glassy pool and a flock of goats and kids, the long sun-light streaks and shadows falling among the trees. It looked as if nature had spread her loveliest coverlid, had grown her freshest flowers to deck the pall, and throw on the grave of Memphis. I have seen nothing like this palm forest in the East. And in the middle, in a grassy hollow, by the side of a bright pool of water, lies a statue of the great Rameses, the most beautiful sculpture we have yet seen. I must even confess that there is nothing at Ipsamboul to compare with it. I never felt so much the powerfulness of words. There he lies upon his face, as if he had just lain down weary; you speak low that you may not wake him to see the desolation of his land, yet there is nothing dreary, but all is still. It is the most beautiful tomb-stone for the grave of a nation I ever saw. I felt as if God had placed it there himself, and said—

"Very dear to me thou wert, my land of Memphis, and thou shalt have a fitting monument—the sweet green grass above thee spread, and one of the most glorious statues in the world to mark the place." I could have cried when I heard them talk of turning it round upon its back,—as if God had placed it there, and it should not be touched by man. This statue was given to the English. It is well indeed we did not take it. We went down into the hollow to see the features; they are composed, serene, purified beyond anything I ever saw; with such a smile on the mouth, and such an intellect in the brow. I had rather look upon that face again than upon anything in Egypt. The art is so perfect that the stone has all the softness of flesh: you are really afraid to touch those colossal stone features, the high blood nostril, the short upper lip, the moulded brow, for fear of insulting him; and he lies so calmly upon his pillow—the pillow of his mother earth. Nothing is broken but the legs. In either hand is a papyrus, with his cartouche upon it. Though the eyes are open, there is the most perfect appearance of repose. But I am ashamed to speak about the art, when such an expression is there—the spiritualized, transfigured expression, not indeed of a Christ in his transfiguration, but of an Æschylean creation, a Prometheus, or an Abdiel of Milton. This was the colossal standing statue, which perhaps stood before the great temple of Phthah.

Photograph after a painting by Herbert Wellcome.

At some hundred yards distance is a cluster of three mounds, about a mile round, with walls of crude brick, varying from twelve to twenty-four feet thick. This we fixed upon in our own minds as the site of the temple of Phthah, that wonder of ancient times. I brought away (for the school) a crude brick, full of straw, which mayhap the Israelites may have made. At all events, it is part of no Arab building, but of a real old Egyptian one; but I felt as if I had lived so intimately with Moses and Rameses for the last three months, that I did not care much about their bricks, when I had themselves.

Today I walked with Moses, under the palms; through the desert, where he killed the Egyptian—about the palace, where he lived as the grandson of the king—round the temple, where he derived his ideas of a pure worship, and (sifting the chaff from the wheat) thought how he could retain the spirit of the religion, while getting rid of the worship of animals. I forget whether it is Manetho or Strabo, who says that "Moyses" was a priest of Heliopolis, who wished to change the worship of brutes in Egypt; and I have often thought he may have tried the Egyptians first, and failing, gone to the Hebrews. I looked at the line of hills and of Pyramids which he had looked at, and thought that probably the hills were more altered than the Pyramids. How grieved he must have been to leave Memphis,—guilty of ingratitude, as he must have seemed, towards his princess-mother, who had so tenderly and wisely reared him, and given him the means of learning all he valued so much, as the way of raising his brethren—that great, that single instance in history as far as I know, of a learned man, a philosopher, and a gentleman, forming the plan of himself educating savages, and devoting himself to it. It was like Sir Isaac Newton keeping school among the Nubians—Charles James Fox turning missionary. There was more of the Roman Catholic, of the Jesuit, in Moses, than of the Protestant. We should have said, what a waste! to squander such talents among miserable slaves, who won't understand you; keep in your own sphere; you will do much more good among educated men like yourself. I do not know any man in all history with whom I sympathise so much as with Moses—his romantic devotion—his disappointments—his aspirations, so much higher

than anything he was able to accomplish, always striving to give the Hebrews a religion they could not understand.

Well, we rode on through palm groves and corn fields, and by a small lake where once the famous sacred lake of Memphis was, over which the dead were ferried, to the edge of the desert, where once was the necropolis of Memphis, and which we call the desert of Sakhara, a desert covered with whitened bones, mummy cloths, and fragments, and full of pits; not here and there; not in one place and then in another, but strewed like a battlefield, so as really to look like the burial place of the world. Of all the mighty world not one living man has remained to us, only this valley of their bones. Here Ezekiel might have seen his vision of the dry bones, and passed by them round about; for there were very many in the open valley, and lot they were very dry.

Here the Pyramids lost their vulgarity—their come, look-at-me appearance, and melted away into a fitting part and portion of this vast necropolis, subdued by the genius of the place. Hardly anything can be imagined more vulgar, more uninteresting than a Pyramid in itself, set up upon a tray, like a clipt yew in a public house garden; it represents no idea; it appeals to no feeling; it tries to call forth no part of you, but the vulgarest part—astonishment at its size—at the expense. Surely size is a very vulgar element of the sublime,—duration, you will say, is a better, that is true, but this is the only idea it presents—a form without beauty, without ideal, devised only to resist time, to last the longest; and age is an idea one is so familiar with in Egypt, that if a thing has nothing but age to recommend it, you soon learn to pass by it to the children of Savak and Athor, of Time and of Beauty. No, the Pyramids are a fit emblem of the abominable race they represented and overthrew. Have they a thought in them? it is a thought of tyranny. And what earthly good they ever did to any human being, but upsetting the wretches who built them, I never could find out,—except determining, by the mathematical accuracy of their position that, in 6000 years the axis of the earth has not changed an iota of its direction. As a monument of time, then, the earth is as good as the Pyramids.

Well, I had been very loth to see the Pyramids; but here we stood at the bottom of the oldest monument of man in the known world, the large

Pyramid of Sakhara, which is now believed to have been the family tomb of the first of the third dynasty, Sesorchris I, 3500 years before Christ. There is nothing left to testify of man's existence before this. It is not above 300 feet high, and has a chamber excavated beneath it in the rock 100 feet deep, into which you descend by a well. I should like to have seen this mysterious cave, but it was impossible. This Pyramid, unlike the others, is made of five great steps.

I ran up a mound near it, from which I could see the whole of this necropolis of the world Sprinkled about the churchyard stood the nine Pyramids of Sakhara. On my left, to the south, the two of Dashoor, of which the nearest is almost as large (by thirty feet) as the Great Pyramid of Gizeh—both these are supposed to be of the third dynasty—near them the two brick pyramids—mere ruins. On my right, to the north, the three Pyramids of Abousir, of the three last kings of the third dynasty, and beyond them, but seeming quite near, the two Giants of Gizeh, with the smaller one of the Holy Mycerinus (all of the fourth dynasty, 3229 B.C.) Above my head was the great Pyramid of Sakhara, 3453 B.C. But their ugliness was softened away by the shadow of death, which reigned over the place—as moonlight makes everything look beautiful. I could have wandered about that desert and those tombs for hours, but fatigue and those screeching Arabs, the two great Egyptian evils, drove us away.

We stopped as we went at the tomb of Psammeticus II, a modern of 600 years before Christ, the predecessor of the Pharaoh Hophra of the Bible—who was the predecessor of Amasis, the patron of Pythagoras and Solon, and friend of Polycrates, of the twenty-sixth dynasty. This was a series of chambers, excavated in the ground, to which you descended by a pit. The chambers were valuted, and had pits in them. The hieroglyphs were clear; they were of the decadence.

A granite sarcophagus here, an ibis pit there, stopped us, as we rode away from the Arabs, and back to Memphis, by the long palm grove and village of Sakhara. Again we stopped, and had a long look at out Rameses, whom we found still sleeping on the turf of the valley. I never saw anything which affected me so much. I do not believe there is anything like it in the world, except the Santa Cecilia decollate in Trastevere at Rome. We clambered over the mounds, and thought we made out two gigantic clusters of what must have been temples. Here and there we found an Athor capital, a granite figure of an official, bearing on his shoulders one of those slaves with king's heads, which were carried in processions. Otherwise the city of three thousand six hundred and odd years before Christ, founded by Menes himself, lay asleep under the green sod and the palm trees—"At her head a green grass turf, at her feet a stone."

The difficulty of writing about Egypt is, that one feels ashamed of talking about one's own impressions at such a deathbed as this; and yet, to describe the place itself,—one cannot—there are no words big enough. Memphis has wound itself round my heart—made itself a place in my imagination. I have walked there with Moses and Rameses, and with them I shall always return there.

*   *   *

I told you how Saturday morning Mr. B—and I rode into the town from old Cairo, about two miles (I always feel so proud when mounted like a caliph on my ass); how he deposited me with Madame Francois, my friend and hotel keeper, how I walked up and down the dreary sandy large high room, with no furniture, but mosquito curtains, and getting impatient looked out of the window into the white unwindowed street; how one solitary individual came down the street, who, looking up at the same moment that I was looking out, turned out to be the mad Count we met on the Nile, who gave us birds and books, but whose name we never knew; how I was very near jumping out of the window, but remembering I should have to give back the books, refrained; how Mr. B came back with only one letter—how Mr. Legros followed with a new pair of primrose coloured gloves, put on for us, in which he looked like a dear old bear in satin shoes; how he fell about our necks—how he wanted me to go and see the hippopotamus—how I, getting uneasy about wished to go back—how he mounted us on our asses; how Mr. B., at the door of our consulate, remembered he must go to the Greek merchant; how I rode into the consulate, ass and all, taking her with me as a sufficient chaperone, and a quite maternal protector, even though she could not speak, how at this moment two handfuls of letters arrived—how I snatched—how Mr. Legros said, "Won't you get off to read your letters?"—how I did it, but remembering in the house the gross impropriety I had been guilty of in leaving my ass, and coming in without her, implored to go into the garden; how I climbed up upon a white wall to be modest and retiring, and read my letters; how shocked I was when wine and biscuits arrived, and were deposited by a dumb Arab in beautiful trousers before me (if it had been coffee I might have had fewer scruples); how I crawled down again, and remounting our asses, for Mr. B. had by this time come back, we embraced Mr. Legros, and ambled away to old Cairo at a pace caliphs might have envied.

Well, we fetched and spent the afternoon in Fostat (old Cairo), very interesting, though differing from Memphis. First, we went through narrow, narrow streets, with threads, not gleams, of sun through them, where the Moorish balconies not only met, but overlapped, overhead, to a Coptish church in the Roman fortress, where a Coptic funeral was going on—women couchant on the floor and howling—the coffin a mere shallow tray with the body in it, covered by a pink gauze—a priest chanting; and when he had done, the finery torn off the corpse, which galloped away, followed by the women howling.

Below the church we went down into a grotto or crypt, supported by four slips of columns on either side, making three aisles, very small and low, about eight paces by seven, certainly the oldest Christian place of worship I ever was in, without excepting the catacombs of Rome. Mr. B. thought it older than any church at Jerusalem. Here, it is said, a serpent was worshipped by the Egyptians, till the Virgin and Child made it their abode, when it disappeared. Certain it is that all sects, however inimical, Copt, Catholic, Greek, Maronite, believe in the tradition, and each says mass there. I cannot help, like Robertson, believing in tradition, with one's own reservations. It is astonishing how much more difficulty we have in believing in an antiquity one thousand eight hundred years old than in one of six thousand. We have lately been so intimate with buildings of thousands of years, and cannot now believe in one of hundreds.

But however that may be, it is certain that many martyrs suffered here— that it served as a Roman dungeon in Diocletian's time. It is within the Roman camp of Fostat, and near the gate where the Prætorium was. It is certain that Mary was in Old Cairo, and I shall believe that it was here she lived till further notice.____ says it could not be, because it is so near the Prætorium; but it was much more likely that Mary should put herself under the protection of the Romans, who cared for no religion (till the Christians persecuted them), than under the enthusiastic bigoted Egyptians, who, like us, hated and despised every nation but their own. The insignificant Mary could be of no importance to the Romans, except as a Roman subject, for what were they likely to know of Herod's quarrels?

From hence we went to a Coptic convent, still on the site of the Roman fortress, of which the church is of the third century, full of beautiful Moorish screens and ivory work, with saints which work all sorts of miracles—one a "patriarch Abraham", who with the help of a believing shoemaker saved the Christians' lives by making a mountain move, to convince a hardly believing caliph. They showed us his and the shoemaker's picture, and the mark on the pillar where he rested his head when he prayed. Is it not curious? Evidently some mixture of the visit of Abraham to Memphis, with "Christians" substituted in the tradition; also a picture of the Virgin and Child by St. Mark, and a St. Onofrio, whose shrine was covered with bits of hair nailed under his picture by believing toothaches, who, having done this, are cured. We went to the rooms at the top of the convent, where sick Copts (among others, Dr. Abbott's wife) come to get well, and the Roman Catholic odours savoured sweet in my nostrils. But I never remember so strange a feeling as looking through a chink in the convent wall (in a great state of rapture at finding myself really again in something like Catholic precincts) and seeing the pyramids as large as life in the plain. Strange incongruity!

After alternating Osiriolatry and Mariolatry (on my part),we took a third dose in the form of Amrou's Mosque, which he built when he took the Roman fortress sixteen years after the Hegira for the Caliph Omar, calling the place Fostat, from his leather tent. He was seven months taking the place: he made it the royal city. Now, his mosque stands among mounds and ruins, desolate to see. But oh! what a beautiful thing it is; an immense open quadrangle, with the octagonal well and water "de rigueur" in the middle; at the further end a colonnade of seven aisles, so light and airy that they look as if they were there for their amusement and were dancing with their shadows, not at all burthened by a sense of their responsibilities, but laughing merrily with the sunbeams. The adjoining side has rows of columns, three deep; the other two one. You never saw anything so pretty, or so gay. The pulpit and reading place, the niche towards Mecca, and Amrou's unhonoured tomb in the corner, are still there. But it looks to me like the place of worship of the Cluricaunes, or where Titanis's mischievous elves make their devotions; not at all where a reasonable Mahometan, like myself, could do so.

We rode home over those desolate mounds—the ancient Rameses of the Egyptians, where the Pharaonic palace stood, only a little more to the south, in which Moses met Pharaoh—the Babylon of the Persians (who christened the re-built city after the Babylon of the East), whence Peter wrote his first epistle (there seems no doubt that this is the Babylon he mentions at the end, and that he came here with Mark, whose stay at Alexandria everyone believes)—the Fostat of Amrou, who built his city at the northern end of the vast Babylon. Then came Salah-e-dien, my old friend Saladin, 500 years later, and moved the city still farther to the north, to Masr-el-Kahirah (the victorious Masr), which we have degraded into Cairo, and upon the citadel are his ruins still seen.

All this story the mounds tell, besides the Roman one; for all the convents we saw are within the Roman fortress, which now contains a Christian village; and five steps away is the Jewish synagogue, which you can only go into on a Saturday, where the oldest copy of the law is found, and which is called the synagogue where Jeremiah was when in Egypt. I think it matters little to the spirit of the thing to verify the exact spot, whether five feet to the right or left, where these men walked and talked. If I can believe that here Jeremiah sighed over the miseries of his fatherland—that here Moses, a stronger character, planned the founding of his—that here the infant eyes opened, which first looked beyond the ideas of "fatherland", and of "the God of Abraham, Isaac, and Jacob", and planned the restoration of the world and the worship of the God of the whole earth, is not that all one wants? There is no want of interest, you see, in Cairo, even after Thebes.

And now, my dearest people, I must put up—very much more comfortable in my mind, I can assure you, since I have had my letters. If you can read this—it is in spite of the Khamsin—at this instant the floor of the cabin is a quarter of an inch deep in sand—our faces are covered like the hippopotamus, and I could write much more easily on the table with my finger than on the paper with my pen. It is almost dark, and to sit in the sitting cabin, which is the outer one, is impossible. Let an European wait till he has seen the Nile in a khamsin before he speaks uncivilly of a London fog. We are come over to the island of Roda for shelter—where the cradle of Moses stuck—but have not been on shore yet.

As to our plans, Zirinia, the great Greek merchant, says there is no difficulty in going to Greece.

In three weeks everything at Athens must be settled between the fleet and Otho, and this dreadful wind over, which will most likely last now all through the equinox.

However, all this is en l'air, or rather en sable, at present. And if you were to see the "sable" on the paper, you would think it a sandy foundation. And the moon has just become visible, all covered with sand. She wants her face washed. We lie here because we are in mortal fear of a party to the Pyramids. People in Cairo are always making parties thither. All the boats from Thebes are coming in. There was such a shaking and bowing after church yesterday, and at Shepheard's Hotel.

* * *

Greek affairs go ill. I cannot very well tell what we shall do. European politics are disgusting, disheartening, or distressing—here there are no politics at all, only harem intrigues, and deep, grinding, brutalizing misery. Let no one live in the East, who can find a corner in the ugliest, coldest hole in Europe. Give me Edinburgh wynds rather than Cairo Arabian Nights. And yet they are such an attaching race, the poor Arabs, vide the tears of our crew at parting with us, their round merry faces a mile long, sobbing outside the door. And all for what? Merely for not having been maltreated. I am sure I could not have imagined what real sorrow it was to part from them. If I had not been crying myself, I should have said what a pretty picture it was yesterday. When they all came up to the hotel to bid us goodbye a second time, they begged to see me, else I should not have done it again, and when I went in they were ranged in two semicircles, all their shoes left outside, one black face learning against the white drapery of the bed, even the stupid old Reis cried, and my particular friend Abool Ali, arrayed in a beautiful new brown zaaboot and clean white turban, was spoiling all his new clothes with wiping his eyes. Then they all pressed forward to salute us, Arab fashion, which kisses your hand and presses it to the heart and to the head, and then they would do it all over again, and after that we parted, and shall never see one another more.

In the evening, three of them, who had done us particular services, came by appointment for a particular conversation. And Abool Ali who is very anxious to marry, but cannot have the 150 piastres necessary to buy a "tob" or garment for the lady,—a saucepan, a mat, and two tin dishes, which is all the father, or any father requires,—agreed with me that he would really save 75 piastres within a year, if I would leave the other 75 piastres with the Consul for him. He further promised he would not beat his wife, which he said he should not have occasion to do, as she was not a Cairene, but of the country, and very steady, and that he would not put her away when he was tired of her; he was not profuse of words, and I believed him; and then he swore, not by my request, but by Allah and his two eyes. Another hand-kissing followed, and so we parted. A crew of more native gentlemen never existed; they never showed any curiosity—never peeped into our cabins, and though not only always kind, but empressés, they yet never intruded themselves. The only thing that disconcerted them was that Mr. B. sometimes left us with strange gentlemen at Thebes, and kept them with him, instead of sending them to mount guard over us.

But I ought to begin my story in order. I must kill a few of these files though unlike Sir Isaac, before I begin. I am getting just as bad as the Egyptians, and let them settle all over my face in black clusters, resigning myself to the will of Allah and the flies.

Well, I have disturbed the flies; but now you must wait another moment while I check the salutatory exercises of a few dozen fleas; but it is of no use, I might as well devote myself to the pleasure of the chase at once and for ever.

On Tuesday it was still khamsin, but there was so little, that all of a sudden, at eight o'clock, we made up our minds to go to the Pyramids of Gizeh; we were tired of playing hide and seek with all our acquaintance at Cairo, who wanted to make a party there; tired, too, of having the boat off Gizeh. Paolo was too ill to go with us, but we thought we could manage with two of our excellent crew. The road from Gizeh is very pretty (though not equal to Memphis), with fields of corn, and acres of that exquisite little dwarf lilac Iris. We went along a causeway between an avenue of tamarisk,—the remains of the old causeway are quite perceptible in it, built to convey the stone, which cases the inside of the Pyramid; the outside is built from the Libyan quarries (refer to your Herodotus). Presently those forms of perfect ugliness loomed upon our view, through a grey fog of sand, not unbecoming however. We reached the desert,—as usual without the slightest warning, and an Egyptian donkey's wont, my ass immediately lay down to roll,—an operation he frequently repeated. In an hour and a half we were at the foot of the Great Pyramid, leaving the Sphinx to our left; but no feeling of awe, not even of wonder, much less of admiration, saluted us: there is nothing to compare the Pyramid with; you remain from first to last insensible of its great size, which, as it is its only quality, is unfortunate. As it was now calm, and the wind might rise, we immediately began to go up. As to the difficulty, people exaggerate it tremendously;—there is none, the Arabs are so strong, so quick,

and I will say so gentlemanly; they drag you in step, giving the signal, so that
you are not pulled up piecemeal. The only part of the plan I did not savour
was the stopping every time you are warm for a chill on a cold stone, so that
I came to the top long before the others. Arrived here, I walked about, trying
to call up a sentiment: the stones certainly were remarkably large—the view
was remarkably large—the European names cut there were remarkably large.
Here are three sentiments; which will you have?

I do not know why the desert of Gizeh is so much less striking than that
of Sakhara. One can, in Egypt, seldom render an account to oneself of any
impression. Perhaps it is that Sakhara looks like the burial-place of the world,
it is so grand and desolate and lone, and so riddled with graves. Gizeh looks
like what it is, the burial-place of a family of kings and their courtiers; the
remains of buildings, too, about the place, give it the look of habitation, make
one think of porters and sextons, and men and women; the utter loneliness
of Sakhara, away from all that one is accustomed to see under the sun, makes
one think of souls, not men,—of another planet set apart to be the churchyard of this which is the dwelling place.

It was not at all cold or windly at the top, and we did not hurry ourselves; then we came down again, but no spirit of Rameses or of Moses helped
me down the steps; only the spirit of Cheops gave me his arm, and very bad
company I found him. About half way is a grotto, formed by a very few stones
having been taken out; and this does give one some idea of size. You stop
a few courses short of the bottom, under the wonderful pointed doorway,
which makes the entrance to the inside; everybody knows it by picture. It
is made of four huge blocks. Here, clad in brown Holland and flannel (one
comfort is that the Arabs look upon this last with very different eyes from the
English, as it is a festive or state garment, and two of our crew, to whom I
gave flannel waistcoats, always wore them outside their mantles or zaaboots),
having taken off your shoes, you are dragged by two Arabs (before you had
three) down one granite drain, up another limestone one, hoisted up a place,
where they broke a passage (how they ever found the real one is a miracle);
you creep along a ledge, and at last find yourself in the lofty groove, I can

call it nothing else, up which you ascend to the king's chamber. This is the most striking part of the whole: you look up to what seems an immeasurable height, for your light does not approach the roof; only the overlappings in the sides, which gradually approach one another as they come nearer the top, give you any measure, and you see nothing but black stone blocks; blocks you should not call them, but surface, for you can barely perceive the joints. Except this, I think the imagination can very well supply your place in the Pyramid. After you have crawled, ramped, and scrambled for two hours in black granite sheaths, without an inscription, without a picture of any kind, but the Arabs fighting for the candle, "the mind", I assure you, "is satisfied". As to the difficulty, here again, there is none: people talk of heat, the Theban tombs are much hotter; of suffocation, I did not even feel the thirst, which in Egypt is no joke; of the slipperiness, it is impossible to fall with those Arabs. The only danger you can possibly run is that of catching an awful cold in your bones; this is unavoidable.

But I suppose, as we have got so far, I must go through with you, though very unwillingly. When I was a rat then, not in Pythagoras' time, but on March 29, 1850, which I can but too well remember, I arrived, after running in my usual manner down one drain and up two others—large airy drains they were for me—to a sort of black thing like a tank with a flat roof, and a lesser granite tank in it without a cover, where they say a very bad rat indeed, and the grandson of a worse, Shafra Chabryes, laid his bones; and he made the rats work so hard to heap up this mound which the Big Rat, his grandfather, had begun, that they would have no more kings of that family. There is a very curious way of getting out of the grandson rat's chamber; it seems the architect thought to stop it up for ever by granite portcullises, which you can still see with their grooves on the four sides of the entrance drain, and to climb out themselves either over the portcullis, or by a passage which, some say, came out under the chin of the great Sphynx, shutting up the drain as they came along. But the portcullises are broken through, and I, for my part, got under very well; some of the native rats with me spitting continually to moisten the stone for our pats. In the great granite tank are outlets to the outside of the rat hill, such as ants practice in their anthills, to let in air. I was very curious about these portcullises, which I thought surprising to have been made by my forefather rats 5000 years ago, and went over them again and again, but could not make out how they were managed; then I ran through a very easy drain without a fall in it, to a room with a gabled roof, just under the middle of the mound. After this, we wanted to run down the lowest drain which burrows almost to the centre of the earth, in the living rock underneath; but the rubbish has filled it up so entirely that even we rats are worsted, and it requires a mole; so we were obliged to give it up, as you know we abhor the infidel race of moles. The drains are so much like one another, that a travelled rat like me, who has seen one, has seen all. The other rats were very good natured in hauling me down the broken drain, and then we ran out above the ground; I, for my part, thinking that the rat who made all this might as well never have lived at all.

As I was leisurely crawling up the last passage, my two Arabs having been left fighting for an end of candle, Abool Ali ran down from the outside, seized my hand, and dragged me up triumphantly to the top with the usual Hel-e-hel, with which they haul up the yard or pole the boat off a sand-bank. With this appropriate introduction, I emerged (oh, could anyone but have seen that scene!) to find a harem from Constantinople; about fifty women, all looking like feather beds in their huge "habarahs", veiled up to the eyes, and three grave Turks, their happy possessors, all sitting over the door of the Pyramid, like a semicircle of vultures, waiting to see me come out (and drinking coffee in that happy prospect), bonnetless, shoeless, in my flannel and brown Holland. If I had had "an umbrella in case of fire, it would have been something": but was my good angel; she had not been in, and, though she could not speak for laughing, she pounced upon me, wrapped me in a shawl, and stuck on my bonnet. The Turks never moved a muscle; they probably thought me some description of sheytan, which are very common, as well as efreets, in Egypt.

Well, my dears, I expect you will murder me. I could almost murder myself: all I can say for myself is, that I have faithfully rendered in blue ink what impressions the Pyramid makes.

And now, what will become of me? That I can never revisit my native country, an outcast from my hearth and home is certain; and—the smallest evil resulting from an ill-timed sincerity—a victim to truth I must remain. In England, where Egypt is considered as a tray for pyramids and little else, where not to have prostrated oneself at the foot of the Pyramid is not to have admired Egypt, where Egypt=Pyr. and Pyr.=Egy., because things which are = the same thing, are = one another, which is out of Euclid; it is mathematically proved that either I have not been in Egypt, or I am no fit inhabitant of the land of England: Q.E.D. Goodbye. You will never see me more. One thing is a comfort, neither will the Pyramids.

But before I sink, a victim to persecution. I will endeavour to atone for my errors by riding round the other Pyramids. The second, built by the first Cheops, 3229 B.C. (abominable man!), is the most perfect in its exterior casing; but we did not go in. The great one is built by the second Cheops, and finished by his grandson, the last of the fourth dynasty. It is no doubt a marvel of mathematical accuracy—the four sides lying to the four points of the compass—no easy matter with that size of building; height:base:: 5:8: ½ base: perpend height:: inclined height: base, &c., &c. All that is very fine, but does not make an impression.

Next we rode round the third and small pyramid, where Mycerinus the Holy, who still lives in songs and hymns, was laid by a grateful people: he was the third of that unlucky dynasty. We have his body and the cover of his sarcophagus in England: there is a beautiful prayer on our lid. Beyond this are three little pyramids, half ruined, where the second Mycerinus and his wife and daughter were laid. Nitocris, the heroine of all the romance of Egypt, finished the third pyramid, in which she lies. She is the original of "Cinderella", of Herodotus' story of "Rhodopis", the "rosy checked", of Strabo's fable of "Naucratis",—her name means Neith the Victorious. She is still seen by the Arabs, a beautiful shade, wandering round her Pyramid. She maintained the throne six years in the name of her murdered husband (2973 B.C. sixth dynasty), finished her Pyramid, invited the murderers to the consecration, when she avenged her husband and then perished by her own hand. But her sarcophagus had disappeared.

Here you can see plainly the two causeways which led from the Pyramids to the river, a rounded head of rock forming one side of something like a great entrance, and near it the Sphynx. People ought to have some conscience; as to the expression of the Sphynx, you might as well talk about the expression of our High Tor. You can make out much more perfect faces there. Well, some people have imaginations, and some have not. Go to. I hope when my portrait is exposed in the same condition as this of Thothmosis IV of blessed memory, people will discover as many marks of profound intellect, great sweetness and propriety of conduct, united with perfection of feature. A wonderful gift is "Einbildungskraft" certainly. May a "portion for seven, and also for eight" thereof be mine before I visit the Sphynx again. It is the more abominable, because Thothmosis IV, being so late as 1509 B.C. has no right to be so defaced. I cannot help it. He is said to be inside; but some may say the Sphynx only contained the outlet for the workmen, who closed the entrance to the great Pyramid. Well, let them all rest in peace, and let me rest too.

As we rode away we saw the tombs hewn in the rock, and another causeway, leading to the Libyan hills. We found our boat, stretching out its motherly arms to us, off the Nilometer at Roda, and dropped down directly to the lower end of the island (where we lay the first night we went on board). There we found Mr. _____, who came on board directly with his charming daughter, a black, and a great friend of mine; and the only pretty picture I had had in my mind all day, she gave me. Years ago she used to sir with her father and his gun in the moonlight on the side of the Pyramid, a few courses up, watching the jackals and wolves run by. Fancy the old white-headed man, the little black dab of a child (the ugliness of the scene softened by the moonlight), watching the troop of jackals whistling by like a rushing wind in the deep shadow.

CHAPTER 3

THE AMUNDSEN-ELLSWORTH POLAR FLIGHT

By Lincoln Ellsworth

Lincoln Ellsworth at Svalbard, circa 1925.

So long as the human ear can hark back to the breaking of waves over deep seas; so long as the human eye can follow the gleam of the Northern Lights over the silent snow fields; then so long, no doubt, will the lure of the unknown draw restless souls into those great Artic wastes.

I sit here about to set down a brief record of our late Polar experience, and I stop to try to recall when it was that my imagination was first captured by the lure of the Arctic. I must have been very young, because I cannot now recall when first it was. Doubtless somewhere in my ancestry there was a restless wanderer with an unappeasable desire to attain the furthest north. And, not attaining it, he passed it on with other sins and virtues to torment his descendants.

The large blank spaces surrounding the North Pole have been a challenge to the daring since charts first were made. For nearly four generations that mysterious plain has been the ultimate quest of numberless adventurers.

Before this adventure of ours, explorers had depended upon ships and dogs. Andrée and Wellman planned to reach the Pole with balloons, but theirs were hardly more than plans. Andrée met with disaster soon after leaving Spitzbergen. Wellman's expedition never left the ground.

What days they were—those ship and dog days! What small returns came to those men for their vast spending of energy and toil and gold! I am filled with admiration for the courage and the hardihood of the men who cut adrift from civilization and set out with dogs or on foot over the tractless ice fields of the Far North. All honor to them! Yet now what utter neglect it seems of the resources of modern science!

No doubt the men who have been through it best realize what a hopeless, heart-breaking quest it was, Peary's land base at Camp Columbia was only 413 miles from the Pole; yet it took him twenty-three years to traverse that 413 miles.

Curiously enough, Peary was the first man with whom I ever discussed the matter of using an airplane for polar work. That was shortly before his death, and he was enthusiastic about the project. Eight years later, in 1924, Captain Amundsen arrived in New York. He had already announced his belief that the Polar Sea could be crossed in a plane, and for those eight years my mind had not freed itself of the idea. We had a long talk and, as the result, I brought Amundsen and my father together. My father, too, became enthusiastic and agreed to buy us two flying boats. Thus the adventure began.

The island of Spitzbergen, lying just halfway between Norway and the North Pole, is ideally situated to serve as a base for Polar exploration. Besides its nearness to the Pole—ten degrees, or 600 nautical miles—a warm current, an offshoot of the Gulf Stream, follows along the western and northern coasts of the island, and has the effect of producing ice-free waters at the highest latitude in the world. These were the principal reasons which prompted Captain

Amundsen and myself to choose Spitzbergen as a base for our aeroplane flight to the Pole.

We wanted to be on the ground early in the spring and to make our flight before the summer fogs should enshroud the Polar pack and hide from view any possible landing place beneath us, for it was our intention to descend at the Pole for observations. From April 19th to August 24th (127 days) the sun never sets in the latitude of King's Bay. Spitzbergen, where we had established our base. Here one may find growing during the long summer days 110 distinct species of flowering plants and grasses. But from October 26th to February 17th is another story; the long Arctic winter is at hand and the sun never shows above the horizon. Many houses have been built along the Spitzbergen coast during the last twenty years by mining companies who annually ship about 300,000 tons of coal, and King's Bay boasts of being the most northerly habitation in the world.

May 21st, 1925, was the day we had long awaited, when, with our two Dornier-Wal flying boats we are ready to take off from the ice at King's Bay to start into the Unknown. We are carrying 7,800 pounds of dead weight in each plane. As this is 1,200 pounds above the estimated maximum lift, we are compelled to leave behind our radio equipment, which would mean an additional 300 pounds. Our provisions are sufficient to last one month, at the rate of two pounds per day per man. The daily ration list per man is:

Pemmican . . . . 400 gr.
Milk Chocolate . . . . 250"
Oatmeal Biscuits . . . . 125"
Powdered Milk . . . . 100"
Malted Milk Tablets . . . . 125"

At 4:15 P.M. all is ready for the start. The 450 H. P. Rolls-Royce motors are turned over for warming up. At five o'clock the full horse power is turned on. We move. The N 25 has Captain Amundsen as navigator. Riiser-Larsen is his pilot, and Feucht mechanic. I am navigator of N 24, with Dietrichson for pilot, and Omdal my mechanic. Six men in all.

The first two hours of our flight, after leaving Amsterdam Islands, we ran into a heavy bank of fog and rose 1,000 meters to clear it. This ascent was glorified by as beautiful a natural phenomenon as I have ever seen. Looking down into the mist, we saw a double halo in the middle of which the sun cast a perfect shadow of our plane. Evanescent and phantom-like, these two multicolored halos beckoned us enticingly into the Unknown. I recalled the ancient legend which says that the rainbow is a token that man shall not perish by water. The fog lasted until midway between latitudes eighty-two and eighty-three. Through rifts in the mist we caught glimpses of the open sea. This lasted for an hour; then, after another hour, the ocean showed, strewn with small ice floes, which indicated the fringe of the Polar pack. Then, to quote Captain Amundsen. "suddenly the mist disappeared and the entire panorama of Polar ice stretched away before our eyes—the most spectacular sheet of snow and ice ever seen by man from an aerial perspective." From our altitude we could overlook sixty

or seventy miles in any direction. The far-flung expanse was strikingly beautiful in its simplicity. There was noting to break the deadly monotony of snow and ice but a network of narrow cracks, or "leads," which scarred this white surface and was the only indication to an aerial observer of the ceaseless movement of the Polar pack. We had crossed the threshold into the Unknown! I was thrilled at the thought that never before had man lost himself with such speed—75 miles per hour—into unknown space. The silence of ages was now being broken for the first time by the roar of our motors.

Roald Amundsen.

We were but gnats in an immense void. We had lost all contacts with civilization. Time and distance suddenly seemed to count for nothing. What lay ahead was all that mattered now.

"Something hideen. Go and find it.

Go and look behind the Rangers—

Something lost behind the Ranges,

Lost and waiting for you. Go!"

On we sped for eight hours, till the sun had shifted from the west to a point directly ahead of us. By all rights we should now be at the Pole, for our dead reckoning shows that we have traveled just one thousand kilometers (six hundred miles), at seventy-five miles per hour, but shortly after leaving Amsterdam Islands we had run into a heavy northeast wind, which had been steadily driving us westward. Our fuel supply was now about half exhausted, and at this juncture, strangely enough, just ahead of us was the first open lead of water that was large enough for an aeroplane to land in that we had encountered on our whole journey north. There was nothing left now but to descend for observations to learn where we were. As Captain Amundsen's plane started to circle for a landing, his rear motor backfired and stopped, so that he finally disappeared among a lot of ice hummocks, with only one motor going.

This was at 1 A.M. on the morning of May 22nd. The lead ran east and west, meeting our course at right angles. It was an awful-looking hole. We circled for about ten minutes, looking for enough open water to land in. The lead was choked up with a chaotic mass of floating ice floes, and it looked as if some one had started to dynamite the ice pack. Ice blocks standing on edge or piled high on top of one another, hummocks and pres-sure-ridges, was all that greeted our eyes. It was like trying to land in the Grand Canyon.

We came down in a little lagoon among the ice-floes, taxied over to a huge ice-cake, and anchoring our plane to it, jumped out with our sextant and artificial horizon to find out where we were. Not knowing what to ex-pect, I carried my rifle, but after our long flight I was a bit unsteady on my legs, tumbled down into the deep snow, and chocked up the barrel. Our eyes were bloodshot and we were almost stone-deaf after listening to the unceasing roar of our motors for eight hours, and the stillness seemed intensified.

Looking around on landing, I had the feeling that nothing but death could be at home in this part of the world and that there could not possibly be any life in such an environment, when I was surprised to see a seal pop up his head beside the plane. I am sure he was as surprised as we were, for he raised himself half out of the water to inspect us and seemed not at all afraid to approach, as he came almost up to us. We had no thought of taking his life, for we expected to be off and on our ways again towards the Pole after our observation. His curiosity satisfied, he disappeared, and we never saw another sign of life in those waters during our entire stay in the ice.

Our observations showed that we had come down in Lat. 87° 44' N., Long. 10° 20' West. As our flight meridian was 12° East, where we landed was, therefore, 22° 20' off our course. This westerly drift had cost us nearly a degree in latitude and enough extra fuel to have carried us to the Pole. As it was, we were just 136 nautical miles from it. At the altitude at which we had been flying just before descending, our visible horizon was forty-six miles; which means that we had been able to see ahead as far as Lat. 88° 30' N., or to within just ninety miles of the North Pole. We had left civilization, and eight hours later we were able to view the earth within ninety miles of the goal that it had taken Peary twenty-three years to reach. Truly "the efforts of one generation may become the commonplace of the next."

When we had finished taking our observation, we began to wonder where N 25 was. We crawled up on all the high hummocks near by and with our field-glasses searched the horizon. Dietrichson remarked that perhaps Amundsen had gone on to the Pole. "It would be just like him," he said. It was not until noon, however, of the 22nd that we spotted them from an especially high hill of ice. The N 25 lay with her nose pointing into the air at an angle of forty-five degrees, among a lot of rough hummocks and against a huge cake of old blue Arctic ice about forty feet thick, three miles away. It was a rough-looking country, and the position of the N 25 was terrible to behold. To us it looked as though she had crashed into this ice.

We of the N 24 were not in too good shape where we were. We had torn the nails loose on the bottom of our plane, when we took off from King's

Bay, so that she was leaking badly; in fact, the water was now above the bottom of the petrol tanks. Also, our forward motor was disabled. In short, we were badly wrecked. Things looked so hopeless to us at that moment that it seemed as though the impossible would have to happen ever to get us out. No words so well express our mental attitude at that time as the following lines of Swinburne's:

> "From hopes cut down across a world of fears,
> We gaze with eyes too passionate for tears,
> Where Faith abides, though Hope be put to flight."

That first day, while Dietrichson and I had tried to reach the N 25, Omdal had been trying to repair the motor. We dragged our canvas canoe up over hummocks and tumbled into icy crevasses until we were thoroughly exhausted. The snow was over two to three feet deep all over the ice, and we floundered through it, never knowing what we were going to step on next. Twice Dietrichson went down between the floes and only by handing onto the canoe was he able to save himself from sinking. After half a mile of this we were forced to give up and return.

We pitched our tent on top of the ice floe, moved all our equipment out of the plane into it, and tried to make ourselves as comfortable as possible. But there was no sleep for us and very little rest during the next five days.

The airship *Norge* in flight after leaving its hangar in 1926.

Omdal was continually working on the motor, while Dietrichson and I took turns at the pump. Only by the most incessant pumping were we able to keep the water down below the gasoline tanks.

Although we had located the N 25, they did not see us till the afternoon of the second day, which was May 23rd. We had taken the small inflated balloons, which the meteorologist had given us with which to obtain data regarding the upper air strata, and after tying pieces of flannel to them set them loose. We hoped that the wind would drift them over to N 25 and so indicate to them in which direction to look for us. But the wind blew them in the wrong direction, or else they drifted too low and got tangled up in the rough ice.

Through all that first day the wind was blowing from the north and we could see quite a few patches of open water. On the second day the wind shifted to the south and the ice began to close in on us. It was as though we were in the grasp of a gigantic claw that was slowly but surely contracting. We had a feeling that soon we would be crushed.

On the third day, May 24th, the temperature was -11.5 c., and we had trouble with our pump freezing. The two planes were now slowly drifting together, and we established a line of communication, so that we knew each other's positions pretty well. It is tedious work, semaphoring, for it requires two men: one with the flag, and the other with a pair of field-glasses to read the signals. It took us a whole hour merely to signal our positions, after which we must wait for their return signals and then reply to them.

On this day, after an exchange of signals, we decided to try to reach Amundsen. We packed our canvas canoe, put it on our sledge, and started across what looked to us like mountainous hummocks. After only going a few hundred yards we had to give up. The labor was too exhausting. With no sleep for three days, and only liquid food, our strength was not what it should have been. Leaving our canvas canoe, we now made up our packs of fifty pounds each, and pushed on. We may or we may not return to our plane again.

According to my diary we traveled the first two miles in two hours and fifteen minutes, when we came upon a large lead that separated us from the

N 25 and which we could see no way to cross. We talked to them by signal and they advised our returning. So, after a seven-hour trip, we returned to our sinking plane, having covered perhaps five and one half miles in about the same length of time it had taken us to fly from Spitzbergen to Lat. 87.44. Arriving at our plane, we pitched camp again and cooked a heavy pemmican soup over our Primus stove. Dietrichson gave us a surprise by producing a small tin of George Washington coffee. We took some of the pure alcohol carried for the Primus stove and put it into the coffee, and with pipes lighted felt more or less happy.

As we smoked in silence, each with his own thoughts, Dietrichson suddenly clasped his hands to his eyes, exclaiming: "Something is the matter with my eyes!" He was snow-blind, but never having experienced this before, did not know what had happened to him. We had been careful to wear our snow-glasses during most of the journey, but perhaps not quite careful enough. After bandaging Dietrichson's eyes, Omdal and I put him to bed and then continued with our smoking and thoughts. It seems strange, when I think back now, that during those days nothing that happened greatly surprised us. Everything that happened was accepted as part of the day's work. This is an interesting sidelight on man's adaptability to his environment.

All our energies were now being bent in getting the N 24 onto the ice floe, for we knew she would be crushed if we left her in the lead. The whole cake we were on was only about 200 meters in diameter, and there was only one level stretch on it of eighty meters. It was laborious work for Dietrichson and myself to try to clear the soggy wet snow, for all we had to work with was one clumsy home-made wooden shovel and our ice-anchor. As I would loosen the snow by picking at it with the anchor, Dietrichson would shovel it away.

Looking through our glasses at N 25, we could see the propellers going, and Amundsen pulling up and down on the wings, trying to loosen the plane from the ice, but she did not budge. On the morning of May 26th, Amundsen signaled to us that if we couldn't save our plane to come over and help them. We had so far succeeded in getting the nose of our plane up onto the ice-cake, but with only one engine working it was impossible to do more. Anyway, she was safe now from sinking, but not from being crushed, should the ice press in on her. During the five days of our separation the ice had so shifted that the two planes were now plainly in sight of each other and only half a mile apart. During all that time the ice had been in continual movement, so that now all the heavy ice had moved out from between the two camps. We signaled to the N 25 that we were coming, and making up loads of eighty pounds per man, we started across the freshly frozen lead that separated us from our companions. We were well aware of the chances we were taking, crossing this new ice, but we saw no other alternative. We must get over to N 25 with all possible speed if we were ever to get back again to civilization.

With our feet shoved loosely into our skis, for we never fastened them on here for fear of getting tangled up, should we fall into the sea, we shuffled along, slowly feeling our way over the thin ice. Omdal was in the lead, myself and Dietrichson—who had recovered from his slight attack of snowblindness the next day—following in that order. Suddenly I heard Dietrichson yelling behind me, and before I knew what it was all about Omdal ahead of me cried out also and disappeared as though the ice beneath him had suddenly opened and swallowed him. The ice under me started to sag, and I quickly jumped sideways to avoid the same fate that had overtaken my companions. There just happened to be some old ice beside me and that was what saved me. Lying down on my stomach, partly on this ledge of old ice, and partly out on the new ice, I reached the skis out and pulled Dietrichson over to where I could grab his pack and partly pull him out onto the firmer ice, where he lay panting and exhausted. Then I turned my attention to Omdal. Only his pallid face showed above the water. It is strange, when I think that both these Norwegians had been conversing almost wholly in their native tongue, that Omdal was now crying in English, "I'm gone! I'm gone!"—and he was almost gone too. The only thing that kept him from going way under was the fact that he kept digging his fingers into the ice. I reached him just in time to pull him over to the firmer ice. I reached him just before he sank and held him by his pack until Dietrichson could crawl over to me and hold him up, while

I cut off the pack. It took all the remaining strength of the two of us to drag Omdal up onto the old ice.

Our companions could not reach us, neither could they see us, as a few old ice hummocks of great size stood directly in front of N 25. They could do nothing but listen to the agonizing cries of their fellowmen in distress. We finally succeeded in getting over to our companions, who gave us dry clothes and hot chocolate, and we were soon all right again, except for Omdal's swollen and lacerated hands. Both men had lost their skis. In view of the probability of being forced to tramp to Greenland, four hundred miles away, the loss of these skis seemed a calamity.

I was surprised at the change only five days had wrought in Captain Amundsen. He seemed to me to have aged ten years. We now joined with our companions in the work of freeing the N 25 from her precarious position. As stated before, when Captain Amundsen's plane had started to come down into the lead, his rear motor back-fired, and he was forced to land with only one motor working, which accounted for the position which we now found N 25 in. She lay half on and half off an ice floe; her nose was up on the cake and her tail down in the sea. Coming down thus had reduced her speed and saved her from crashing into the cake of old blue ice, which was directly ahead. It seemed amazing that whereas five days ago the N 25 had found enough open water to land in, now there was not enough to be seen anywhere sufficient to launch a rowboat in. She was tightly locked in the grip of the shifting ice.

A most orderly routine was being enforced at Amundsen's camp. Regular hours for everything—to work, sleep, eat, smoke and talk; no need to warn these men, as so many explorers had been compelled to do, not to give one another the story of their lives, lest boredom come. These Norwegians have their long periods of silence in which the glance of an eye or the movement of a hand takes the place of conversation. This, no doubt, accounts for the wonderful harmony that existed during the whole twenty-five days of our imprisonment in the ice. One might expect confusion and disorganization under the conditions confronting us. But it was just the reverse. We did everything as if we had oceans of time in which to do it. It was this calm, cool, and unhurried way of doing things which kept our spirits up and eventually got us out of a desperate situation. No one ever got depressed or blue.

We elected Omdal our cook. Although we felt better nourished and stronger after our noon cup pemmican broth, it was always our morning and evening cup of chocolate that we looked forward to most. How warming and cheering that hot draught was! Captain Amundsen remarked that the only time we were happy up there was when either the hot choclate was going down our throats, or else when we were rolled up in our reindeer sleeping bags. The rest of the time we were more or less miserable, but never do I remember a time when we ever lost faith! The after-compartment of our plane—a gaunt hole—served as kitchen, dining-room and sleeping-quarters, but it was draughty and uncomfortable, and it seemed always a relief to get out into the open again after our meals. The cold duralumin metal overhead was coated with hoarfrost which turned into a steady drip as the heat from our little Primus stove, together with that from our steaming chocolate, started to warm up the cabin. Feucht always sat opposite me—I say sat, but he squatted—we all squatted on the bottom of the plane with our chocolate on our knees. I remember how I used to covertly watch him eating his three oatmeal wafers and drinking his chocolate. I always tried to hold mine back so as not to finish before him. I had the strange illusion that if I finished first it was because he was getting more to eat than I. I particularly recall one occasion, two weeks later, after we had cut our rations in half, when I purposely hid my last biscuit in the folds of my parka, and the satisfaction it gave me to draw it out and eat it after Feucht had laid his cup aside. It was the stirring of those primitive instincts which, hidden beneath the veneer of our civilization, lie ever ready to assert themselves upon reversion to primitive conditions. We smoked a pipe apiece of tobacco after each meal, but unfortunately we had taken only a few days' supply of smoking stuff. When that went, we had to resort to Riiser-Larsen's private stock of rank, black chewing twist. It took a real hero to smoke that tobacco after moistening it so as to make it burn slower and thus hold out longer. It always gave us violent hiccoughs.

We were compelled to give up our civilized habits of washing or changing our clothes. It was too cold to undress, and we could not spare the fuel to heat any water after our necessary cooking was done.

During all our stay in the ice I never saw Captain Amundsen take a drink of water. I was always thirsty after the pemmican, and when I called for water, he said he could not understand how I could drink so much water.

Captain Amundsen and I slept together in the pilot's cockpit, which we covered over with canvas to darken it at night. I was never able to get used to the monotony of continuous daylight and found it very wearing. With the exception of Riiser-Larsen the rest of the men slept on their skis stretched across the rear-compartment to keep them off the metal bottom. Riiser-Larsen had the tail all to himself, into which he was compelled to crawl on hands and knees.

It took us a whole day to construct a slip and work our plane up onto the ice-cake. The work was exhausting on our slim rations, and, besides, we had only the crudest of implements with which to work: three wooden shovels, a two-pound pocket safety-ax, and an ice anchor. Through hopeless necessity we lashed our sheath-knives to the end of our ski-sticks, with which we slashed at the ice. It is remarkable, when one considers the scant diet and the work we accomplished with these implements! Captain Amundsen conservatively estimates that we moved three hundred tons of ice during the twenty-five days of our imprisonment up there in order to free our plane.

The floe we were on measured 300 meters in diameter, but we needed a 400-meter course from which to take off. Our best chance, of course, would be to take off in open water, but the wind continued to blow from the south, and the south wind did not make for open water.

Riiser-Larsen was tireless in his search for an ice floe of the right dimensions. While the rest of us were relaxing, he was generally to be seen on the sky-line searching with that tireless energy that was so characteristic of him. Silent and resourceful, he was the rock on which we were building our hopes.

The incessant toil went on. On May 28th the N 25 was safe from the screwing of the pack-ice. On this day we took two soundings, which gave us a depth of 3,750 meters (12,375 feet) of the Polar Sea. This depth corresponds almost exactly to the altitude of Mont Blanc above the village of Chamonix. Up to this time our only thought had been to free the plane and continue on to the Pole, but now, facing the facts as they confronted us, it seemed inadvisable to consider anything else but a return to Spitzbergen. The thermometer during these days registered between −9° c. and −11° c.

On May 29th Dietrichson, Omdal and I, by a circuitous route, were able to reach the N 24 with our canvas canoe and sledge. We must get the remaining gasoline and provisions. Our only hope of reaching Spitzbergen lay in salvaging this fuel from the N 24. We cut out one of the empty tanks, filled it from one of the fresh ones, loaded it in our canoe, put the canoe on the sledge and started back. And now we found that a large lead had opened up behind us, over which we were barely able to get across ourselves, so we had to leave the tank and supplies on the further side over night. The next day the lead had closed again and Dietrichson and Omdal succeeded in getting the gasoline over. The light sledge got slightly broken among the rough hummocks, which was an additional catastrophe, in view of the probability of having to walk to Greenland.

We now had 245 liters additional fuel,—1,500 liters altogether,—or a margin of 300 liters on which to make Spitzbergen, provided we could get off immediately.

On May 31st an inventory of our provisions showed that we had on hand:

285 half-pound cakes of pemmican,

300 cakes of chocolate,

3 ordinary cracker-tins of oatmeal biscuits,

3 20-lb. sacks of powdered milk,

3 sausages, 12 lbs. each,

42 condensed milk tins of Horlick's Malted Milk Tablets,

25 liters of kerosene for our Primus stove (we later used motor fuel for cooking).

Our observations for Latitude and Longitude this day showed our position to be 87.32 N. and 7.30 W. It meant that the whole pack had been steadily drifting southeast since our arrival. It was at least some consolation to know that we were slowly but surely drifting south, where we knew there was game. How we should have liked to have had that seal we saw the first day! We had seen no life of any description since, neither in the water nor in the air, not even a track on the snow to show that there was another living thing in these latitudes but ourselves. It is a land of misery and death.

With a view to working the longest possible time in an attempt to get the N 25 clear, and at the same time having sufficient provisions left with which to reach Greenland, Captain Amundsen felt that it was necessary to cut down our daily rations to 300 grams per man, or just one half pound per man per day. This amounted to one-half the ration that Peary fed his dogs a day on his journey to the Pole. By thus reducing our rations, he figured that our provisions would last for two months longer.

Captain Amundsen now set June 15th as the date upon which a definite decision must be arrived at. On that date something must be done; so a vote was taken, each man having the option of either starting on foot for Greenland on that date, or else sticking by the plane with the hope of open water coming while watching the food dwindle. There was much divided opinion. It seemed absurd to consider starting out on a long tramp when right by our side was 640 horse power lying idle, which could take us back to civilization within eight hours. Captain Amundsen was for staying by the plane. He said with the coming of summer the leads would open. Riiser-Larsen said he would start walking on June 15th. Feucht said he would not walk a foot and that he would stick by the motors. Omdal said he would do what the majority did, and I said I would prefer to wait until June 14th before making a decision.

My own mind was pretty well made up that if I ever succeeded in traveling 100 miles towards Greenland on foot, I would be doing well. Yet sitting down by the plane and watching the last of the food go was a thing that ran counter to my every impulse. I agreed with Captain Amundsen that I should much prefer to "finish it" on my feet. I think that all really believed that in our worn-our condition, carrying thirty pounds on our backs and dragging a canvas canoe along with which to cross open leads, none of us would be able to reach the Greenland coast.

Most of our doubt regarding the tramp to Greenland, of course, came from our not knowing just how far the bad country that we were in extended. Climb up as high as we could, we were never able to see the end of it. Whether it extended to Greenland or not was the question, and that was what made it so hard for us to decide what course to take.

After our evening cup of chocolate Captain Amundsen and I generally would put on our skis and take a few turns around the ice floe we were on before turning into our sleeping-bags. I usually asked him on these occasions what he thought of the situation. His reply was that things looked pretty bad, but he was quick to add that it had always been his experience in life that when things were blackest, there was generally light ahead.

On May 31st there was eight inches of ice in the lead on the far side of the floe we were on. We decided to try a take-off on this new ice. From our ice-cake down into the lead there was a six-foot drop, so that it was necessary to construct a slip upon which to get our plane down into the lead. We built this slip in accordance with standard road-making principles—first heavy blocks of ice, then filling in on top with smaller pieces, and then tiny lumps and loose snow, on top of which we spread a layer of loose snow which froze into a smooth surface. It took us two days to build this slip and to level off the ice ahead for 500 meters.

At this time we had established regular nightly patrols, each man taking his turn at patrolling all night around and around the ice floe, on his skis, looking for open water. The mental strain during this period was terrific, for we never knew when the cake we were on might break beneath us.

On June 2nd, at 5 P.M., we decided that our slip was worthy a trial. We started up the motors and taxied across the floe and down the slip, but we had built our slip too steep, and, therefore, not having enough speed, the plane simply sagged through the ice and for 1,000 meters we merely plowed through it. We shut off the motors and prepared to spend the night in the lead.

At midnight I was awakened by Captain Amundsen yelling that the plane was being crushed. I could plainly hear the pressure against the metal sides. We lost no time in getting everything out onto some solid ice near by, and by working the plane up and down permitted the incoming ice to close in beneath her from both sides. It was a narrow escape. We had expected the plane to be crushed like an egg shell. Riiser-Larsen's only comment after the screwing stopped was, "Another chapter to be added to our look!" Before morning our first heavy fog set in. The Artic summer was upon us. From then or the fog hung like a pall over us and for the remainder of our stay in the Arctic we were never free from it, although we were always able to see the rim or the sum through it and knew that above it the sky was clear and the sun shining brightly, but we could not rise into it. With the coming of the fog the temperature rose to freezing.

We were gradually working our way over toward where the N 24 was lying. During the day we would level off a new course, but there was not sufficient wind in which to rise, and as usual our heavily loaded plane broke through the thin ice,—

"Trailing like a wounded duck, working out her soul.
Felt her lift and felt her sag, betted when she'd break;
Wondered every time she raced if she'd stand the shock."

The N 25 started leaking so badly from the pressure she received the other night that Captain Amundsen and I were obliged to pitch our tent on the floe upon which the N 24 was resting. We were wondering how much more she could stand. N 24 still lay with her nose on the ice floe, as we left her, but she had now listed sideways, so that the tip of one wing was firmly imbedded in the freshly frozen ice around her. During the past few days the ice had been freezing in from both sides, forming a long, narrow lane in front of N 24, but parts of this lane have bent into a curve. It was a narrow, crooked passage, but Riiser-Larsen felt that it offered one more opportunity for a take-off. He taxied N 25 forward, narrowly escaping an accident. As he slowed up to negotiate the curve, the nose broke through the ice with the reduced speed. The plane suddenly stopped and lifted its tail into the air. We jumped out and hacked away the ice until the plane settled on an even keel. We dared not remain where we were because the main body of the pack was fast closing in upon us from both sides.

At two o'clock the next morning we commenced work on an extension of our previous course and continued on throughout the day and on into the following night. It was a tremendous task, as the ice was covered with tightly frozen lumps, old pressure-ridges of uptilted ice cakes. Hacking away with our shot-handled pocket-ax and ice anchor was such back-breaking work that we were compelled to work on our knees most of the time. The sweat was rolling down my face and blurred my snow-glasses, so that I was compelled to take them off for a couple of hours. I paid the penalty by becoming snow-blind in one eye. Dietrichson was not so fortunate. He was badly attacked in both eyes, and had to lie in the tent in his sleeping-bag for two days with his eyes bandaged and suffering acutely from the intense inflammation.

We awoke on the morning of June 5th, tired and stiff, to look upon the level track we had so frantically labored to prepare, but saw in its place a jumbled mass of upturned ice blocks. With the destruction of our fourth course our position was no desperate. But we would hang on till the 15th, when the vital decision would have to be made as to whether or not we should abandon N 25 and make for the Greenland coast while there were yet sufficient provisions left. But we had come here on wings, and I know we all felt only wings could take us back to civilization. If we could only find a floe of sufficient area from which to take off. That was our difficulty.

In the early morning of June 6th Riiser-Larsen and Omdal started out into the heavy fog with the grim determination of men who find themselves in deperate straits, to search for what seemed to us all the unattainable. We saw no more of them till evening. Out of the fog they came, and we knew by their faces, before they uttered a word, that they had good news. Yes, they had found a floe! They had been searching through the fog, stumbling through the rough country. Suddenly the sun broke through and lit up one end of a floe, as Riiser-Larsen puts it, which became our salvation. It was a half mile off, and it would be necessary to build a slip to get out of the lead and bridge two ice cakes before reaching the desired floe.

The main body of the pack was now only ten yards away. Immediately behind the N 25 a huge ice wall was advancing slowly, inch by inch, and fifteen minutes after we started the motors the solid ice closed in over the spot where our plane had lain. We were saved.

We worked our way slowly up to where we meant to build the slip, using a saw to cut out the ice ahead where it was too heavy for the plane to break through. After six hours of steady toil we had constructed our slip and had the plane safe up on floe No. 1. That night of June 6th we slept well, after the extra cup of chocolate that was allowed us to celebrate our narrow escape.

The next morning began the most stupendous task we had yet undertaken: cutting a passage through a huge pressure-ridge,—an ice wall fifteen feet thick which separated floe No. 1 from floe No. 2,—and then bridging between floe No. 1 and floe No. 2 two chasms fifteen feet wide and ten feet deep, separating the two floes from one another. In our weakened condition this was a hard task, but we finished it by the end of the second day. Crossing the bridges between the floes was exciting work. The sustaining capacity of such ice blocks as we could manage to transport and lay in the water could not be great. The heavier blocks which we used for a foundation were floated into place in the sea and left to freeze—as we hoped they would—into a solid mass during the night. When the time came, we must cross at full speed, if we were not to sink into the sea, and then instantly stop on the other side, because we had taken no time to level ahead, so great was our fear that the ice floes might drift apart during the operation of bridging. We made the passages safely and were at last upon the big floe. In order to take advantage of the south wind, which had continued to blow ever since the day of our landing, we leveled a course across the shortest diameter of this cake, which offered only 300 meters for a take-off. But before we completed our work the wind died down. Nevertheless we made a try, but merely bumped over it and stopped just short of the open lead ahead. Our prospects did not look good. The southerly winds had made the deep snow soft and soggy. But it was a relief to know that we were out of the leads, with our plane safe from the screwing of the pack-ice.

It was June 9th, and now began the long grind of constructing a course upon which our final hopes must rest. If we failed there was nothing left. My diary shows the following entry for June 10th:—"The days go by. For the first time I am beginning to wonder if we must make the great sacrifice for our great adventure. The future looks so hopeless. Summer is on. The snows are getting too soft to travel over and the leads won't open in this continually shifting ice."

Riiser-Larsen looked the ground over and decided that we must remove the two and a half feet of snow right down to the solid ice and level a track twelve meters wide and four hundred meters long. It was a heartbreaking task to remove this wet summer snow with only our clumsy wooden shovels. It must be thrown clear an additional six meters to either side, so as not to interfere with the wing stretch. After but a few shovelfuls we stood weak and panting gazing disheartened at the labor ahead.

One problem was how to taxi our plane through the wet snow and get it headed in the right direction. We dug down to the blue ice, and now we were confronted with a new difficulty. The moist fog, which came over us immediately, melted the ice as soon as it was exposed. We found that by working our skis underneath the plane we were able finally to get her to turn, but after splitting a pair of skis we decided to take no more chances that way. In desperation we now tried stamping down the snow with our feet and found that it served the purpose admirably. By the end of our first day of shoveling down to the blue ice, we had succeeded in clearing a distance of only forty meters, while with the new method we were able to make one hundred meters per day. We adopted a regular system in stamping down this snow. Each man marked out a square of his own, and it was up to him to stamp down every inch in this area. We figured that at this rate we would have completed our course in five days.

During the first day's work we saw our first sign of animal life since the seal popped his head up out of the lead where we first landed. Somebody looked up from his work of shoveling snow to see a little auk flying through the fog overhead. It came out of the north and was headed northwest. Next day two weary geese flopped down beside the plane. They must have thought that dark object looming up through the fog in all that expanse of desolate white looked friendly. They seemed an easy mark for Dietrichson, but the rich prize was too much for his nerves and he missed. The two geese ran over the snow a long distance as if they did not seem anxious to take wing again. The coo came from the north and disappeared into the northwest. We wondered if there could be land in that direction. It was an interesting speculation.

On the 14th our course was finished. Then Riiser-Larsen paced it again and was surprised to find that instead of four hundred meters it was five hundred. When he informed Amundsen of this fact, the Captain was quick to remark that one million dollars couldn't buy that extra hundred meters from him, and we all agreed that it was priceless. And so it proved to be.

On the evening of the 14th, after our chocolate, and with a southerly wind still blowing—this was a tail-wind on this course and of no help to us—we decided to make a try. But we only bumped along and the plane made no effort to rise. What we needed to get off with was a speed of 100 kilometers per hour. During all our previous attempts to take off, forty kilometers had been the best we could do. On this trial we got up to sixty, and Riiser-Larsen was hopeful. It was characteristic of the man to turn in his seat as we jumped out and remark to me: "I hope you are not disappointed, Ellsworth. We'll do better next time." That calm, dispassionate man was ever the embodiment of hope.

That night it was my watch all night. Around and around the ice-cake I shuffled, with my feet thrust loosely into the ski straps and a rifle slung over my shoulder, on the alert for open water. Then, too, we were always afraid that the ice-cake might break beneath us. It was badly crevassed in places. Many times during that night, on my patrol, I watched Riiser-Larsen draw himself up out of the manhole in the top of the plane to see how the wind was blowing. During the night the wind had shifted from the south and in the morning a light breeze was blowing from the north. This was the second time during our twenty-five days in the ice that the wind had blown from the north. We had landed with a north wind—but were we to get away with a north wind? That was the question. The temperature during the night was—1.5° c. and the snow surface was crisp and hard in the morning. We now were forced to dump everything that we could spare. We left one of our canvas canoes, rifles, cameras, field-glasses; we even discarded sealskin parkas and heavy ski-boots, replacing them with moccasins. All we dare retain was half of our provisions, one canvas canoe, a shotgun and one hundred rounds of ammunition.

Then we all climbed into the plane and Riiser-Larsen started up. Dietrichson was to navigate. The plane began to move! After bumping for four hundred meters the plane actually lifted in the last hundred meters. When I could feel the plane lifting beneath me I was happy, but we had had so many cruel disappointments during the past twenty-five days that our minds were in a state where we could feel neither greater elation nor great suffering. Captain Amundsen had taken his seat beside Riiser-Larsen, and I got into the tail.

For two hours we had to fly through the thick fog, being unable either to get above to below it. During all this time we flew slowly, with a magnetic compass, a thing heretofore considered to be an impossibility in the Arctic. Dietrichson dropped down for drift observations as frequently as possible. The fogs hung so low that we were compelled to fly close to the ice, at one time skimming over it at a height of but one hundred feet. Finally we were able to rise above the fog and were again able to use our "Sun Compass."

Southward we flew! Homeward we flew! One hour—two hours—four, six hours. Then Feucht yelled back to me in the tail. "Land!" I replied, "Spitzbergen?"—"No Spitzbergen, no Spitzbergen!" yells back Feucht in his broken English. So I made up my mind that it must be Franz-Josefs-Land. Anyway, it was land, and that meant everything!

Our rationing regulations were now off, and we all started to munch chocolate and biscuits.

For an hour Riiser-Larsen had noticed that the stabilization rudders were becoming more and more difficult to operate. Finally they failed to work completely and we were forced down on the open sea, just after having safely passed the edge of the Polar pack. We landed in the sea, after flying just eight hours, with barely ninety liters of gasoline in our tanks, one half hour's fuel supply. The sea was rough, and we were forced to go below and cover up the man-holes, for the waves broke over the plane

I had eaten seven cakes of chocolate when Feucht yelled, "Land ahead!" But I was now desperately ill and cared little what land it was so long as it was just land. After thirty-five minutes of taxi-ing through the rough sea, we reached the coast.

In we came—"in the wash of the wind-whipped tide."

"Overloaded, undermanned, meant to founder, we Euchred God Almighty's storm, bluffed the Eternal Sea!"

How good the solid land looked! We threw ourselves down on a large rock, face upward to the sun, till we remembered that we had better take an observation and know for sure where we were.

It seems remarkable, when I think about it now, how many narrow escapes we really had. Again and again it looked like either life or death, but something always just turned up to help us out. Caption Amundsen's answer was, "You can call it luck if you want, but I don't believe it."

We got out our sextant and found that one of our position lines cut through the latitude of Spitzbergen. While we were waiting to take our second observation for an intersection, three hours later, some one yelled, "A sail!"—and there, heading out to sea, was a little sealer. We shouted after them and put up our flag, but they did not see us, and so we jumped into our plane and with what fuel we had left taxied out to them. They were after a wounded walrus that they had shot seven times in the head, otherwise they would have been gone long before. They were over-joyed to see us. We tried to tow the plane, but there was too much headwind, so we beached her in Brandy Bay, North Cape, North-East-Land, Spitzbergen, one hundred miles east of our starting point at King's Bay.

We slept continuously during the three days in the sealer, only waking to devour the delicious seal meat steaks smothered in onions and the eider-duck egg omelets prepared for us.

The homage that was accorded us upon our return to civilization will ever remain the most cherished memory of our trip. We took steamer from King's Bay for Norway on June 25th, after putting our plane on board, and nine days later arrived at Horten, the Norwegian Naval Base, not far from Oslo.

On July 5th, with the stage all set, we flew N 25 into Oslo. It was difficult to realize that we were in the same plane that had so recently been battling in the midst of the Arctic ice. Good old N 25! We dropped down into the Fjord amid a pandemonium of frantically shrieking river craft and taxied on through he wildly waving and cheering throngs, past thirteen fully manned British battleships, and as I listened to the booming of the salute from the Fort and looked ahead at the great silent expectant mass of humanity that waited to greet us, I was overcome with emotion and the tears rolled down my face. At that moment I felt paid in full for all that I had gone through.

CHAPTER 4

CHILOE AND CONCEPCION

By Charles Darwin

Photograph of Charles Darwin taken around 1874 by Leonard Darwin.

On January the 15th we sailed from Low's Harbour, and three days afterwards anchored a second time in the bay of S.Carlos in Chiloe. On the night of the 19th the volcano of Osorno was in action. At midnight the sentry observed something like a large star, which gradually increased in size till about three o'clock, when it presented a very magnificent spectacle. By the aid of a glass, dark objects, in constant succession, were seen, in the midst of a great glare of red light, to be thrown up and to fall down. The light was sufficient to cast on the water a long bright reflection. Large masses of molten matter seem very commonly to be cast out of the craters in this part of the Cordillera. I was assured that when the Corcovado is in eruption, great masses are projected upwards and are seen to burst in the air, assuming many fantastical forms, such as trees: their size must be immense, for they can be distinguished from the high land behind S. Carlos, which is no less than ninety-three miles from the Corcovado. In the morning the volcano became tranquil.

I was surprised at hearing afterwards that Aconcagua in Chile, 480 miles northwards, was in action on the same night; and still more surprised to hear that the great eruption of Coseguina (2700 miles north of Aconcagua), accompanied by an earthquake felt over a 1000 miles, also occurred within six hours of this same time. This coincidence is the more remarkable, as Coseguina had been dormant for twenty-six years; and Aconcagua most rarely shows any signs of action. It is difficult even to conjecture whether this coincidence was accidental, or shows some subterranean connection. If Vesuvius, Etna, and Hecla in Iceland (all three relatively nearer each other than the corresponding points in South America), suddenly burst forth in eruption on the same night, the coincidence would be thought remarkable; but it is far more remarkable in this case, where the three vents fall on the same great mountain-chain, and where the vast plains along the entire eastern coast, and the upraised recent shells along more than 2000 miles on the western coast, show in how equable and connected a manner the elevatory forces have acted.

Captain Fitz Roy being anxious that some bearings should be taken on the outer coast of Chiloe, it was planned that Mr. King and myself should ride to Castro, and thence across the island to the Capellade Cucao, situated on the west coast. Having hired horses and a guide, we set out on the morning of the 22nd. We had not proceeded far, before we were joined by a woman and two boys, who were bent on the same journey. Every one on this road acts on a "hail fellow well met" fashion; and one may here enjoy the privilege, so rare in South America, of traveling without firearms. At first, the country consisted of a succession of hills and valleys: nearer to Castro it became very level. The road itself is a curious affair; it consists in its whole length, with the exception of very few parts, of great logs of wood, which are either broad and laid longitudinally, or narrow and placed transversely. In summer the road is not very bad; but in winter, when the wood is rendered slippery from rain, traveling is exceedingly difficult. At that time of the year, the ground on each side becomes a morass, and is often overflowed: hence it is necessary that the longitudinal logs should be fastened down by transverse poles, which are pegged on each side into the earth. These pegs render a fall from a horse dangerous, as the chance of alighting on one of them is not small. It is remarkable, however, how active custom has made the Chilotan horses. In crossing bad parts, where the logs had been displaced, they skipped from one to the other, almost with the quickness and certainty of a dog. On both hands the road is bordered by the lofty forest-trees, with their bases matted together by canes. When occasionally a long reach of this avenue could be beheld, it presented a curious scene of uniformity: the white line of logs, narrowing in perspective, became hidden by the gloomy forest, or terminated in a zigzag which ascended some steep hill.

Although the distance from S. Carlos to Castro is only twelve leagues in a straight line, the formation of the road must have been a great labour. I was told that several people had formerly lost their lives in attempting to cross the forest. The first who succeeded was an Indian, who cut his way through the canes in eight days, and reached S. Carlos: he was rewarded by the Spanish government with a grant of land. During the summer, many of the Indians wander about the forests (but chiefly in the higher parts, where the woods are not quite so thick) in search of the half-wild cattle which live on the leaves of the cane and certain trees. It was one of these huntsmen who by chance discovered, a few years since, an English vessel, which had been wrecked on the outer coast. The crew beginning to fail in provisions, and it is not probable that, without the aid of this man, they would ever have extricated themselves from these scarcely penetrable woods. As it was, one seaman died on the march, from fatigue. The Indians in these excursions steer by the sun; so that if there is a continuance of cloudy weather, they can not travel.

The day was beautiful, and the number of trees which were in full flower perfumed the air; yet even this could hardly dissipate the effects of the gloomy dampness of the forest. Moreover, the many dead trunks that stand like skeletons, never fail to give to these primeval woods a character of solemnity, absent in those of countries long civilized. Shortly after sunset we bivouacked for the night. Our female companion, who was rather good-looking, belonged to one of the most respectable families in Castro: she rode, however, astride, and without shoes or stockings. I was surprised at the total want of pride shown by her and her brother. They brought food with them, but at all out meals sat watching Mr. King and myself whilst eating, till we were fairly shamed into feeding the whole party. The night was cloudless; and while lying in our beds, we enjoyed the sight (and it is a high enjoyment) of the multitude of stars which illumined the darkness of the forest.

January 23rd.—We rose early in the morning, and reached the pretty quiet town of Castro by o' clock. The old governor had died since our last visit, and a Chileno was acting in his place. We had a letter of introduction to Don Pedro, whom we found exceedingly hospitable and kind, and more disinterested than is usual on this side of the continent. The next day Don Pedro procured us fresh horses, and offered to accompany us himself. We proceeded to the south—generally following the coast, and passing through several hamlets, each with its large barn-like chapel built of wood. At Vilipilli, Don Pedro asked the commandant to give us a guide to Cucao. The old gentleman offered to come himself; but for a long time nothing would persuade him that two Englishmen really wished to go to such an out-of-the—way place as Cucao. We were thus accompanied by the two greatest aristocrats in the country, as was plainly to be seen in the manner of all the poorer Indians towards them. At Chonchi we struck across the island, following intricate winding paths, sometimes passing through magnificent forests, and sometimes through pretty cleared spots, abounding with corn and potato crops. This undulating woody country, partially cultivated, reminded me of the wilder parts of England, and therefore had to my eye a most fascinating aspect. At Vilinco, which is situated on the borders of the lake of Cucao, only a few fields were cleared; and all the inhabitants appeared to be Indians. This lake is twelve miles long, and runs in an east and west direction. From local circumstances, the sea-breeze blows very regularly during the day, and during the night it falls calm: this has given rise to strange exaggerations, for the phenomenon, as described to us at S. Carlos, was quite a prodigy.

The road to Cucao was so very bad that we determined to embark in a periagua. The commandant, in the most authoritative manner, ordered six Indians to get ready to pull us over, without deigning to tell them whether they would be paid. The periagua is a strange rough boat, but the crew were still stranger. I doubt if six uglier little men ever got into a boat together. They pulled, however, very well and cheerfully. The stroke-oarsman gabbled Indian, and uttered strange cries, much after the fashion of a pig-driver driving his pigs. We started with a light breeze against us, but yet reached the Capella de Cucao before it was late. The country on each side of the lake was one unbroken forest. In the same periagua with us, a cow was embarked. To get so large an animal into a small boat appears at first a difficulty, but the Indians managed it in a minute. They brought the cow along side the boat, which was heeled towards her; then placing two oars under her belly, with their ends resting on the gunwale, by the aid of these levers they fairly tumbled the poor beast heels over head into the bottom of the boat, and then lashed her down with ropes. At Cucao we found an uninhabited hovel (which is the residence of the padre when he pays this Capella a visit), where, lighting a fire, we cooked our supper, and were very comfortable.

The district of Cucao is the only inhabited part on the whole west coast of Chiloe. It contains about thirty or forty Indian families, who are scattered along four or five miles of the shore. They are very much secluded from the rest of Chiloe, and have scarcely any sort of commerce except sometimes in a little oil, which they get from seal-blubber. They are tolerably dressed in clothes of their own manufacture, and they have plenty to eat. They seemed, however, discontented, yet humble to a degree which it was quite painful to witness. These feelings are, I think, chiefly to be attributed to the harsh and authoritative manner in which they are treated by their rulers. Our companions, although so very civil to us, behaved to the poor Indians as if they had been slaves, rather than free men. They ordered provisions and the use of their horses, without ever condescending to say how much, or indeed whether the owners should be paid at all. In the morning, being left alone with these poor people, we soon ingratiated ourselves by presents of cigars and mate. A lump of white sugar was divided between all present, and tasted with the greatest curiosity. The Indians ended all their complaints by saying, "And it is only because we are poor Indians, and know nothing; but it was not so when we had a King."

The next day after breakfast, we rode a few miles northward to Punta Huantamo. The road lay along a very broad beach, on which, even after so many fine days, a terrible surf was breaking. I was assured that after a heavy gale, the roar can be heard at night even at Castro, a distance of no less than twenty-one sea-miles across a hilly and wooded country. We had some difficulty in reaching the point, owing to the intolerably bad paths; for everywhere in the shade the ground soon becomes a perfect quagmire. The point itself is a bold rocky hill. It is covered by a plant allied, I believe, to Bromelia, and called by the inhabitants Chepones. In scrambling through the beds, our hands were very much scratched. I was amused by observing the precaution our Indian guide took, in turning up his trousers, thinking that they were more delicate than his own hard skin. This plant bears a fruit, in shape like an artichoke, in which a number of seed-vessels are packed: these contain a pleasant sweet pulp, here much esteemed. I saw at Low's Harbour the Chilotans making chichi, or cider, with this fruit: so true is it, as Humboldt remarks, that almost everywhere man finds means of preparing some kind of beverage from the vegetable kingdom. The savages, however, of Tierra del Fuego, and I believe of Australia, have not advanced thus far in the arts.

The coast to the north of Punta Huantamo is exceedingly rugged and broken, and is fronted by many breakers, on which the sea is eternally roaring. Mr. King and myself were anxious to return, if it had been possible, on foot along this coast; but even the Indians said it was quite impracticable. We were told that men have crossed by striking directly through the woods from Cucao to S. Carlos, but never by the coast. On these expeditions, the Indians carry with them only roasted corn, and of this they eat sparingly twice a day.

January 26th.—Re-embarking in the periagua, we returned across the lake, and then mounted our horses. The whole of Chiloe took advantage of this week of unusually fine weather, to clear the ground by burning. In every direction volumes of smoke were curling upwards. Although the inhabitants were so assiduous in setting fire to every part of the wood, yet I did not see a single fire which they had succeeded in making extensive. We dined with our friend the commandant, and did not reach Castro till after dark. The next morning we started very early. After having ridden for some time, we obtained from the brow of a steep hill an extensive view (and it is a rare thing on this road) of the great forest. Over the horizon of trees, the volcano of Corcovado, and the great flattopped one to the north, stood out in proud preeminence: scarcely another peak in the long range showed its snowy summit. I hope it will be long before I forget this farewell view of the magnificent Cordillera fronting Chiloe. At night we bivouacked under a cloudless sky, and the next morning reached S. Carlos. We arrived on the right day, for before evening heavy rain commenced.

February 4th.—Sailed from Chiloe. During the last week I made several short excursions. One was to examine a great bed of now-existing shells, elevated 350 feet above the level of the sea: from among these shells, large forest-trees were growing. Another ride was to P. Huechucucuy. I had with me a guide who knew the country far too well; for he would pertinaciously tell me endless Indian names for every little point, rivulet, and creek. In the same manner as in Tierra del Fuego, the Indian language appears singularly well adapted for attaching names to the most trivial features of the land. I believe every one was glad to say farewell to Chiloe; yet if we could forget the gloom and ceaseless rain of winter, Chiloe might pass for a charming island. There is also something very attractive in the simplicity and humble politeness of the poor inhabitants.

We steered northward along shore, but owing to thick weather did not reach Valdivia till the night of the 8th. The next morning the boat proceeded to the town, which is distant about ten miles. We followed the course of the river, occasionally passing a few hovels, and patches of ground cleared out of the otherwise unbroken forest; and sometimes meeting a canoe with an Indian family. The town is situated on the low banks of the stream, and is so completely buried in a wood of apple-trees that the streets are merely paths in an orchard. I have never seen any country where apple-trees appeared to thrive so well as in this damp part of South America: on the borders of the roads there were many young trees evidently self-grown. In Chiloe the inhabitants possess a marvellously short method of making an orchard. At the lower part of almost every branch, small, conical, brown, wrinkled points project: these are always ready to change into roots, as may sometimes be seen, where any mud has been accidentally splashed against the tree. A branch as thick as a man's thigh is chosen in the early spring, and is cut off just beneath a group of these points, all the smaller branches are lopped off, and it is then placed about two feet deep in the ground. During the ensuing summer the stump throws the long shoots, and sometimes even bears fruit: I was shown one which had produced as many as twenty-three apples, but this was thought very unusual. In the third season the stump is changed (as I have myself seen) into a well-wooded tree, loaded with fruit. An old man near valdivia illustrated his motto, "Necesidad es la madre del invencion," by giving an account of the several useful things he manufactured from his apples. After making cider, and likewise wine, he extracted from the refuse a white and finely flavoured spirit; by another process he procured a sweet treacle, or, as he called it, honey. His children and pigs seemed almost to live, during this season of the year, in his orchard.

February 11th.—I set out with a guide on a short ride, in which, however, I managed to see singularly little, either of the geology of the country or of its inhabitants. There is not much cleared land near Valdivia: after crossing a river at the distance of a few miles, we entered the forest, and then passed only one miserable hovel, before reaching our sleeping place for the night. The short difference in latitude, of 150 miles, has given a new aspect to the forest compared with that of Chiloe. This is owing to a slightly different proportion in the kinds of trees. The evergreens do not appear to be quite so numerous, and the forest in consequence has a brighter tint. As in Chiloe, the lower parts are matted together by canes: here also another kind (resembling the bamboo of Brazil and about twenty feet in height) grows in clusters, and ornaments the banks of some of the streams in a very pretty manner. It is with this plant that the Indians make their chuzos, or long tapering spears. Our resting-house was so dirty that I preferred sleeping outside: on these journeys the first night is generally very uncomfortable, because one is not accustomed to the tickling and biting of the fleas. I am sure, in the morning, there was not a space on my legs the size of a shilling which had not its little red mark where the flea had feasted.

February 12th.—We continued to ride through the uncleared forest; only occasionally meeting an Indian on horseback, or a troop of fine mules bringing alerce-planks and corn from the southern plains. In the afternoon one of the horses knocked up: we were then on a brow of a hill, which commanded a fine view of the Llanos. The view of these open plains was very refreshing, after being hemmed in and buried in the wilderness of trees. The uniformity of a forest soon becomes very wearisome. This west coast makes me remember with pleasure the free, unbounded plains of Patagonia; yet, with the true spirit of contradiction, I cannot forget how sublime is the silence of the forest. The Llanos are the most fertile and thickly peopled parts of the country, as they possess the immense advantage of being nearly free from trees. Before leaving the forest we crossed some flat little lawns, around which single trees stood, as in an English park: I have often noticed with surprise, in wooded undulatory districts, that the quite level parts have been destitute of trees. On account of the tired horse, I determined to stop at the Mission of Cudico, to the friar of which I had a letter of introduction. Cudico is an intermediate district between the forest and the Llanos. There are a good many cottages, with patches of corn and potatoes, nearly all belonging to Indians. The tribes dependent on Valdivia are "reducidos y cristianos." The Indians farther northward, about Arauco and Imperial, are still very wild, and not converted; but they have all much intercourse with the Spaniards. The padre said that the Christian Indians did not much like coming to mass, but that otherwise they showed respect for religion. The greatest difficulty is in making them observe the ceremonies of marriage. The wild Indians take as many wives as they can support, and a cacique will sometimes have more than ten: on entering his house, the number may be told by that of the separate fires. Each wife lives a week in turn with the cacique; but all are employed in weaving ponchos, etc., for his profit. To be the wife of a cacique, is an honour much sought after by the Indian women.

The men of all these tribes wear a coarse woolen poncho: those south of Valdivia wear short trousers, and those north of it a petticoat, like the chilipa of the Gauchos. All have their long hair bound by a scarlet fillet, but with no other covering on their heads. These Indians are good-sized men; their cheek-bones are prominent, and in general appearance they resemble the great American family to which they belong; but their physiognomy seemed to me to be slightly different from that of any other tribe which I had before seen. Their expression is generally grave, and even austere, and possesses much character: this may pass either for honest bluntness or fierce determination. The long black hair, the grave and much-lined features, and the dark complexion, called to my mind old portraits of James I. On the road we met with none of that humble politeness so universal in Chiloe. Some gave their "mari-mari" (good morning) with promptness, but the greater number did not seem inclined to offer any salute. This independence of manners is probably a consequence of their long wars, and the repeated victories which they alone, of all the tribes in America, have gained over the Spaniards.

I spent the evening very pleasantly, talking with the padre. He was exceedingly kind and hospitable; and coming from Santiago, had contrived to surround himself with some few comforts. Being a man of some little education, he bitterly complained of the total want of society. With no particular zeal for religion, no business or pursuit, how completely must this man's life be wasted! The next day, on our return, we met seven very wild-looking Indians, of whom some were caciques that had just received from the Chilian government their yearly small stipend for having long remained faithful. They were fine-looking men, and they rode one after the other, with most gloomy faces. An old cacique, who headed them, had been, I suppose, more excessively drunk than the rest, for he seemed extremely grave and very crabbed. Shortly before this, two Indians joined us, who were traveling from a distant mission to Valdivia concerning some lawsuit. One was a good-humoured old man, but from his wrinkled beardless face looked more like an old woman than a man. I frequently presented both of them with cigars; and though ready to receive them, and I dare say grateful, they would hardly condescend to thank me. A Chilotan Indian would have taken off his hat, and given his "Dios le page!" The traveling was very tedious, both from the badness of the roads, and from the number of great fallen trees, which it was necessary either to leap over or to avoid by making long circuits. We slept on the road, and next morning reached Valdivia, whence I proceeded on board.

A watercolour by HMS *Beagle's* draughtsman, Conrad Martens. Painted during the survey of Tierra del Fuego.

A few days afterwards I crossed the bay with a party of officers, and landed near the fort called Niebla. The buildings were in a most ruinous state, and the gun-carriages, quite rotten. Mr. Wickham remarked to the commanding officer, that with one discharge they would certainly all fall to pieces. The poor man, trying to put a good face upon it, gravely replied, "No, I am sure, sir, they would stand two!" The Spaniards must have intended to have made this place impregnable. There is now lying in the middle of the court-yard a little mountain of mortar, which rivals in hardness the rock on which it is placed. It was brought from Chile, and cost 7000 dollars. The revolution having broken out, prevented its being applied to any purpose, and now it remains a monument of the fallen greatness of Spain.

I wanted to go to a house about a mile and a half distant, but my guide said it was quite impossible to penetrate the wood in a straight line. He offered, however, to lead me, by following obscure cattle-tracks, the shortest way: the walk, nevertheless, took no less than three hours! This man is employed in hunting strayed cattle; yet, well as he must know the woods, he was not long since lost for two whole days, and had nothing to eat. These facts convey a good idea of the impracticability of the forests of these countries. A question often occurred to me—how long does any vestige of a fallen tree remain? This man showed me one which a party of fugitive royalists had cut down fourteen years ago; and taking this as a criterion, I should think a bole a foot and a half in diameter would in thirty years be changed into a heap of mould.

February 20th.—This day has been memorable in the annals of Valdivia, for the most severe earthquake experienced by the oldest inhabitant. I happened to be on shore, and was lying down in the wood to rest myself. It came on suddenly, and lasted two minutes, but the time appeared much longer. The rocking of the ground was very sensible. The undulations appeared to my companion and myself to come from due east, whilst others thought they proceeded from south-west: this shows how difficult it sometimes is to perceive the directions of the vibrations. There was no difficulty in standing upright, but the motion made me almost giddy: it was something like the movement of a vessel in a little cross-ripple, or still more like that felt by a person skating over thin ice, which bends under the weight of his body. A bad earthquake at once destroys our oldest associations: the earth, the very emblem of solidity, had moved beneath our feet like a thin crust over a fluid;—one second of time has created in the mind a strange idea of insecurity, which hours of reflection would not have produced. In the forest, as a breeze moved the trees, I felt only the earth tremble, but saw no other effect. Captain Fitz Roy and some officers were at the town during the shock, and there the scene was more striking; for although the houses, from being built of wood, did not fall, they were violently shaken, and the boards creaked and rattled together. The people rushed out of doors in the greatest alarm. It is these accompaniments that create that perfect horror of earthquakes, experienced by all who have thus seen, as well as felt, their effects. Within the forest it was a deeply interesting, but by no means an awe-exciting phenomenon. The tides were very curiously affected. The great shock took place at the time of low water; and an old woman who was on the beach told me that the water flowed very quickly, but not in great waves, to high-water mark, and then as quickly returned to its proper level; this was also evident by the line of wet sand. The same kind of quick but quiet movement in the tide happened a few years since at Chiloe, during a slight earthquake, and created much causeless alarm. In the course of the evening there were many weaker shocks, which seemed to produce in the harbour the most complicated currents, and some of great strength.

March 4th.—We entered the harbour of Concepcion. While the ship was beating up to the anchorage, I landed on the island of Quiriquina. The major-domo of the estate quickly rode down to tell me the terrible news of the great earthquake of the 20th:—"That not a house in Concepcion or Talcahuano (the port) was standing; that seventy villages were destroyed; and that a great wave had almost washed away the ruins of Talcahuano." Of this latter statement I soon saw abundant proofs—the whole coast being strewed over with timber and furniture as if a thousand ships had been wrecked. Besides chairs, tables, book-shelves, etc., in great numbers, there were several roofs of cottages, which had been transported almost whole. The storehouses at Talcahuano had been burst open, and great bags of cotton, yerba, and other valuable merchandise were scattered on the shore. During my walk round the island, I observed that numerous fragments of rock, which, from the marine productions adhering to them, must recently have been lying in deep water, had been cast up high on the beach; one of these was six feet long, three broad, and two thick.

The island itself as plainly showed the overwhelming power of the earthquake, as the beach did that of the consequent great wave. The ground in many parts was fissured in north and south lines, perhaps caused by the yielding of the parallel and steep sides of this narrow island. Some of the fissures near the cliffs were a yard wide. Many enormous masses had already fallen on the beach; and the inhabitants thought that when the rains commenced far greater slips would happen. The effect of the vibration on the hard primary slate, which composes the foundation of the island, was still more curious: the superficial parts of some narrow ridges were as completely shivered as if they had been blasted by gunpowder. This effect, which was rendered conspicuous by the fresh fractures and displaced soil, must be confined to near the surface, for otherwise there would not exist a block of solid rock through out Chile; nor is this improbable, as it is known that the surface of a vibrating body is affected differently from the central part. It is, perhaps, owing to this same reason, that earthquakes do not cause quite such terrific havoc within deep mines as would be expected, I believe this convulsion has been more effectual in lessening the size of the island of Quiriquina, than the ordinary wear-and-tear of the sea and weather during the course of a whole century.

The next day I landed at Talcahuano, and afterwards rode to Concepcion. Both towns presented the most awful yet interesting spectacle I ever beheld. To a person who had formerly known them, it possibly might have been still more impressive; for the ruins were so mingled together, and the whole scene possessed so little the air of a habitable place, that it was scarcely possible to imagine its former condition. The earthquake commenced at half-past eleven o'clock in the forenoon. If it had happened in the middle of the night, the greater number of the inhabitants (which in this one province must amount to many thousands) must have perished, instead of less than a hundred: as it was, the invariable practice of running out of doors at the first trembling of the ground, alone saved them. In Concepcion each house, or row of houses, stood by itself, a heap or line of ruins; but in Talcahuano, owing to the great wave, little more than one layer of bricks, tiles, and timber with here and there part of a wall left standing, could be distinguished. From this circumstance Concepcion, although not so completely desolated, was a more terrible, and if I may so call it, picturesque sight. The first shock was very sudden. The major-domo at Quiriquina told me, that the first notice he received of it, was finding both the horse he rode and himself, rolling together on the ground. Rising up, he was again thrown down. He also told me that some cows which were standing on the steep side of the island were rolled into the sea. The great wave caused the destruction of many cattle; on one low island near the head of the bay, seventy animals were washed off and drowned. It is generally thought that this has been the worst earthquake ever recorded in Chile; but as the very severe ones occur only after long intervals, this cannot easily be known; nor indeed would a much worse shock have made any difference, for the ruin was now complete. Innumerable small tremblings followed the great earthquake, and within the first twelve days no less than three hundred were counted.

After viewing Concepcion, I cannot understand how the greater number of inhabitants escaped unhurt. The houses in many parts fell outwards; thus forming in the middle of the streets little hillocks of brickwork and rubbish.

Mr. Rouse, the English consul, told us that he was at breakfast when the first movement warned him to run out. He had scarcely reached the middle of the court-yard, when one side of his house came thundering down. He retained presence of mind to remember, that if he once got on the top of that part which had already fallen, he would be safe. Not being able from the motion of the ground to stand, he crawled up on his hands and knees; and no sooner had he ascended this little eminence, than the other side of the house fell in, the great beams sweeping close in front of his head. With his eyes blinded, and his mouth choked with the cloud of dust which darkened the sky, at last he gained the street. As shock succeeded shock, at the interval of a few minutes, no one dared approach the shattered ruins, and no one knew whether his dearest friends and relations were not perishing from the want of help. Those who had saved any property were obliged to keep a constant watch, for thieves prowled about, and at each little trembling of the ground, with one hand they beat their breasts and cried "Misericordia!" and then with the other filched what they could from the ruins. The thatched roofs fell over the fires, and flames burst forth in all parts. Hundreds knew themselves ruined, and few had the means of providing food for the day.

Earthquakes alone are sufficient to destroy the prosperity of any country. If beneath England the now inert subterranean forces should exert those powers, which most assuredly in former geological ages they have exerted, how completely would the entire condition of the country be changed! What would become of the lofty houses, thickly packed cities, great manufactories, the beautiful public and private edifices? If the new period of disturbance were first to commence by some great earthquake in the dead of the night, how terrific would be the carnage! England would at once be bankrupt; all papers, records, and accounts would from that moment be lost. Government being unable to collect the taxes, and failing to maintain its authority, the hand of violence and rapine would remain uncontrolled. In every large town famine would go forth, pestilence and death following in its train.

Shortly after the shock, a great wave was seen from the distance of three or four miles, approaching in the middle of the bay with a smooth outline;

but along the shore it tore up cottages and trees, as it swept onwards with irresistible force. At the head of the bay it broke in a fearful line of white breakers, which rushed up to a height of 23 vertical feet above the highest spring-tides. Their force must have been prodigious; for at the Fort a cannon with its carriage, estimated at four tons in weight, was moved 15 feet inwards. A schooner was left in the midst of the ruins, 200 yards from the beach. The first wave was followed by two others, which in their retreat carried away a vast wreck of floating objects. In one part of the bay, a ship was pitched high and dry on shore, was carried off, again driven on shore, and again carried off. In another part, two large vessels anchored near together were whirled about, and their cables were thrice wound round each other; though anchored at a depth of 36 feet, they were for some minutes aground. The great wave must have traveled slowly, for the inhabitants of Talcahuano had time to run up the hills behind the town; and some sailors pulled out seaward, trusting successfully to their boat riding securely over the swell, if they could reach it before it broke. One old woman with a little boy, four or five years old, ran into a boat, but there was nobody to row it out: the boat was consequently dashed against an anchor and cut in twain; the old woman was drowned, but the child was picked up some hours afterwards clinging to the wreck. Pools of salt-water were still standing amidst the ruins of the houses, and children, making boats with old tables, and chairs, appeared as happy as their parents were miserable. It was, however, exceedingly interesting to observe, how much more active and cheerful all appeared than could have been expected. It was remarked with much truth, that from the destruction being universal, no one individual was humbled more than another, or could suspect his friends of coldness—that most grievous result of the loss of wealth. Mr. Rouse, and a large party whom he kindly took under his protection, lived for the first week in a garden beneath some apple-trees. At first they were as merry as if it had been a picnic; but soon afterwards heavy rain caused much discomfort, for they were absolutely without shelter.

In Captain Fitz Roy's excellent account of the earthquake, it is said that two explosions, one like a column of smoke and another like the blowing of a great whale, were seen in the bay. The water also appeared everywhere to be boiling; and it "became black, and exhaled a most disagreeable sulphureous smell." The latter circumstances were observed in the Bay of Valparaiso during the earthquake of 1822; they may, I think, be accounted for, by the disturbance of the mud at the bottom of the sea containing organic matter in decay. In the Bay of Callao, during a calm day, I noticed, that as the ship dragged her cable over the bottom, its course was marked by a line of bubbles. The lower orders in Talcahuano thought that the earthquake was caused by some old Indian women, who two years ago, being offended, stopped the volcano of Antuco. This silly belief is curious, because it shows that experience has taught them to observe, that there exists a relation between the suppressed action of the volcanos, and the trembling of the ground. It was necessary to apply the witchcraft to the point where their perception of cause and effect failed; and this was the closing of the volcanic vent. This belief is the more singular in this particular instance, because, according to Captain Fitz Roy, there is reason to believe that Antuco was noways affected.

The town of Concepcion was built in the usual Spanish fashion, with all the streets running at right angles to each other; one set ranging S.W. by W., and the other set N.W. by N. The walls in the former direction certainly stood better than those in the latter; the greater number of the masses of brickwork were thrown down towards the N.E. Both these circumstances perfectly agree with the general idea, of the undulations having come from the S.W., in which quarter subterranean noises were also heard; for it is evident that the walls running S.W. and N.E. which presented their ends to the point whence the undulations came, would be much less likely to fall than those walls which, running N.W. and S.E., must in their whole lengths have been at the same instant thrown out of the perpendicular; for the undulations, coming from the S.W., must have extended in N.W. and S.E. waves, as they passed under the foundations. This may be illustrated by placing books edgeways on a carpet, and then, after the manner suggested by Michell, imitating the undulations of an earthquake: it will be found that they fall with more or less readiness, according as their direction more or less nearly coincides with the line of the waves. The fissures in the ground generally, though not uniformly, extended in a S.E. and N.W. direction, and therefore corresponded to the lines of undulation or of principal flexure. Bearing in mind all these circumstances, which so clearly point to the S.W. as the chief focus of disturbance, it is a very interesting fact that the island of S. Maria, situated in that quarter, was, during the general uplifting of the land, raised to nearly three times the height of any other part of the coast.

The different resistance offered by the walls, according to their direction, was the N.E. presented a grand pile of ruins, in the midst of which door-cases and masses of timber stood up, as if floating in a stream. Some of the angular blocks of brickwork were of great dimensions; and they were rolled to a distance on the level plaza, like fragments of rock at the base of some high mountain. The side walls (running S.W. and N.E.), though exceedingly fractured, yet remained standing; but the vast buttresses (at right angles to them, and therefore parallel to the walls that fell) were in many cases cut clean off, as if by a chisel, and hurled to the ground. Some square ornaments on the coping of these same walls, were moved by the earthquake into a diagonal position. A similar circumstance was observed after an earthquake at Valparasio, Calabria, and other places, including some of the ancient Greek temples. This twisting displacement, at first appears to indicate a vorticose movement beneath each point thus affected; but this is highly improbable. May it not be caused by a tendency in each stone to arrange itself in some particular position, with respect to the lines of vibration,—in a manner somewhat similar to pins on a sheet of paper when shaken? Generally speaking, arched doorways or windows stood much better than any other part of the buildings. Nevertheless, a poor lame old man, who had been in the habit, during trifling shocks, of crawling to a certain doorway, was this time crushed to pieces.

I have not attempted to give any detailed description of the appearance of Concepecion, for I feel that it is quite impossible to convey the mingled feelings which I experienced. Several of the officers visited it before me, but their strongest language failed to give a just idea of the scene of desolation. It is a bitter and humiliating thing to see works have cost man so much time and labour, overthrown in one minute; yet compassion for the inhabitants was almost instantly banished, by the surprise in seeing a state of things produced in a moment of time, which one was accustomed to attribute to a succession of ages. In my opinion, we have scarcely beheld, since leaving England, any sight so deeply interesting.

In almost every severe earthquake, the neighbouring waters of the sea are said to have been greatly agitated. The disturbance seems generally, as in the case of Concepcion, to have been of two kinds: first, at the instant of the shock, the water swells high up on the beach with a gentle mortion, and then as quietly retreats; secondly, some time afterwards, the whole body of the sea retires from the coast, and then returns in waves of overwhelming force. The first movement seems to be an immediate consequence of the earthquake affecting differently a fluid and a solid, so that their respective levels are slightly deranged: but the second case is a far more important phenomenon. During most earthquakes, and especially during those on the west coast of America, it is certain that the first great movement of the waters has been a retirement. Some authors have attempted to explain this, by supposing that the water retains its level, whilst the land oscillates upwards; but surely the water close to the land, even on a rather steep coast, would partake of the motion of the bottom: moreover, as urged by Mr. Lyell, similar movements of the sea have occurred at islands far distant from the chief line of disturbance, as was the case with Juan Fernandez during this earthquake, and with Madeira during the famous Lisbon shock. I suspect (but the subject is a very obscure one) that a wave, however produced, first draws the water from the shore, on which it is advancing to break: I have observed that this happens with the little waves from the paddles of a steam-boat. It is remarkable that whilst Talcahuano and Callao (near Lima), both situated at the head of large shallow bays, have suffered during every severe earthquake from great waves, Valparaiso, seated close to the edge of profoundly deep water, has never been overwhelmed, though so often shaken by the severest shocks. From the great wave not immediately following the earthquake, but sometimes after the interval of even half an hour, and from distant islands being affected similarly with the coasts near the focus of the disturbance, it appears that the wave first rises in the offing; and as this is of general occurrence, the cause must be general: I suspect we must look to the line, where the less disturbed waters of the deep ocean join the water nearer the coast, which has partaken of the movements of the land, as the place where the great wave is first generated; it would also appear that the wave is larger or smaller, according to the extent of shoal water which has been agitated together with the bottom on which it rested.

The most remarkable effect of this earthquake was the permanent elevation of the land, it would probably be far more correct to speak of it as the cause. There can be no doubt that the land round the Bay of Concepcion was upraised two or three feet; but it deserves notice, that owing to the wave having obliterated the ole lines of tidal action on the sloping sandy shores, I could discover no evidence of this fact, except in the united testimony of the inhabitants, that one little rocky shoal, now exposed, was formerly covered with water. At the island of S. Maria (about thirty miles distant) the elevation was greater; on one part, Captain Fitz Roy founds beds of putrid mussel-shells still adhering to the rocks, ten feet above high-water mark: the inhabitants had formerly dived at lower-water spring-tides for these shells. The elevation of this province is particularly interesting, from its having been the theatre of several other violent earthquakes, and from the vast numbers of sea-shells scattered over the land, up to a height of certainly 600, and I believe, of 1000 feet. At Valparaiso, as I have remarked, similar shells are found at the height of 1300 feet: it is hardly possible to doubt that this great elevation has been effected by successive small uprisings, such as that which accompanied or caused the earthquake of this year, and likewise by an insensibly slow rise, which is certainly in progress on some parts of this coast.

The island of Juan Fernandez, 360 miles to the N.E., was, at the time of the great shock of the 20th, violently shaken, so that the trees beat against each other, and a volcano burst forth under water close to the shore: these facts are remarkable because this island, during the earthquake of 1751, was then also affected more violently than other places at an equal distance from Concepcion, and this seems to show some subterranean connection between these two points. Chiloe, about 340 miles southward of Concepcion, appears to have been shaken more strongly than the intermediate district of Valdivia, where the volcano of Villarica was noways affected, whilst in the Cordillera in front of Chiloe, two of the volcanos burst forth at the same instant in violent action. These two volcanos, and some neighbouring ones, continued for a long time in eruption, and ten months afterwards were again influenced by an earthquake at Concepcion. Some men, cutting wood near the base of one of these volcanos, did not perceive the shock of the 20th, although the whole surrounding Province was then trembling; here we have an eruption relieving and taking the place of an earthquake, as would have happened at Concepcion, according to the belief of the lower orders, if the volcano at Antuco had not been closed by witchcraft. Two years and three-quarters afterwards, Valdivia and Chiloe were again shaken, more violently than on the 20th, and an island in the Chonos Archipelago was permanently elevated more than eight feet. It will give a better idea of the scale of these phenomena, if (as in the case of the glaciers) we suppose them to have taken place at corresponding distances in Europe:—then would the land from the North Sea to the Mediterranean have been violently shaken, and at the same instant of time a large tract of the eastern coast of England would have been permanently elevated, together with some outlying islands,—a train of volcanos on the coast of Holland would have burst forth in action, and an eruption taken place at the bottom of the sea, near the northern extremity of Ireland—and lastly, the ancient vents of Auvergne, Cantal, and Mont d' Or would each have sent up to the sky a dark column of smoke, and have long remained in fierce action. Two years and three-quarters afterwards, France, from its centre to the English Channel, would have been again desolated by an earthquake and an island permanently upraised in the Mediterranean.

The space, from under which volcanic matter on the 20th was actually erupted, is 720 miles in one line, and 400 miles in another line at right angles to the first: hence, in all probability, a subterranean lake of lava is here stretched out, of nearly double the area of the Black Sea. From the intimate and complicated manner in which the elevatory and eruptive forces were shown to be connected during this train of phenomena, we may confidently come to the conclusion, that the forces which slowly and by little starts uplift continents, and those which at successive periods pour forth volcanic matter fro open orifices, are identical. From many reasons, I believe that the frequent quakings of the earth on this line of coast are caused by the rending of the strata, necessarily consequent on the tension of the land when upraised, and their injection by fluidified rock. This rending and injection would, if repeated often enough (and we know that earthquakes repeatedly affect the same areas in the same manner), form a chain of hills;—and the linear island of S. Mary, which was upraised thrice the height of the neighbouring country, seems to be undergoing this process. I believe that the solid axis of a mountain, differs in its manner of formation from a volcanic hill, only in the molten stone having been repeatedly injected, instead of having been repeatedly ejected. Moreover, I believe that it is impossible to explain the structure of great mountain-chains, such as that of the Cordillera, where the strata, capping the injected axis of plutonic rock, have been thrown on their edges along several parallel and neighbouring lines of elevation, except on this view of the rock of the axis having been repeatedly injected, after intervals sufficiently long to allow the upper parts or wedges to cool and become solid;—for if the strata had been thrown into their present highly inclined, vertical, and even inverted positions, by a single blow, the very bowels of the earth would have gushed out; and instead of beholding abrupt mountain-axes of rock solidified under great pressure, deluges of lava would have flowed out at innumerable points on every line of elevation.

CHAPTER 5

EXCERPT FROM
THE TRAVELS OF MARCO POLO

By Marco Polo

Marco Polo wearing a native outfit of
the Tartar people, date unknown.

Know reader, that the time when Baldwin II was Emperor of Constantinople, where a magistrate representing the Doge of Venice
then resided, and in the year of our Lord 1250, Nicolo Polo, the
father of the said Marco, and Maffeo, the brother of Nicolo, respectable and
well-informed men, embarked in a ship of their own, with a rich and varied

cargo of goods, and reached Constantinople in safety. After mature deliber-
ation on the subject of their proceedings, it was dertermined, as the measure
most likely to improve their trading capital, that they should prosecute their
voyage into the Euxine or Black Sea. With this view they made purchases of
many fine and costly jewels, and taking their departure from Constantinople, navigated that sea to a port name Soldaia, from whence they travelled
on horseback many days until they reached the court of a powerful chief of
the Western Tartars, named Barka VI who dwelt in the cities of Bolgara and
Assara, and had the reputation of being one of the most liberal and civilized
princes hitherto known amongst the tribes of Tartary. He expressed much
satisfaction at the arrival of these travelers, and received them with marks of
distinction. In return for which courtesy, when they had laid before him the
jewels they brought with them, and perceived that their beauty pleased him,
they presented them for his acceptance. The liberality of this conduct on the
part of the two brothers struck him with admiration; and being unwilling
that they should surpass him in generosity, he not only directed double the
value of the jewels to be paid to them, but made them in addition several
other rich presents.

The brothers having resided a year in the dominions of this prince, they
became desirous of revisiting their native country, but were impeded by the
sudden breaking out of a war between him and another chief, named Alaù,
who ruled over the Eastern Tartars. In the fierce and very bloody battle that
ensued between their respective armies, Alaù was victorious, in consequence
of which, the roads being rendered unsafe for travellers, the brothers could
not attempt to return by the way they came; and it was recommended to
them as the only practicable mode of reaching Constantinople, to proceed
in an easterly direction, by an unfrequented route, so as to skirt the limits of Barka's territories. Accordingly they made their way to a town named
Oukaka, situated on the confines of the kingdom of the Western Tartars.
Leaving that place, and advancing still further, they crossed the Tigris, one
of the four rivers of Paradise, and came to a desert, the extent of which was
seventeen days' journey, wherein they found neither town, castle, nor any

substantial building, but only Tartars with their herds, dwelling in tents on the plain. Having passed this tract, they arrived at length at a well-built city called Bokhara, a province of that name belonging to the dominions of Persia, and the noblest city of that kingdom, but governed by a prince whose name was Barak. Here, from inability to proceed further, they remained three years.

It happened while these brothers were in Bokhara, that a person of consequence and gifted with eminent talents made his appearance there. He was proceeding as ambassador from Alaù before mentioned, to the Grand Khan, supreme chief of all the Tartars named Kublai, whose resident was at the extremity of the continent, in a direction between north-east and east. Not having ever before had an opportunity, although he wished it, of seeing any natives of Italy, he was gratified in a high degree at meeting and conversing with these brothers, who had now become proficients in the Tartar language; and after associating with them for several days, and finding their manners agreeable to him, he proposed to them that they should accompany him to the presence of the Great Khan, who would be pleased by their appearance at his court, which had not hitherto been visited by any person from their country; adding assurances that they would be honourably received, and recompensed with many gifts. Convinced as they were that their endeavours to return homeward would expose them to the most imminent risks, they agreed to this proposal, and recommending themselves to the protection of the Almighty, they set out on their journey in the suite of the ambassador, attended by several Christian servants whom they had brought with them from Venice. The course they took at first was between the north-east and north, and an entire year was consumed before they were enabled to reach the imperial residence, in consequence of the extraordinary delays occasioned by the snows and the swelling of the rivers, which obliged them to halt until the former had melted and the floods had subsided. Many things worthy of admiration were observed by them in the progress of their journey, but which are here omitted, as they will be described by Marco Polo, in the sequel of the book.

Being introduced to the presence of the Grand Khan, Kublaï, the travelers were received by him with the condescension and affability that belonged to his character, and as they were the first Latins who had made their appearance in that country, they were entertained with feasts and honoured with other marks of distinction. Entering graciously into conversation with them, he made earnest inquiries on the subject of the western parts of the world, of the emperor of the Romans, and of other Christian kings and princes. He wished to be informed of their relative consequence, the extent of their possessions, the manner in which justice was administered in their several kingdoms and principalities, how they conducted themselves in warfare, and above all he questioned them particularly respecting the Pope, the affairs of the church, and the religious worship and doctrine of the Christians. Being well instructed and discreet men, they gave appropriate answers upon all these points, and as they were perfectly acquainted with the Tartar (Moghul) language, they expressed themselves always in becoming terms; insomuch that the Grand Khan, holding them in high estimation, frequently commanded their attendance.

When he had obtained all the information that the two brothers communicated with so much good sense, he expressed himself well satisfied, and having formed in his mind the design of employing them as his ambassadors to the Pope, after consulting with his ministers on the subject, he proposed to them, with many kind entreaties, that they should accompany one of his officers, named Khogatal, on a mission to the see of Rome. His object, he told them, was to make a request to his holiness that he would send to him a hundred men of learning, thoroughly acquainted with the principles of the Christian religion, as well as with the seven arts, and qualified to prove to the learned of his dominions, by just and fair argument, that the faith professed by Christians is superior to, and founded upon more evident truth than, any other; that the gods of the Tartars and the idols worshipped in their houses were only evil spirits, and that they and the people of the East in general were under an error in reverencing them as divinities. He moreover signified his pleasure that upon their return they should bring with them, from Jerusalem, some of the holy oil from the lamp which is kept burning over the sepulchre of our Lord Jesus Christ, whom he professed to hold in veneration and to consider as the true God. Having heard these commands addressed to them by the Grand Khan, they humbly prostrated themselves before him, declaring their willingness and instant readiness to perform, to the utmost of their ability, whatever might be the royal will. Upon which he caused letters, in the Tartarian language, to be written in his name to the Pope of Rome; and these he delivered into their hands. He likewise gave orders that they should be furnished with a golden tablet displaying the imperial cipher, according to the usage established by his majesty; in virtue of which the person bearing it, together with his whole suite, are safely conveyed and escorted from station to station by the governors of all places with the imperial dominions, and are entitled, during the time of their residing in any city, castle, town, or village, to a supply of provisions and everything necessary for their accommodation.

Being thus honourably commissioned they took their leave of the Grand Khan, and set out on their journey, but had not proceeded more than twenty days when the officer, named Khogatal, their companion, fell dangerously ill, in the city named Alau. In this dilemma it was determined, upon consulting all who were present, and with the approbation of the man himself, that they

An artistic rendering of one of the many stops in Marco Polo's travels, circa 1215.

should leave him behind. In the prosecution of their journey they derived essential benefit from being provided with the royal tablet, which procured them attention in every place through which they passed. Their expenses were defrayed, and escorts were furnished. But notwithstanding these advantages, so great were the natural difficulties they had to encounter, from the extreme cold, the snow, the ice, and the flooding of the rivers, that their progress was unavoidably tedious, and three years elapsed before they were enabled to reach a seaport town in the lesser Armenia, named Laiassus. Departing from thence by sea, they arrived at Acre in the month of April, 1269, and there learned, with extreme concern, that Pope Clement the Fourth was recently dead. A legate whom he had appointed, named M. Tebaldo de'Vesconti di Piacenza, was at this time resident in Acre, and to him they gave an account of what they had in command from the Grand Khan of Tartary. He advised them by all means to wait the election of another Pope, and when that should take place, to proceed with the objects of their embassy. Approving of this counsel, they determined upon employing the interval in a visit to their families in Venice. They accordingly embarked at acre in a ship bound to Negropont, and from thence went on to Venice, where Nicolo Polo found that his wife, whom he had left with child at his departure, was dead, after having been delivered of a son, who received the name of Macro, and was now of the age of nineteen years. This is the Marco by whom the present work is composed, and who will give therein a relation of all those matters of which he has been an eye-witness.

In the meantime the election of a Pope was retarded by so many obstacles, that they remained two years in Venice, continually expecting its accomplishment; when at length, becoming apprehensive that the Grand Khan might be displeased at their delay, or might suppose it was not their intention to revisit his country, they judged it expedient to return to Acre; and on this occasion they took with them young Marco Polo. Under the sanction of the legate they made a visit to Jerusalem, and there provided themselves with some of the oil belonging to the lamp of the Holy Sepulchre, conformably to the directions of the Grand Khan. As soon as they were furnished with his letters addressed to that prince, bearing testimony to the fidelity with which they had endeavoured to execute his commission, and explaining to him that the Pope of the Christian church had not as yet been chosen, they proceeded to the before-mentioned port of Laiassus. Scarcely however had they taken their departure, when the legate received messengers from Italy, dispatched by the College of Cardinals, announcing his own elevation to the Papal Chair; and he thereupon assumed the name of Gregory the Tenth. Considering that he was now in a situation that enabled him fully to satisfy the wishes of the Tartat sovereign, he hastened to transmit the letters to the king of Armenia, communicating to him the event of his election, and requesting, in case the two ambassadors who were on their way to the court of the Grand Khan should not have already quitted his dominions, that he would give directions for their immediate return. These letters found them still in Armenia, and with great alacrity they obeyed the summons to repair once more to Acre; for which purpose the king furnished them with an armed galley; sending at the same time an ambassador from himself, to offer his congratulations to the Sovereign Pontiff.

Upon their arrival, His Holiness received them in a distinguished manner, and immediately despatched them with letters papal, accompanied by two friars of the order of Preachers, who happened to be on the spot; men of letters and of science, as well as profound theologians. One of them was named Fra Nicola da Vicenza, and the other, Fra Guielmo da Tripoli. To them he gave licence and authority to ordain priests, to consecrate bishops, and to grant absolution as fully as he could do in his own person. He also charged them with valuable presents, and among these, several handsome vases of crystal, to be delivered to the Grand Khan in his name, and along with his benediction. Having taken leave, they again steered their course to the port of Laiassus, where they landed, and from thence proceeded into the country of Armenia. Here they received intelligence that the soldan of Babylonia, named Bundokdari, had invaded the Armenian territory with a numerous army, and had overrun and laid waste the country to a great extent. Terrified at these accounts, and apprehensive for their lives, the two friars determined not to proceed further, and delivering over to the Venetians the letters and presents entrusted to them by the Pope, they placed themselves under the protection of the Master of the Knights Templars, and with him returned directly to the coast. Nicolo, Maffeo, and Marco, however, undismayed by perils or difficulties (to which they had long been inured), passed the borders of Armenia, and prosecuted their journey. After crossing deserts of several days' march, and passing many dangerous defiles, they advanced so far, in a direction between north-east and north, that at length they gained information of the grand khan, who then had his residence in a large and magnificent city named Clemen-fu. Their whole journey to this place occupied no less than three years and a half; but, during the winter months, their progress had been inconsiderable. The Grand Khan having notice of their approach whilst still remote, and being aware how much they must have suffered from fatigue, sent forward to meet them at the distance of forty days' journey, and gave orders to prepare in every place through which they were to pass, whatever might be requisite to their comfort. By these means, and through the blessing of God, they were conveyed in safety to the royal court.

Upon their arrival they were honourably and graciously received by the Grand Khan, in a full assembly of his principal officers. When they drew nigh to his person, they paid their respects by prostrating themselves on the floor. He immediately commanded them to rise, and to relate to him the circumstances of their travels, with all that had taken place in their negotiation with His Holiness the Pope. To their narrative, which they gave in the regular order of events, and delivered in perspicuous language, he listened with attentive silence. The letters and the presents from Pope Gregory were then laid before him, and, upon hearing the former read, he bestowed much commendation on the fidelity, the zeal, and the diligence of his ambassadors; and receiving with due reverence the oil from the holy sepulchre, he gave directions that it should be preserved with religious care. Upon his observing Marco Polo, and inquiring who he was, Nicolo made answer, "This is your servant, and my son;" upon which the Grand Khan replied, "He is welcome, and it pleases me much," and he caused him to be enrolled amongst his attendants of honour. And on account of their return he made a great feast and rejoicing; and as long as the said brothers and Marco remained in the court of the Grand Khan, they were honoured even above his own courtiers.

Marco was held in high estimation and respect by all belonging to the court. He learnt in a short time and adopted the manners of the Tartars, and acquired a proficiency in four different languages, which he became qualified to read and write. Finding him thus accomplished, his master was desirous of putting his talents for business to the proof, and sent him on an important concern of state to a city named Karazan situated at the distance of six months' journey from the imperial residence; on which occasion he conducted himself with so much wisdom and prudence in the management of the affairs entrusted to him, that his services became highly acceptable. On his part, perceiving that the Grand Khan took a pleasure in hearing accounts of whatever was new to him respecting the customs and manners of people, and the peculiar circumstances of distant countries, he endeavoured, wherever he went, to obtain correct information on these subjects, and made notes of all he saw and heard, in order to gratify the curiosity of his master. In short, during seventeen years that he continued in his service, he rendered himself so useful, that he was employed on confidential missions to every part of the empire and its dependencies; and sometimes also he travelled on his own private account, but always with the consent, and sanctioned by the authority, of the Grand Khan. Under such circumstances it was that Marco Polo had the opportunity of acquiring a knowledge, either by his own observation, or what he collected from others, of so many things, until his time unknown, respecting the eastern parts of the world, and which he diligently and regularly committed to writing, as in the sequel will appear. And by this means he obtained so much honour, that he provoked the jealousy of the other officers of the court.

Our Venetians having now resided many years at the imperial court, and in that time having realized considerable wealth, in jewels of value and in gold, felt a strong desire to revisit their native country, and, however honoured and caressed by the sovereign, this sentiment was ever predominant in

their minds. It became the more decidedly their object, when they reflected on the very advanced age of the Grand Khan, whose death, if it should
happen previously to their departure, might deprive them of that public assistance by which alone they could expect to surmount the innumerable difficulties of so long a journey, and reach their homes in safety; which on the
contrary, in his lifetime, and through his favour, they might reasonably hope
to accomplish. Nicolo Polo accordingly took an opportunity one day, when
he observed him to be more than usually cheerful, of throwing himself at his
feet, and soliciting on behalf of himself and his family to be indulged with his
majesty's gracious permission for their departure. But far from showing himself disposed to comply with the request, he appeared hurt at the application,
and asked what motive they could have for wishing to expose themselves to
all the inconveniences and hazards of a journey in which they might probably
lose their lives. If gain, he said, was their object, he was ready to give them
the double of whatever they possessed, and to gratify them with honours to
the extent of their desires; but that, from the regard he bore to them, he must
positively refuse their petition.

It happened, about this period, that a queen named Bolgana, the wife of
Arghun, sovereign of India, died, and as her last request (which she likewise
left in a testamentary writing) conjured her husband that no one might succeed to her place on his throne and in his affections, who was not a descen-
dant of her own family, now settled under the dominion of the Grand Khan,
in the country of Kathay. Desirous of complying with this solemn entreaty,
Arghun deputed three of his nobles, discreet men, whose names were Ulatai,
Apusca, and Goza, attended by a numerous retinue, as his ambassadors to
the grand khan, with a request that he might receive at his hands a maiden
to wife, from among the relatives of his deceased queen. The application was
taken in good part, and under the directions of his majesty, choice was made
of a damsel aged seventeen, extremely handsome and accomplished, whose
name was Kogatin, and of whom the ambassadors, upon her being shown to
them, highly approved. When everything was arranged for their departure,
and a numerous suite of attendants appointed, to do honour to the future

consort of king Arghun, they received from the grand khan a gracious dismissal, and set out on their return by the way they came. Having travelled for eight months, their further progress was obstructed and the roads shut up against them, by fresh wars that had broken out amongst the Tartar princes. Much against their inclinations, therefore, they were constrained to adopt the measure of returning to the court of the Grand Khan, to whom they stated the interruption they had met with.

About the time of their reappearance, Marco Polo happened to arrive from a voyage he had made, with a few vessels under his orders, to some parts of the East Indies, and reported to the Grand Khan the intelligence he brought respecting the countries he had visited, with the circumstances of his own navigation, which, he said, was performed in those seas with the utmost safety. This latter observation having reached the ears of the three ambassadors, who were extremely anxious to return to their own country, from whence they had now been absent three years, they presently sought a conference with our Venetians, whom they found equally desirous of revisiting their home; and it was settled between them that the former, accompanied by their young queen, should obtain an audience of the Grand Khan, and represent to him with what convenience and security they might effect their return by sea, to the dominions of their master; while the voyage would be attended with less expense than the journey by land, and be performed in a shorter time; according to the experience of Marco Polo, who had lately sailed in those parts. Should His Majesty incline to give his consent to their adopting that mode of conveyance, they were then to urge him to suffer the three Europeans, as being persons well skilled in the practice of navigation, to accompany them until they should reach the territory of King Arghun. The Grand Khan upon receiving this application showed by his countenance that it was exceedingly displeasing to him, averse as he was to parting with the Venetians. Feeling nevertheless that he could not with propriety do otherwise than consent, he yielded to their entreaty. Had it not been that he found himself constrained by the importance and urgency of this peculiar case, they would never otherwise have obtained permission to withdraw themselves from his service. He sent for them however, and addressed them with much kindness and conde-scension, assuring them of his regard, and requiring from them a promise that when they should have resided some time in Europe and with their own fam-ily, they would return to him once more. With this object in view he caused them to be furnished with the golden tablet (or royal chop), which contained his order for their having free and safe conduct through every part of his do-minions, with the needful supplies for themselves and their attendants. He likewise gave them authority to act in the capacity of his ambassadors to the Pope, the kings of France and Spain, and other Christian princes.

At the same time preparations were made for the equipment of fourteen ships, each having four masts, and capable of being navigated with nine sails, the construction and rigging of which would admit of ample description; but to avoid prolixity, it is for present omitted. Among these vessels there were at least four or five that had crews of two hundred and fifty or two hundred and sixty men. On them were embarked the ambassadors, having the queen under their protection together with Nicolo, Maffeo, and Marco Polo, when they had first taken their leave of the Grand Khan, who present-ed them with many rubies and other handsome jewels of great value. He also

An aerial view of the island of Java, in modern-day Indonesia.

gave directions that the ships should be furnished with stores and provisions for two years.

After a navigation of about three months, they arrived at an island which lay in a southerly direction, named Java, where they saw various objects worthy of attention, of which notice shall be taken in the sequel of the work. Taking their departure from thence, they employed eighteen months in the Indian seas before they were enabled to reach the place of their destination in the territory of King Arghun; and during this part of their voyage also they had an opportunity of observing many things, which shall, in like manner, be related hereafter. But here it may be proper to mention, that between the day of their sailing and that of their arrival, they lost by deaths, of the crews of the vessels and others who were embarked, about six hundred persons; and of the three ambassadors, only one, whose name was Goza, survived the voyage; while of all the ladies and female attendants one only died.

Upon landing they were informed that King Arghun had died some time before, and that the government of the country was then administered, on behalf of his son, who was still a youth, by a person of the name of Ki-ako-to. From him they desired to receive instructions as to the manner in which they were to dispose of the princess, whom, by the orders of the late King, they had conducted thither. His answers was, that they ought to present the lady to Kasan, the son of Arghun, who was then at a place on the borders of Persia, which has its denomination from the Arbor secco, where an army of sixty thousand men was assembled for the purpose of guarding certain passes against the irruption of the enemy. This they proceeded to carry into execution, and having effected it, they returned to the residence of Ki-akato, because the road they were afterwards to take lay in that direction. Here, however, they reposed themselves for the space of nine months. When they took their leave he furnished them with four golden tablets, each of them a cubit in length, five inches wide, and weighing three or four marks of gold.

Their inscription began with invoking the blessing of the Almighty upon the Grand Khan, that his name might be held in reverence for many years, and denouncing the punishment of death and confiscation of goods to all whop should refuse obedience to the mandate. It then proceeded to direct that the three ambassadors, as his representatives, should be treated throughout his dominions with due honour, that their expensed should be defrayed, and that they should be provided with the necessary escorts. All this was fully complied with, and from many places they were protected by bodies of two hundred horse; nor could this have been dispensed with, as the government of Ki-akato was unpopular, and the people were disposed to commit insults and proceed to outrages, which they would not have dared to attempt under the rule of their proper sovereign. In the course of their journey our travelers received intelligence of there (Kublai) having departed this life; which entirely put an end to all prospect of their revisiting those regjons. Pursuing, therefore, their intended route, they at length reached the city of Trebizond, from whence they proceeded to Constantinople, then to Negropont, and finally to Venice, at which place, in the enjoyment of health and abundant riches, they safely arrived in the year 1295. On this occasion they offered up their thanks to God, who had now been pleased to relieve them from such great fatigues, after having preserved them from innumerable perils.

CHAPTER 6

THREE MONTHS
IN UNINHABITED LANDS

By Sven Hedin

Sven Hedin in *McClure's Magazine*,
December 1897.

O n a summer's night in 1906 I settled myself comfortably on the
grass under the ancient plane trees of Ganderbal. The moderately
warm breezes of Kashmir caressed the trunks and whispered in the
crowns, but the grove was dark and the silence was broken only intermittently
by nocturnal sounds, after the day had gone to rest.

Why had they not arrived yet, I pondered. Perhaps they would not appear before the new day had risen over the mountains?

"Hello," I called to the five oarsmen, who had brought me here and who were still busy with their long, slender canoe, "Light a fire so that the caravan may find us."

Dried branches crackled and cracked and tongues of flame fluttered as golden pennants in a wind. The plane trees towered in a ring of gray specters, while the crowns turned as green as the enamel in a Mohammedan mosque. The stars that had just peeped through the leafy arches were extinguished, but the grove was flooded with light as for a temple festival, and the smoke ascended like a sacrificial tribute from an incense-burner.

I lit my pipe and mused. Another march of conquest was about to begin through Tibet. The long journey through Europe, the Caucasus, Asia Minor, Persia, Seistan and Baluchistan had been completed to Simla, where Viceroy Lord Minto informed me that London had refused permission to use India as a starting-point for a march into the forbidden country. Therefore I had been forced to revise my whole plan. I had gone to Srinagar, whence I would continue to Leh in Ladakh and join the main caravan route to Chinese Turkestan, detour in uninhabited regions and, unnoticed turn eastward. The British residentiary in Srinagar had notified me that the road to Chinese territory was also closed to me, unless I had a Chinese passport. My telegraphic request had been successful, with Swedish diplomatic assistance, and the passport arrived in good time. The first caravan was assembled in Srinagar, led by Kashmirians and escorted by two well armed Afghans and two Rajputs. Robert, a young Eurasian, was to be my secretary and the Hindoo, Manuel, my cook. We purchased thirty six fine asses from the Maharajah of Poonch, but the baggage was to be carried to Leh by hired horses. Our travel fund consisted of gold and silver rupees, current in Tibet.

The horses were loaded in my yard in Srinagar on the sixteenth of July and the long train vanished in a cloud of dust on the road to Ganderbal. Alone I walked to the bank of a canal, where a canoe was in readiness with its oarsmen. I took my place at the rudder. The highly polished boat glided like an eel through the water that seethed around the stern. The broad blades of the oars were bent by sinewy arms. Picturesque houses with any balconies lined the banks. Children played at landings and bridges, while women were washing linen. One house was built like a bridge across the canal, and the quaint perspectives succeeded each other so rapidly that we could not digest them before new ones were opened up as we traveled on our narrow waterway. Now we were in the shade, and now the sun scorched between groves of trees and houses. Ducks and geese rooted in the slime and gnats were having their evening dance over the water.

The sun sank and twilight spread over the enchanted region. The last houses disappeared, the outlines of parks and groves suggested dark phantoms on both sides of the canal. The night was raven-black as the oarsmen slowed down and the canoe glided toward the landing at Ganderbal.

And here I was by the fire under the plane trees awaiting the caravan. There was a rustling in the bushes. By the light of the fire I recognized one of the Afghans. He whistled shrilly. Robert and Manuel also appeared, accompanied by a long row of Kashmirians.

New fires crackled. A few of the men hurried back with resinous torches in their hands to light up the trail among the trees for the missing ones.

At the midnight hour all were here. What a din, what a buzz of voices and cries! The escorts were shouting their commands, Kashmirians wrangled and quarreled, horses were neighing for their bags of corn, mules kicked and fires crackled. But, gradually, it became comparatively quiet and the white turbans were grouped around the camp fires in front of the tents. Wild faces, browned to a copper color by India's sun, glistened like metal in the glare of the fire.

Dinner was served and for the first time I entered my tent which was shared with two cute puppies, Brown and White Puppy.

At last I was ready for bed and snuffed the candle. Sleep was slow in coming. Reflections from the fires danced on the tent canvas, and the murmur of voices was audible for a long time.

A new expedition had started. In fancy I heard the roar of mighty rivers, howling of raging snowstorms and temple songs in adoration of Buddha. Endless Asia was stretching yonder, waiting for me, and mysterious Tibet with its last geographic secrets, its temple cities, Lamas and incarnated gods. My head was like the workshop of a smith, where marvelous conquests and wild adventures were being hammered out. I knew which parts of earth's highest and most expansive mountain region had remained absolutely inexplored by the Western World. The most recent maps of Tibet still showed three large white areas, in the north, in the center, and in the south, marked "unexplored." The southern area of 65,000 square miles, situated north of the Brahmaputra, was the largest, and was exceeded in size only by the Polar Regions and interior Arabia. I wanted to cross these unknown expanses and fill out the blank spaces on the map with mountains, rivers and lakes and I had an ambition to be the first white man to stand at the source of the Indus, which Alexander the Macedonian believed he had discovered 2300 years ago. I also dreamed of going through to Tashi-lunpo, the monastic citadel, where the holiest man of Tibet resides, the Tashi Lama. In the previous year he had visited India and its Viceroy, who had given me a most sympathetic account of him. By the course which I had outlined, I could not reach the Tashi Lama's holy temple-city without traversing the three white areas. In 1904 the Dalai Lama had fled to Urga and Peking, when the British army of invasion under Younghusband forced itself into Lhasa, leaving four thousand slain Tibetans along the way. The Tashi Lama was now the foremost man in Tibet. I had an almost superstitious conviction that he alone had the power to open all gates for me. Thinking upon these matters did not induce sleep. I also wondered what would be the fate of all the men and animals that I had taken with me upon these roads of great adventures. Little could I then divine that not a man not an animal now stirring noisily around my tent, would be with me upon my return to Simla, two years and two months later. They were scattered as chaff before the wind. But now, as the fires died and silence enveloped the grove, all of them slept peacefully under the plane trees of Ganderbal. Our winding road led among willow, walnut and apricot trees up through the valley of the Sind and rural villages, over swaying bridges to the music of the roaring white-foamed river. Alternately, the sun burned, or darkness

Mount Kalish, the highest peak in modern Tibet. Hedin is the first known European to have reached this mountain.

followed the rapid marshaling of masses of clouds by the monsoon. We were refreshed by soft summer filled the air. At night we listened to the mournful howls of jackals and, by day, to the tinkling bells of the caravan. The march was ever upward toward snow-capped peaks that were dyed in purple as the day dawned.

In hundreds of precipitous bends of the mountain road, we moved up the pass, Zoji-la. It became necessary to reorganize the caravan completely in the village of Kargil on the other side. The Kashmirians and Afghans, who, in true bandit fashion, had stolen sundry articles from peaceable villagers along the road, were now dismissed together with their horses. Other men were engaged and seventy-seven horses were hired for the journey to Leh.

We were now at the Indus, where we rode on narrow, breakneck paths. The Himalayas were in the rear and we were getting deeper and deeper into new labyrinths of magnificent mountains. We had left the world of Hindoos and Mohammedans and were now riding through sections where Lamaism is supreme. Here and there we passed by a picturesquely located Lamaistic monastery. Along the road long stone walls had been erected, capped with slabs of green slate, in which the sacred phrase had been inscribe: Om mani padme hum. Lizards, as green as the slabs, darted unconcernedly over the sacred words.

I had ridden over this road twice previously, but in winter, when the ground was covered with snow. Now, the mountains were caressed by warm breezes and foaming, white, wild brooks tumbled from their sides into the Indus, to die in its embrace. I cast longing glances along the course of the mighty river and wondered if fortune would favor me by raising my tent up yonder by its source. No white man had ever been there.

Leh is one of the most charming cities of Asia, situated at no great distance from the banks of the Indus and surrounded by regal mountains. The old picturesque royal castle rises high above its stone houses, Lamaistic temples, mosques, bazaars and poplars. The body of the main caravan of invasion was to be set up and organized here, in which work I had the invaluable assistance of the Joint Commissioner, Captain Paterson, and of the lovable Moravian missionaries, who had become my friends in earlier expeditions.

But the greatest help came from Mohammed Isa, who had traveled with several European expeditions in innermost Asia and who was to be the leader of my caravan. He spoke Tibetan, enjoyed a good reputation in entire Ladakh, maintained excellent discipline, but was also good-natured and had a sense of humor. I greeted him in a friendly manner and within five minutes he was enlisted in my employ. He was given the following order:

"Engage twenty-five reliable Ladakhs, buy about sixty prime horses and provisions for at least three months."

On the following day my yard was transformed into a market and we were soon the owners of fifty-eight horses. The caravan also numbered thirty-six mules, thirty hired horses and seven yaks, that were led by their owners.

A few days later Mohammed Isa announced that twenty-five men were on exhibition in the yard for inspection. Eight were Mussulmans, seventeen acknowledged faith in Buddha and the holy men of the Lamaistic religion. Guffaru, the oldest man in the company at sixty-two years, had brought his own funeral shroud to be assured of honorable obsequies in the event of being overtaken by death during the journey. Tsering, a brother of Mohammed Isa, also advanced in years, was to be my cook. The others will be introduced later, as they appear in their own rôles. All were Ladakhs, with the exception of Rub Das, who was a Gurkha from Nepal. All spoke Tibetan and East Turkish. During the years I had become sufficiently familiar with the latter language to express myself and could therefore use any one of my servants as interpreter.

Gulam Rasul, a rich merchant in Leh, helped us to make our purchases for the men and animals. My yard was a workshop, packsaddles were sewed for the animals, tents were made for the men, rice, flour, barley, corn, brick-tea, preserves and numberless other articles were weighed and put in sacks, while the bells tinkled and the men talked. The sunshine filtered through the leaves of the apricot trees and cast green shadows on my floor. On an appointed day the excitement of the camp rose higher than usual. The bells on the mules gave the signal for the departure of the first division under Tsonam Tsering. Mohammed Isa followed with the main caravan.

On the fourteenth of August I started with a few men and nine baggage horses. The whole city was out to bid us farewell. Our road led out through the gate of the city by the Mohammedan burial place. Two horses shied, threw off their burdens and ran away among the markers on the graves, under which the sons of Islam await resurrection and the joys of Paradise.

After this incident all went well. Majestic mountains were rising to the left, at the right was the mighty waterway of the Indus.

From this point we penetrated the wilderness. On the pass, Marsimik-la, 18,340 feet above the sea, the first horse collapsed. The next pass was called Chang-lung-yogma and had an altitude of 18,960 feet. The ascent was incredibly steep and hours were needed to climb the dizzy height.

The view, that opens to the south, defeats any attempt of description by words. The valley that we had followed narrows into a mere furrow in a confusion of cliffs and ridges. The silver-white, sun-lit peaks of Himalaya tower over and we were on the mountain chain Karakorum. Toward the south we beheld Himalaya, in the north, Kuen-lun, the border-wall to Chinese Turkestan. Desolate Tibet expanded toward the east and southeast.

This wonderful scenery was quickly blotted out by chilling snowstorm, while the long dark line of the caravan proceeded to the Tibetan Highland. We encamped on a spot as desolate as the surface of the moon, twenty-five hundred feet higher than the peak of Mt. Blanc. Not a blade of grass grows here. The rainfall in the area does not reach the Indus, but runs into small basins without any outlets. Geographical names are totally wanting and I shall designate our camping places by numerals.

The tents had already been pitched at the base of Tikse, a Lamaistic monastery, and Muhammed Isa pointed out the arrangement of the camp and the long rows of pack animals standing there, munching grain from their feed-bags. Night came with rest, and silence was broken only by the songs of the sentinels.

The train proceeded deeper into Asia. On the crest of the pass, Chang-la, 17,580 feet above sea-level, a cairn stood, with sacrificial sticks, covered with tattered streamers, torn by the wind. Skulls of antelopes and yaks adorned the cairn. When hailstorms beat upon the whitened foreheads, the illusion was almost complete of the whining and moaning of the dead animals.

Villages were less frequent and finally there were none. In the last ones we purchased thirty sheep, ten goats and a pair of large half-wild watch dogs. The two puppies from Srinagar, irritated by the first snowfall, stood in the opening of the tent and barked themselves hoarse at the falling flakes.

In the very last village the men of Ladakh celebrated a farewell feast in honor of their homeland. The entire population gathered around our camp fire. Men played flutes and beat drums while the women danced.

Only a few days before we had enjoyed summer. We had now been received by the most inhospitable winter. We were wrapped in darkness in the middle of the day while hail pelted us and finally turned to snow. We marched in four columns quite close to each other. The animals with their burdens and the men on their horses were chalky white—we resembled sculptures in alabaster. We were able to see our nearest neighbor only, and simply followed the tinkling of the closest bell.

All changed in a few days. The weather cleared to radiance and the ground dried. We even suffered from the lack of water, but later discovered a spring at the foot of a mountain to the northeast, glistening like silver in the sunlight.

Our chosen course then led eastward in a valley, twenty miles wide, where antelopes and wild asses had undisturbed grazing and where our own animals found nourishment. We were not yet in an unknown land.

We camped several days on the western shore of a large lake that was discovered by Captain Wellby in 1896. While here we dismissed the owners of the hired horses and yaks, as well as the men from India, who could not stand the severe climate. And now the final tie that bound me to the outer world was severed. The returning men carried my last mail back with them.

The large lake is ablong, running east and west. Kuen-lun rises in the north, while in the south is a chain of wild, precipitous cliffs, changing in red and flaming yellow colors with the same wild intensity as in the Grand Canyon at sunset, The peaks are shaped like pyramids and cupolas with shining caps of eternal snow and in the valleys between the mountains, blue and green glaciers extend their armors of ice toward the lake. The sky is turquoise blue; not even the slightest breeze ruffles the lake, whose smooth surface reflects the fantastic contours and brilliant colors of the mountains.

We moved our camp to the north shore. While Mohammed Isa was conducting the caravan to the east end of the lake, we put our boat in condition. I sat at the helm and Rehim Ali was my oarsman. The distance to the south shore looked to be short. I should have time to make a series of soundings and reach the camp at the eastern shore before nightfall. A signal fire was to be kept burning in the camp if we were delayed.

The Tibetan highlands of Hedin's treks.

We started off. The depth was one hundred and sixty feet. A little later the sounding-lead of the line, two hundred and thirteen feet long, did not touch bottom.

A deathly silence surrounded us, broken only by the splash of the oars and the ripples around the stern. The smooth mirror-like sheet was cut by the boat. We were gliding along in a landscape of dreams. It was perplexingly difficult to determine where the fiery-red Mountains ended and the reflection began. The mirrored image of the heavens at nadir was just as exquisitely blue as in zenith. One became dizzy and had the sensation of soaring through crystal-clear space within a ring of glowing volcanoes. Finally we reached the desolate shore. It was late in the afternoon. We again put out and steered toward the east. An hour passed, Rehim Ali looked uneasy. Upon my question about the reason, he answered: "Storm."

I turned around. The horizon in the west darkened and yellowish-gray dust clouds swept over the mountains. A roar was heard in the distance.

The lake was still as smooth as glass. But the heralds of the storm were over us.

"Hoist the mast and sail." The boat was rigged in a moment. I grasped the sheet and the tiller. At the first gust of wind the sail filled and our light craft shot like a frightened duck over waves that soon grew to billows. Swiftly as an arrow we glided by the flat sandy points that jutted out from the shore. A flock of wild geese sat on one of the points amazed at the big bird that used only one motionless wing.

The next point extended far out into the lake, encircled by seething breakers. If we failed to clear it, we would be shipwrecked, for the oiled canvas was stretched like a drumhead over the wooden braces and would be rent in colliding with the bottom in this mad speed. The storm raged in all its fury. The mast was bent like a bow. Foam-crested waves raced by us and the water in our wake seethed in millions of boiling bubbles.

The atmosphere had cleared. The sinking sun resembled a ball of glittering gold. Scarlet skies were driving eastward. As if illuminated from within, the mountains glowed like rubies. The storm atomized the foam on the waves and scarlet plumes floated like flying veils over the lake. Shadows were lengthened, only the highest peaks still being gilded by the setting sun.

Over the fore-top the white breakers were seen around a new point. We must veer to starboard and land alee to await dawn. But the maneuver was impossible. The sea was too high and the wind too strong. In a few seconds the booming around the point was inaudible, for we were being driven out on endless wastes of water, over which the wings of night were spread.

The moon rose over the mountains to give a silvery touch to the foamy wreaths on the crests of the waves, which were chasing one another like threatening specters. We were flying directly, east. The life belts were ready, for if the boat were filled it would immediately be drawn down by the center board.

All my strength was needed to prevent the boat from steering against the wind. I looked in vain for the beacon fire. The moon set. The darkness was impenetrable, the stars alone twinkled. It was killing cold. The spray from the crests of the waves turned into an armor of ice on our garments. The whole night was ahead of us; in the east an unknown shore, where we might be hurled against perpendicular rocks and crushed in the darkness and breakers.

A dull roar was heard over the foretop. It was from the breakers on the beach. We were hurled ashore by the roll and suction of the waves. Everything was saved. We were soaking wet. It was −16 C. We tilted the boat against an oar and had shelter. We kindled a small fire with difficulty. My feet had become numb and Rehim Ali rubbed them.

We were hungry, tired and nearly frozen, when we heard the hoof-beats of horses. Mohammed Isa and two men had come to our rescue. They had believed us drowned in the storm and had just started out to look for us.

A few days later we camped again on the west shore of a bitterly salt lake, which also had to be sounded. Supplied with provisions, sweet water, and warm clothing, Robert, Rehim and I rowed across to the north shore in glorious weather and had our breakfast.

The greatest depth was only fifty-two feet. The shores were low and the bottom consisted of a deposit mixed with salt in hard, keen-edged cakes. A row of these blocks of salt extended out into the lake at our landing place. We walked on them and drew our boat into somewhat deeper water.

We stepped aboard. At that moment the western sky took on a threatening aspect. We raised the mast and the first gust of wind caused the sail to flutter.

"Perhaps it is safer to spend the night here." We had provisions and fur-coats and would have time to gather yak-dung before it was dark.

As we were about to land we saw two large light gray wolves standing on the shore at a distance of fifty feet with dripping tongues and eyes aglow with hunter and bloodthirstiness. Neither the fluttering soil, nor the rocks of salt that we threw, frightened them away. They seemed to understand that we had not brought weapons to a lake of salt water, where no fowl are found. I had previous proofs of the wolf's unlimited audacity and if these two specimens were the heralds of a whole pack we might have an uncomfortable night on the shore.

The wolves paced back and forth impatiently. The storm increased and the waves rose high and white. Our choice was between the wolves and the storm. A sudden squall moved the boat from the shore. My oarsmen took their places. The wolves contemplated us with disappointment and anger and trotted eastward along the shore, sensing that sooner or later we must land.

With wind and waves from starboard we crossed the lake and fought for our lives. The greatest peril was landing among the sharp salt-slabs where the boat would be split like paper. As the depth was only six feet, I intended to turn and take a chance on the open water among rolling, silvery waves, rather than to suffer shipwreck on the shore.

In that moment the undulations ceased and we discovered that we were in calm water. A salt point that we had not noticed gave us shelter. That night, spent on this wet shore of salt in a biting cold, I prefer to pass over in silence. It was beastly, and endlessly long. On the following morning we found the camp, where we had hot tea, wrapped ourselves in furs and slept like the dead for a whole day.

We had now come to the stage where hardly a day elapsed that we did not lost one of our animals. Eighteen horses and two mules had died. A pack of wolves followed us faithfully and gorged itself on the fallen martyrs. A death watch of six ravens had followed us for six weeks. The black birds of death laughed hoarsely at the attempts of the puppies to drive them away. When a storm approached they sounded cries of alarm. As soon as a horse had died, they pecked his eyes out. Nevertheless, we would have missed them, if they had deserted us.

The herd of sheep was soon gone. Tundup Sonam, the hunter, provided us with daily meat. He sometimes killed a yak with one ball straight to the heart. Once he killed two wild sheep. Quite often he came lugging an antelope, whose meat was better than that of other animals.

We halted for a day or two at fairly good pastures. Our pack animals were not tethered at night, but were guarded on account of wolves. The mules were more sensitive to the cold than the horses. On the night of October

seventh when the temperature sank to –24 C a few mules stationed themselves at the door of my tent. They knew that the tent gave shelter against the
cold.

We once missed three horses. Robsang started out afoot and alone to
look for them. He was absent three days. I feared that the wolves had devoured him, but in the evening he returned with two horses. The third horse
had been driven by the wolves to the shore of a small salt lake, that was still
open, where they expected that he would turn back to become the victim of
their fangs. The horse, however, as his tracks indicated, had jumped into the
lake to swim to the other shore, but strength failed him and he was drowned.
Robsang believed that the tracks of the wolves betrayed their confusion and
disappointment.

Mohammed Isa started off with the horses in the direction I had indicated. After breakfast I rode on with Robert and Rehim Ali, who held my horse
at all stops. When we came by dried yak-dung, we built a fire to warm my
hands sufficiently to take notes and sketches.

Tsering was always the last person to leave. He was responsible for my
tent and for the baggage that I needed daily. His little caravan usually passed
me at one of the resting places. Once I caught up with him on a pass, where
he exerted himself to build a cairn.

"What good will that do? We are the last ones in the train."

"To appease the mountain spirit and give us a safe pilgrimage to
Tashi-lumpo," he answered.

All the Lamaists were just as desirous as I that the pilgrimage would be
made successfully.

Winter was now setting in. On October seventeenth the cold was –2C.
At that time I had an equal number of men, horses and mules, or twenty-sev-
en of each kind. Superfluous baggage was discarded. I gave up several books.
In two months we had not seen the trace of a human being.

Tsering sat by the fire preparing my dinner in a violent snowstorm.
In the meanwhile he told stories to the others. Snowflakes sputtered in the
fire.

By October twentieth the whole country was white. The caravan proceeded to a pass. I trailed, as usual. The snow became deeper. There, a horse had fallen! The ravens had already pecked his eyes out. The wind had driven the snow up against his back. He lay as though resting on a bed of white sheets.

The pass was 18,400 feet above sea level. Icy winds. Ten degrees cold, impenetrable snowstorm. Confused by the snowstorm, Mohammed Isa had chosen the wrong course. We must remain together. It would be perilous to lose each other after all tracks had been obliterated. I followed his tracks in the snow and we camped in an abyss, almost snowed in. We hoped for Nomads who could sell us yaks and horses.

In the morning one mule was dead at the camp and two horses had collapsed near by. At Camp Number 46 there was no grazing. The horses chewed each other's tails and packsaddles. The latter were stuffed with hay. Forty days' rations of rice were reserved for the men, the balance, as well as barley and corn, was fed to the pack-animals. Mohammed reconnoitered the nasty labyrinth of snow covered mountains into which we had been misled. He had discovered level ground with pasture in the southeast. At twilight he asked for permission to conduct the caravan there. I remained with Tsering and three other men.

The cold sank to –27 C. In the morning one mule was dead—frozen stiff. If we had raised him, he would have stood like a horse in a gymnasium. Another one died as the sun rose and the reflection of the rays gave almost a sign of life to the open eye.

I started out with the shattered wreck. We met Tundup Sonam, who had been sent to show us the road. The caravan had lost its way in the night and became divided. Four mules had died; herder and sheep had disappeared. The caravan was facing destruction. If we could not find Nomads soon, we would be compelled to throw the baggage away and continue on foot. We were piloted by the hunter in biting cold and a blinding snowstorm. In time we reached the plain, built a fire so that we would not freeze to death. A little later we met a scout, who directed us to the division that was led by Sonam

Tsering. Nine pack animals had died in this terrible night. Twenty-one ema-
ciated horses and twenty mules in the same pitiful condition remained. We
could not proceed far under such conditions. Four hundred miles separated
us from Dangra-yun-tso, the lake, to which I had asked the private secretary
of the Viceroy to dispatch my mail by special courier. The goals I had set
seemed to be out of reach.

The other part of the divided caravan was reassembled. The herder had
tethered the sheep in a ravine and sat among them to keep from freezing to
death. By a miracle they had escaped the wolves.

Wooden boxes were burned in the evening fires, dispensable cooking
utensils, felt-carpets and horseshoes were discarded. The other articles were
put in sacks. Tundup Sonam shot three antelopes, one of which had been
devoured by wolves before we could get him.

A short day's march led us to a small deeply frozen lake. Late in the
evening a flock of wild geese flew on its way to warmer regions. Their chorus
of honks indicated that they had intended to settle by a spring at the shore.
When they saw their rendezvous occupied they rose higher and their honks
died away in the distance. Their forbears had traveled the same course in falls
and springs. They journeyed in snow storms and sunshine, night and day. By
light of moon and stars they saw the little lake gleam like a shield of silver.
I envied them. In a few days and nights they traversed the entire Tibet and
lifted themselves over the highest mountain chains on earth, while we needed
months and our animals were perishing.

Wherever Tibet is crossed, wild geese may be seen every spring and fall.
Separate colonies travel on different, traditional, direct routes. Do they select
the time of the full moon for their flight, when the earth is illumined? Tibetans have a touching reverence for the wild geese, not the least because these
winged Nomads of the air practice monogamy. A Tibetan would rather die of
starvation than do violence to a wild goose.

The wolves became holder and howled just outside of our tents. The
night-guard was increased. One night Tundup lay in ambush and shot a wolf
that limped out on the ice and lay down to die.

On another occasion Tundup shot a yak that had two Tibetan balls in its body. He surprised a herd of yaks in a glen. They all fled with the exception of a bull who stopped and was wounded. Foaming with rage, the animal charged. In the last moment the hunter swung himself up on a terrace from which he aimed straight to the heart and the yak fell. We erected our tents on this spot and had meat for several days.

On a day when my usual companions and I were about two hundred meters away from the camp, Mohammed Isa fired a bullet into a herd of yaks that was grazing near by. Instead of venting his fury on the marksman, a stately bull charged with full speed directly at Robert, Rehim Ali and me. Foaming with rage the yak lowered his horns to raise me and my horse in the air. I removed my fur coat to throw it over the yak's head in the last second. But Rehim Ali had stumbled and fallen and the yak selected him as victim, rushed over him and continued his flight. I rode back to the prostrate man in the belief that he had been gored to death. He had escaped with a bloody streak on one leg and torn clothing. As a result of shock to his nervous system in the terrifying experience, Rehim Ali showed signs of an unbalanced mind for a time.

***

At last we were getting nearer to human beings. We noticed several old fireplaces and a placer mining camp, where gold prospectors had occupied a score of tents. One night our last horses and mules were chased northward by a pack of hungry wolves, but were overtaken and saved in time.

Tundup returned from a hunting expedition on November tenth and related that he had discovered a black tent in a valley towards the west. Upon closer investigation we learned that the tent was inhabited by a woman, who had two husbands, both of whom were away hunting. They had neither yaks, horses nor provisions for sale.

Three horses died and only thirteen remained. A report was made to me on November twelfth: "Sir, Tundup Sonam is returning from the valley with two Tibetans." Seeing our tents they were frightened and wanted to flee, but Tundup reassured them. They laid down their guns at a proper distance and followed Mohammed Isa with lagging steps to his tent, where they were offered tea and tobacco.

Afterward they came to my tent, fell on their knees and sers had come to the camp and improved our prospects at one stroke. They carried all kinds of articles inside of their baggy coats, dried chunks of meat, wooden bowls for tsamba and tea. Tobacco pouch, pipe, steel, bodkins and knoves dangled from belts in rhythm with their steps. Their black coarse hair hung in tufts around the greasy coat-collar and the lice that inhabited these primeval forests had never in their lives run the risk of being caught in a comb. Musketoons and bifurcated props were strapped over the shoulders, the belt held broad swords and the men rode small, chubby, long-haired horses with bright, lively eyes.

They call themselves Changpas or Northmen and spend their winters in the desolate regions of Chang-tang in northern Tibet to eke out a living by hunting. Cows furnish them milk, butter, cheese and cream. From big game they secure meat, skins and fur. They prefer the meat when it is raw, hard, dry and old. They may often be seen taking out the rib of a yak or a wild ass, more like a blackened stick of wood, from the ample folds of their fur coats, and carving it with their sharp case knives. Chinese brick-tea is the chief delicacy among the good things of life, especially if it has an abundance of leaves and stems. A lump of butter swims the wooden bowl like oil among driftwood. In this count even the horses eat meat on account of the scarcity of pasture. It seems strange to see small grass-eating animals stand a munch the strips of meat, until the saliva hangs in long icicles from their mouths.

Not even a person of refined taste need turn up his nose the menu placed before him in the tent of a yak-hunt: goat's milk with fat, yellow cream; yak kidneys browned in fat; yak-marrow, toasted over dung-fire; small, fat pieces of the tender meat along the spine of the antelope, or its head held by the long horns in the flames until the skin has be burned away and it all looks like a mass of soot. Table salt found in inexhaustible quantities on the shores of lakes.

Normads and hunters, in common with wild geese, are migratory and know all springs and pastures. They rest and hunt where their forebears have tented and hunted. They lay their traps for antelopes or lie in ambush for wild asses on a stone wall that perhaps has stood since time immemorial. Quietly and stealthily the hunter steals up on the yak against the wind and knows by experience just when to stop and shoot. Then he strikes sparks with the steel against the flint. The burning tinder lights the end of a cord that is brought in contact with the touch-hole by the hammer, after the bead has been drawn. He does not shoot until he is sure of hitting the mark, for he must save powder and lead. The yak falls, the meat is cut up and preserved under the folds of the tent. The pelts of yaks, wild asses, antelopes and wild sheep are tanned and utilized. Boots, harness, straps and many other articles are made from them and the sinews serve as thread.

When the Changpa men are on the hunt, the women care for the domestic animals and as the hunter returns at sunset the ruminating yaks are lying down in front of the tent. There they lie all night and the Nomads need not go far for dung, their only fuel. The sheep are herded into a circular fold of stone, and wolves are kept at a distance by large wild dogs.

As darkness falls the family is seated around the fire over which the teakettle is boiling. The long pipe moves from mouth to mouth. The conversation touches upon the success of the hunt, the care of the herds and the removal to better pasture. Worn-out soles are repaired and hides are tanned by hand. A woman churns butter in a wooden stoup, while her small naked children are playing in the light of the fire. Each one retires to his own lair of furs and before the rising sun has gilded the mountain tops the bellows are blowing to revive the fire.

Thus they live and thus they roam and thus it has been generation after generation, for uncounted centuries. Chang-tang is their poor homeland, where they live bravely and largely in God's free air, struggling against poverty and dangers. They have no fear of the roar of the storm: the clouds are their brothers. They share dominion over mountains and valleys only with the beasts of the wilderness, and the eternal stars twinkle over their tents by night.

They love the icy cold, the dancing drift-snow and the white moonlight in quiet Tibetan wintry nights.

During his whole life the Nomad has the deepest reverence for the spirits of the mountains, lakes and springs. He is convinced that the hunt will be unsuccessful if he does not read devoutly his "Om mani padme hum." He knows that the spirits of the air, unless due veneration be accorded them, will bury all pastures under heaps of snow,—the doom of inevitable starvation of sheep and goats, and he may well fear an unfortunate end to his wandering if he does not add a new stone to the old cairn on the mountain passes as he goes by. He does not have the slightest idea of the splendor of temple halls and of the blue smoke that circles up to the faces of the gilded gods. A pilgrimage to the great monastic cities is the privilege of rich Nomads. He believes in transmigration and is convinced that all evil deeds will be punished in the next existence, when he reappears in the form of a pack animal, a dog, or a vulture.

Some day death will stand at the tent door and peer through. The storm is howling outside, fire burns in the hearth and silence is broken only by the everlasting prayer "Om mani padme hum." The dying man reviews his long, laborious, joyless life. He is afraid of the evil spirits, who are waiting for his departure to lead the soul on its dismal wandering into the great unknown. Unless he has appeased them while living, it is now too late. He resigns himself hopelessly to their power and caprice. Bent, wrinkled and gray, the old hunter finishes his course. The hunting ground, where he has lived his days, vanishes back of him and he takes the first step out into the uncertain darkness. His nearest relatives carry the body to a mountain where it is laid, naked and frozen, as food for wolves and birds of prey. In life he had no continuing city and no grave after death. His grandchildren do not know where he was laid. Perhaps that is best, for where dead men's bones whiten, evil spirits dwell.

When we resumed the march, we took the two Nomads along as pilots and I could begin to insert names on my map again. They told us everything they knew about the region, roads and the roaming of their friends. Four days later they informed us that their knowledge of the country was exhausted. I paid them four rupees a day each for the time they had been with us. Kashmir gave each one of them a case knife and an armful of empty cigarette tins. Our generosity amazed them and they declared it beyond belief that such kind people existed.

It was severely cold and the temperature went down to –3 C at night. Our solitary travel would soon be ended. Beyond the threshold of a pass we noticed large herds of sheep, yaks and six black tents. A pack of half-wild dogs barked themselves hoarse and the inhabitants were astonished when we raised our tents near by on the shore of lake Dungtsa-tso.

Lobsang Tsering, the beardless and weather-beaten chief of the tent village, snuffed, laughed and chattered. Evidently he had received no orders from Lhasa. We purchased five yaks of him and once more our twenty-five veterans were given assistance. The useful yaks had come to us a veritable Godsend.

Alternately, I rode the dapper gray horse that I mounted at Leh, or a small, lively white animal from Ladakh. The winter storms had begun. We stiffened in the saddles. Our eyes watered and the tears congealed. Garments became gray from the flying dust. Lips cracked, especially if we laughed, but there were few appeals to risibilities in a temperature of –33 C. We wanted to get into our tents and to a fire. The storm whizzed and howled.

Four mules died. Wolves were on the spot almost before we left it.

Mohammed Isa attempted to buy yaks in a tent village. A man approached and roared in an authoritative voice.

"A European is among you. We will sell you no yaks. Turn back, or it will fare you ill."

In the night of December first the temperature was –31 C. One mule lay dead between the tents and had nearly been devoured by wolves before the place was out of our sight. Camp Number 77 was located in a valley among wild cliffs. Two men in many-colored furs wearing ivory rings and sacred silver caskets around their necks appeared. They carried guns and swords in silver scabbards, studded with turquoises and corals. They were members of a group of thirty-five pilgrims who, with their herds of one hundred yaks and six hundred sheep, had been at the sacred mountain (Kailas) and the sacred lake (Manasarowar). They had seen me, my Cossacks and Lama, five years ago, when the Governor of Naktsong compelled me to change course to Ladakh.

Early in the dark, rough morning I was awakened by the rattling of guns and swords as they came to sell yaks. They gave us the following information: "Orders to stop you are being circulated south of the next pass."

Consequently, we were to face the same opposition as formerly! Nearly all of our baggage was borne by eighteen yaks. A new world spread itself in the south from a pass, but it was soon enveloped in a snowstorm. We plodded on through the snow. Three men rode toward us on snorting horses, put a few questions to us, and went over to Mohammed Isa.

The summons were therefore in full action! While we were encamped a few days later on the shore of Bogtsang-tsangpo, a group of Tiberans came to my tent. Their "Gova," or chief, recognized me from 1901 and must make an immediate report to the Governor of Naktsong. He pleaded in vain with us to remain, and as we continued our journey, he accompanied us down the river for five days. We caught excellent fishes through the wakes. The Tibetans believe that lizards and snakes are equally suitable food. Karma Tamding in Tang-yung, also recognized me from my previous visit, five years ago. At that time the whole country had talked about my journey. All attempts to preserve my incognito were futile. He sold three yaks to us. Another mule died just as the first stars became visible. We now had only two mules and eleven horses. All the veterans were relieved of burden-bearing.

Karma Tamding returned, accompanied by twelve Nomads, with a large quantity of provisions. We bought toasted meal and corn for sixty-eight rupees. Two women were with him, well clothed as a protection against the paralyzing wind. We did not see much of them, but the little we saw was very dirty.

We shortened the days marches in order to pitch camp before we were thoroughly frozen. On the morning before Christmas an old mendicant Lama sat outside of my tent singing and swinging his magic wand which was literally covered with colored pieces of cloth, tassels and gimcracks. He had wandered all over Tibet, begged from tent to tent, danced with his magic wand and sung his incantations for food.

Our Christmas camp was raised on the shore of a small lake, Dumbok-tso. For dinner Tsering offered us a pan of superb sour milk, juicy mutton roasted over the coals, fresh wheat bread and tea. I fancied hearing church bells ringing far away and the jingle of sleigh-bells in the Swedish forests. The tent was illuminated, my Ladakhs sang, and the Tibetans must have thought that we were performing sacrificial rites and singing to unknown gods. Before the last candle had been extinguished. I read the Bible texts for the day. The stars of Orion sparkled with incomparable brilliance out yonder in the night. We pitched our camp on the north shore of Lake Ngang-tse-tso, altitude, 15,640 feet. We decided to rest here for a season. I wanted to chart and sound the lake. From this point southward to Tsang-po, the country was unknown. Our tired animals also needed rest. The only anxiety was caused by a possibility that the alert watchmen in Lhasa should anticipate us and prevent us from continuing. We had eight horses and one mule left, and the twenty-one yaks were beginning to be footsore. We simply must give the animals a rest.

I spent nine days on the ice of the lake and sounded through the wakes. The greatest depth was only thirty-three feet. Two Ladakhs pulled me along the ice sixty-six miles on an improved sled. Seven Ladakhs carried provisions. Our camps were pitched on the shore.

The ice of the lake was covered with fine powdered salt. Wrapped in a sheepskin coat, I sat on the sled. We moved rapidly as my two Ladakhs ran from wake to wake. One day a snowstorm raged straight in our faces. The two men were blown over and the sled was swept away by the storm and raced on until it was upset in a crack. That runaway ride was glorious while it lasted, for the wind was not felt. But, after the tumble, I faced it again. We resumed our journey. I could scarcely see the two men ten feet ahead. The powdered salt swept over the smooth ice and gave the illusion that we were moving at a dizzy speed.

We made much better time later with the wind. We rested a day in a ravine on the shore. A messenger from Mohammed Isa arrived, half dead of fatigue. He had been seeking us on the ice fifty-four hours.

He reported that, on January first, six armed horsemen had arrived at our stationary camp and made the usual investigation. They had returned on the following day with reinforcements and a message from the Governor of Naktsong to remain where we were and that I must go back to the camp and personally answer the Governor's questions so that he could dispatch a report to Lhasa.

Had we not endured enough? Had we not lost almost our entire caravan? I imagined hearing once more the creaking of the copper gates as they closed, shutting us out from the land of sacred books, the forbidden land.

After the messenger had rested, I sent him back with the declaration that if the chief of the patrol wished to talk to me, he and his entire cavalcade would be welcome to do so on the ice.

On the following day stones and stems were white with hoarfrost. The smooth ice had become wavy as watered silk from the powder. We sounded in new wakes. Mohammed Isa and two men found us on January sixth. My competent leader of the caravan reported:

"Sir, we had intended moving the camp today to the shore so as to be nearer to you, when three Tibetans, who were encamped close by, appeared and compelled us to unload the caravan which was ready to start, and prohibited us from taking one step southward. The Governor is expected within three days. Mounted couriers are in constant motion between him and the patrol. They repeatedly ask why you are out on the ice and seem to think that it is of no importance how deep Lake Ngangtse-tso may be. They suspect that you are greeting gold from the bottom through the wakes and have just sent patrols along the shores."

Mohammed Isa returned and we continued our soundings and camped on the shore, which was already occupied by a herd of wild asses and a wolf.

Early the following morning a courier was sent to the stationary camp for my mount. When I arrived at the tent city the Tibetans sat in the doors of their tents, looking out like so many marmouts in their burrows. The chiefs were eventually informed that I would receive them in Mohammed Isa's tent. They came, humbly saluting and with congress hanging out of their mouths. The leader, dressed in a red band around his head, dark blue fur coat and with a sword in his belt, had been a member of Hlaje Tsering's suite in 1901, when we tented together on the shore of Chargut-tso.

A long conversation ensued and the chieftains confirmed that it was my old friend Hlaje Tsering, who personally would be here in a few days to pass judgment upon me and my caravan.

"Will he be accompanied by five hundred horsemen, as upon the former occasion?" I queried.

"No, Bombo Chimbo, he noticed that troops of horsemen did not frighten you. He now hopes that you will comply with his wishes."

"I have neither time nor disposition to remain here and wait for Hlaje Tsering," I answered.

"Bombo Chimbo, if the Governor does not arrive within three days, you may cut our throats."

Towards evening on the eleventh of January a body of horsemen was outlined on the hills in the east and new tents were erected around us. One of them was more ornamental than the others, made of white and blue canvas. A new troop of horsemen came shortly thereafter. The foremost man was old, bent and was wrapped in fluffy expensive furs and wore a red fur-lined bashlik on his head. After dismounting they laid their guns on the ground and crawled into the tents.

The old man was really Hlaje Tsering! I realized the weakness of my present position. I knew how hopeless it was to persuade a Tibetan Governor, either by a friendly attitude, or by intimidation, to open the roads to the sacred cities.

Bitter regret tortured me because I had not followed the original plan of proceeding to Dangra-yum-tso! It grieved me to contemplate that the large white space on the map began immediately south of Ngangtse-tso and that I must turn back from its very threshold.

True, we had traversed the unknown land to the north, discovered several lakes and mountains, sounded and charted Ngangtse-tso. But all these things were insignificant in comparison with the objective of this expedition, the exploration of the unknown land to the south and discovery of the source of the Indus.

CHAPTER 7

SOUTH COAST DISCOVERY

by Ernest Scott

Ernest Scott (left) standing
outside the Old Law building,
University of Melbourne.

That part of the coast lying between the south-west corner of the continent and Fowler's Bay, in the Great Australian Bight, had been traversed prior to this time. In 1791 Captain George Vancouver, in the British ship Cape Chatham, sailed along it from Cape Leeuwin to King George's Sound, which he discovered and named. He anchored in the harbour, and remained there for a fortnight. He would have liked to pursue the discovery of this unknown country, and did sail further east, as far as the neighbourhood of Termination Island, in longitude 122 degrees, 8 minutes. But, meeting with adverse winds, he abandoned the research, and resumed his voyage to north-west America across the Pacific. In 1792, Bruny Dentrecasteaux, with the French ships Recherche and Esperance, searching for tidings of the lost Laperouse, followed the line of the shore more closely than Vancouver had done, and penetrated much further eastward. His instructions, prepared by Fleurieu, had directed him to explore the whole of the southern coast of Australia; but he was short of water, and finding nothing but sand and rock, with no harbour, and no promise of a supply of what he so badly needed, he did not continue further than longitude 131 degrees, 38½ minutes east, about two and a half degrees east of the present border line of Western and South Australia. These navigators, with the Dutchman Pieter Nuyts, in the early part of the seventeenth century, and the Frenchman St. Alouarn, who anchored near the Leeuwin in 1772, were the only Europeans known to have been upon any part of these southern coasts before the advent of Flinders; and the extent of the voyage of Nuyts is by no means clear.

Flinders laid it down as a guiding principle that he would make so complete a survey of the shores visited by him as to leave little for anybody to do after him. He therefore commenced his work immediately when he touched land, constructing his own charts as the ship slowly traversed the curves of the coast. The result was that many corrections and additions to the charts of Vancouver and Dentrecasteaux were made before the entirely new discoveries were commenced. In announcing this fact, Flinders, always generous in his references to good work done by his predecessors, warmly praised the charts prepared by Beautemps-Beaupre, "geographical engineer" of the Recherche. "Perhaps no chart of a coast so little known as this is, will bear a comparison with its original better than this of M. Beaupre," he said. His own charts were of course fuller and more precise, but he made no claim to superiority on this account, modestly observing that he would have been open to reproach if, after following the coast with an outline of M. Beaupre's chat before him, he had not effected improvements where circumstances did not permit so close an examination to be made in 1792.

King George's Sound.

Several inland excursions were made, and some of the King George's Sound aboriginals were encountered. Flinders noted down some of their words, and pointed out the difference from words for the same objects used by Port Jackson and Van Diemen's Land natives. An exception to this rule was the word used for calling to a distance—cai-wah! (come here). This is certainly very like the Port Jackson cow-ee, whence comes the one aboriginal word of universal employment in Australia to-day, the coo-ee of the townsman and the bushman alike, a call entered in the vocabulary collected by Hunter as early as 1790.

The method of research adopted by Flinders was similar to that employed on the Norfolk voyage. The ship was kept all day as close inshore as possible, so that water breaking on the shore was visible from the deck, and no river or opening could escape notice. When this could not be done, because the coast retreated far back, or was dangerous, the commander stationed himself at the masthead with a glass. All the bearings were laid down as soon as taken, whilst the land was in sight; and before retiring to rest at night Flinders made it a practice to finish up his rough chart for the day, together with his journal of observations. The ship hauled off the coast at dusk, but especial care was taken to come upon it at the same point next morning, as soon after daylight as practicable, so that work might be resumed precisely where it had been dropped on the previous day. "This plan," said Flinders, "to see and lay down everything myself, required constant attention and much labour, but was absolutely necessary to obtaining that accuracy of which I was desirous." When bays or groups of islands were reached, Flinders went ashore with the theodolite, took his angles, measured, mapped, and made topographical notes. The lead was kept busy, making soundings. The rise and fall of the tides were observed; memoranda on natural phenomena were written; opportunities were given for the naturalists to collect specimens, and for the artist to make drawings. The net was frequently drawn in the bays for examples of marine life. Everybody when ashore kept a look out for plants, birds, beasts, and insects. In short, a keenness for investigation, an assiduity in observation, animated the whole ship's company, stimulated by the example of the commander, who never spared himself in his work, and interested himself in that of others.

As in a drama, "comic relief" was occasionally interposed amid more serious happenings. The blacks were friendly, though occasionally shy and suspicious. In one scene the mimicry that is a characteristic of the aboriginal was quaintly displayed. The incident, full of colour and humour, is thus related by Flinders:

> Our friends, the natives, continued to visit us: and an old man with several others being at the tents this morning, I ordered the party of marines on shore, to be exercised in their presence. The red coats and white crossed belts were greatly admired, having some resemblance to their own manner of ornamenting themselves; and the drum, but particularly the fife, excited their astonishment; but when they bright muskets, drawn up in a line, they absolutely screamed with delight; nor were their wild gestures and vociferation to be silenced but by commencing the exercise, to which they paid

the most earnest and silent attention. Several of them moved their hands, involuntarily, according to the motions; and the old man placed himself at the end of the rank, with a short staff in his hand, which he shouldered, presented, grounded, as did the marines their muskets, without, I believe, knowing what he did. Before firing, the Indians were made acquainted with what was going to take place; so that the volleys did not excite much terror.

Seaman Smith was naturally much interested in the aboriginals, whose features were however to him "quite awful, having such large mouths and long teeth." They were totally without clothing, and "as soon as they saw our tents they run into the bushes with such activity that would pawl any European to exhibit. Because our men would not give them a small tommy-hawk they began to throw pieces of wood at them, which exasperated our men; but orders being so humane towards the natives that we must put up with anything but heaving spears." Furthermore, "they rubbed their skin against ours, expecting some mark of white upon their's, but finding their mistake they appeared surprised."

Pleasures more immediately incidental to geographical discovery—those pleasures which eager and enterprising minds must experience, however severe the labour involved, on traversing portions of the globe previously unknown to civilised mankind—commenced after the head of the Great Bight was passed. From about the vicinity of Fowler's Bay (named after the first lieutenant of the Investigator) the coast was virgin to geographical science. Comparisons of original work with former charts were no longer possible. The ship was entering unnavigated waters, and the coasts delineated were new to the world's knowledge. The quickening of the interest in the work in hand, which touched both officers and men of the expedition, can be felt by the reader of Flinder's narrative. There was a consciousness of having crossed a line separating what simply required verification and amplification, from a totally fresh field of research. Every reach of coastline now traversed was like a cable, long buried in the deep of time, at length hauled into daylight, with its oozy deposits of seaweed, shell and mud lying thick upon it.

Contingent upon discovery was the pleasure of naming important features of the coast. It is doubtful whether any other single navigator in history
applied names which are still in use to so many capes, bays and islands, upon
the shores of the habitable globe, as Flinders did. The extent of coastline
freshly discovered by him was not so great as that first explored by some of
his predecessors. But no former navigator pursued extensive new discoveries
so minutely, and, consequently, found so much to name; while the precision
of Flinders' records left no doubt about the places that he named, when in
later years the settlement of country and the navigation of seas necessitated
the use of names. Compare, for instance, in this one respect, the work of
Cook and Dampier, Vasco da Gama and Magellan, Tasman and Quiros, with
that of Flinders. Historically their voyages may have been in some respects
more important; but they certainly added fewer names to the map. There
are 103 names on Cook's charts of eastern Australia from Point Hicks to
Cape York; but there are about 240 new names on the charts of Flinders
representing southern Australia and Tasmania. He is the Great Denominator
among navigators. He named geographical features after his friends, after his
associates on the Investigator, after distinguished persons connected with the
Navy, after places in which he was interested. Fowler's Bay, Point Brown,
Cape Bauer, Franklin's Isles, Point Bell, Point Westall, Taylor's Isle, and Thistle Island, commemorate his shipmates. Spencer's Gulf was named "in honour of the respected nobleman who presided at the Board of Admiralty when
the voyage was planned and the ship was put in commission," and Althorp
Isles celebrated Lord Spencer's heir. Cockburn, Nomenclature of South Australia, is mistaken in speculating that "there is a parish of Althorp in Flinders'
native country in Lincolnshire which probably accounts for the choice of
the name here." Althorp, which should be spelt without a final "e," is not in
Lincolnshire, but in Northampton-shire. St. Vincent's Gulf was named "in
honour of the noble admiral" who was at the head of the Admiralty when the
Investigator sailed from England, and who had "continued to the voyage that
countenance and protection of which Earl Spencer had set the example." To
Yorke's Peninsula, between the two gulfs, was affixed the name of the Right

Hon. C.P. Yorke, afterwards Lord Hardwicke, the First Lord who authorised the publication of Flinders' Voyage. Thus, the ministerial heads of the Admiralty in three Governments (Pitt's, Addington's, and Spencer Perceval's) came to be commemorated. It may be remarked as curious that a naval officer so proud of his service as Flinders was, should nowhere have employed the name of the greatest sailor of his age, Nelson. There is a Cape Nelson on the Victorian coast, but the name was given by Grant.

In Spencer's Gulf we come upon a group of Lincolnshire place-names, for Flinders, his brother Samuel, the mate, Fowler, and Midshipman John Franklin, all serving on this voyage, were Lincolnshire men. Thus we find Port Lincoln, Sleaford Bay, Louth Bay, Cape Donington, Stamford Hill, Surfleet Point, Louth Isle, Sibsey Isle, Stickney Isle, Spilsby Isle, Partney Isle, Revesby Isle, Point Boston, and Winceby Isle. Banks' name was given to a group of islands, and Coffin's Bay must not be allowed to suggest any gruesome association, for it was named after Sir Issac Coffin, resident naval commissioner at Sheerness, who had given assistance in the equipment of the Investigator. A few names, like Streaky Bay, Lucky Bay, and Cape Catastrophe, were applied from circumstances that occurred on the voyage. A poet of the antipodes who should, like Wordsworth, be moved to write "Poems on the Naming of Places," would find material in the names given by Flinders.

Interest in this absorbing work rose to something like excitement on February 20th, when there were indications, from the set of the tide, that an unusual feature of the coast was being approached. "The tide from the north-eastward, apparently the ebb, ran more than one mile an hour, which was the more remarkable from no set of the tide worthy to be noticed having hitherto been observed upon this coast." The ship had rounded Cape Catastrophe, and the land led away to the north, whereas hitherto it had trended east and south. What did this mean? Flinders must have been strongly reminded of his experience in the Norfolk in Bass Strait, when the rush of the tide from the south showed that the north-west corner of Van Diemen's Land had been turned, and that the demonstration of the Strait's existence was complete. There were many speculations as to what the signs indicated. "Large rivers, deep inlets, inland seas and passages into the Gulf of Carpentaria, were terms frequently used in our conversations of this evening, and the prospect of making an interesting discovery seemed to have infused new life and vigour into every man in the ship." The expedition was, in fact, in the bell-mouth of Spencer's Gulf, and the next few days were to show whether the old surmise was true—that Terra Australis was cloven in twain by a strait from the Gulf of Carpentaria to the southern ocean. It was, indeed, a crisis-time of the discovery voyage.

But before the gulf was examined, a tragedy threw the ship into mourning. On the evening of Sunday, February 21st, the cutter was returning from the mainland, where a party had been searching for water in charge of the Master, John Thistle. She carried a midshipman, William Taylor, and six sailors. Nobody on the ship witnessed the accident that happened; but the cutter had been seen coming across the water, and as she did not arrive when darkness set in, the fear that she had gone down oppressed everybody on board. A search was made, but ineffectually; and next day the boat was found floating bottom uppermost, stove in, and bearing the appearance of having been dashed against rocks. The loss of John Thistle was especially grievous to Flinders. The two had been companions from the very beginning of his career in Australia. Thistle had been one of Bass's crew in the whaleboat; he had been on the Norfolk when Van Diemen's Land was circumnavigated; and he had taken part in the cruise to Moreton Bay. His memory lives in the name of Thistle Island, on the west of the entrance to the gulf, and in the noble tribute which his commander paid to his admirable qualities. It would be wrong to deprive the reader of the satisfaction of reading Flinder's eulogy of his companion of strenuous years:

> The reader will pardon me the observation that Mr. Thistle was truly a valuable man, as a seaman, an officer, and a good member of society. I had known him, and we had mostly served together, from the year 1794. He had been with Mr. Bass in his perilous expedition in the whaleboat, and with me in the voyage round Van Diemen's Land, and in the succeeding expedition to Glass House and Hervey's Bays. From his merit and prudent conduct, he was promoted from

before the mast to be a midshipman and afterwards a master in His Majesty's service. His zeal for discovery had induced him to join the Investigator when at Spit-head and ready to sail, although he had returned to England only three weeks before, after an absence of six years. Besides performing assiduously the duties of his situation. Mr. Thistle had made himself well acquainted with the practice of nautical astronomy, and began to be very useful in the surveying department. His loss was severely felt by me, and he was lamented by all on board, more especially by his messmates, who knew more intimately the goodness and stability of his disposition." (In a letter to Banks from Spithead on June 3rd, 1801, Flinders had written: "I am happy to inform you that the Buffalo has brought home a person formerly of the Reliance whom I wish to have as master. He volunteers, the captain of the ship agrees, and I have made application by to-day's post and expect his appointment by Friday." The reference was evidently to John Thistle.)

Taylor's Isle was named after the young midshipman of this catastrophe, and six small islands in the vicinity bear the names of the boat's crew. It is a singular fact that only two of the eight sailors drowned could swim. Even Captain Cook never learnt to swim!

Before leaving the neighbourhood, Flinders erected a copper plate upon a stone post at the head of Memory Cove, and had engraved upon it the names of the unfortunates who had perished, with a brief account of the accident. Two fragments of the original plate are now in the museum at Adelaide. In later years it was beaten down by a storm, and South Australian Government erected a fresh tablet in Memory Cove to replace it.

A thorough survey of Port Lincoln was made while the ship was being replenished with water. Some anxiety had been felt owing to the lack of this necessity, and Flinders showed the way to obtain it by digging holes in the white clay surrounding a brackish marsh which he called Stamford Mere. The water that drained into the holes was found to be sweet and wholesome, though milky in appearance. As the filling of the casks and conveying them to the ship—to a quantity of 60 tons—occupied several days, the surveying and scientific employments were pursued diligently on land.

The discovery of Port Lincoln was in itself an event of consequence, since it is a harbour of singular commodiousness and beauty, and would, did it but possess a more prolific territory at its back, be a maritime station of no small importance. Nearly forty years later, Sir John Franklin, then Governor of Tasmania, paid a visit to Port Lincoln, expressly to renew acquaintance with a place in the discovery of which he had participated in company with a commander whose memory he honoured; and he erected on Stamford Hill, at his own cost, an obelisk in commemoration of Flinders. In the same way, on his first great overland arctic journey in 1821, Franklin remembered Flinders in giving names to discoveries.

It was on March 6th that the exploration of Spencer's Gulf commenced. As the ship sailed along the western shore, the expectations which had been

Spencer's Gulf, present day south Austraila.

formed of a strait leading through the continent to the Gulf of Carpentaria faded away. The coast lost its boldness, the water became more and more shallow, and the opposite shore began to show itself. The gulf was clearly tapering to an end. "Our prospects of a channel or strait cutting off some considerable portion of Terra Australis grew less, for it now appeared that the ship was entering into a gulph." On the 10th, the Investigator having passed Point Lowly, and having on the previous day suddenly come into two-and-a-half fathoms, Flinders decided to finish the exploration in a rowing boat, accompanied by Surgeon Bell. They rowed along the shore till night fell, slept in the boat, and resumed the journey early next morning (March 11th). At ten o' clock, the oars touched mud on each side, and it became impossible to proceed further. They had reached the head of the gulf, then a region of mangrove swamps and flat waters, but now covered by the wharves of Port Augusta, and within view of the starting point of the transcontinental railway.

The disappointment was undoubtedly great at not finding even a large river flowing into the gulf. The hope of a strait had been abandoned as the continually converging shores, shallow waters, and diminishing banks made it clear, long before the head was reached, that the theory of a bifurcated Terra Australis was impossible. But as Flinders completed his chart and placed it against the outline of the continent, he might fairly enjoy the happiness of having settled an important problem and of taking one more stride towards completing the map of the world.

The Investigator traveled down by the eastern shore, once hanging upon a near bank for half an hour, and by March 20th was well outside. The length of the gulf, from the head to Gambier Island, Flinders calculated to be 185 miles, and its width at the mouth, in a line from Cape Catastrophe, 48 miles. At the top it tapered almost to a point. The whole of it was personally surveyed and charted by Flinders, who was able to write that for the general exactness of his drawing he could "answer with tolerable confidence, having seen all that is laid down, and, as usual, taken every angle which enters into the construction."

The next discovery of importance was that of Kangaroo Island, separated from the foot-like southern projection of Yorke's Peninsula by Investigator

Strait. The Island was named an account of the quantity of kangaroos seen and shot upon it; for a supply of fresh meat was very welcome after four months of salt pork. Thirty-one fell to the guns of the Investigator's men. Half a hundredweight of heads, forequarters and tails were stewed down for soup, and as much kangaroo steak was available for officers and men as they could consume "by day and night." It was declared to be a "delightful regale."

The place where Flinders is believed to have first landed on Kangaroo Island is now marked by a tall cairn, which was spontaneously built by the inhabitants, the school children assisting, in 1906. An inscription on a faced stone commemorates the event. The white pyramid can be seen from vessels using Backstairs Passage.

A very short stay was made at Kangaroo Island on this first call. On March 24th Investigator Strait was crossed, and the examination of the mainland was resumed. The ship was steered north-west, and, the coast being reached, no land was visible to the eastward. The conclusion was drawn that another gulf ran inland, and the surmise proved to be correct. The new discovery, named St. Vincent's Gulf, was penetrated on the 27th, and was first explored on the eastern shore, not on the western as had been the case with Spencer's Gulf. Mount Lofty was sighted at dawn on Sunday, March 28th. The nearest part of the coast was there leagues distant at the time, "mostly low, and composed of sand and rock, with a few small trees scattered over it; but at a few miles inland, where the back mountains rise, the country was well clothed with forest timber, and had a fertile appearance. The fires bespoke this to be a part of the continent." The coast to the northward was seen to be very low, and the soundings were fast decreasing. From noon to six o'clock the Investigator ran north thirty miles, skirting a sandy shore, and at length dropped anchor in five fathoms.

On the following morning land was seen to the westward, as well as eastward, and there was "a hummocky mountain, capped with clouds, apparently near the head of the inlet." Wind failing, very little progress was made till noon, and at sunset the shores appeared to be closing round. The absence of tide gave no prospect of finding a river at the head of the gulf. Early on the morning of the 30th Flinders went out in a boat, accompanied by Robert Brown, and rowed up to the mud-flats at the head of the gulf. Picking out a narrow channel, it was found possible to get within half a mile of dry land. Then, leaving the boat, Flinders and Brown walked along a bank of mud and sand to the shore, to examine the country. Flinders ascended one of the foothills of the range that forms the backbone of Yorke's Peninsula, stretching north and south upwards of two hundred miles.

At dawn on March 31st the Investigator was gotten under way to proceed down the eastern side of Yorke's Peninsula. The wind was contrary, and the work could be done only "partially," though, of course, sufficiently well to complete the chart. The peninsula was described as "singular in form, having some resemblance to a very ill-shaped leg and foot." Its length from Cape Spencer to the northern junction with the mainland was calculated to be 105 miles. On April 1st Flinders was able to write that the exploration of St. Vincent's Gulf was finished.

The general character of the country, especially on the east, he considered to be superior to that on the borders of Spencer's Gulf; and the subsequent development of the State of South Australia has justified his opinion. He would assuredly have desired to linger longer upon the eastern shore, could he have foreseen that within forty years of the discovery there would be laid there the foundations of the noble city of Adelaide, with its fair and fruitful olive-groves, vineyards, orchards and gardens, and its busy port, whither flow the wheat of vast plains and the wool from a million sheep leagues upon leagues away.

A second visit to Kangaroo Island was necessitated by a desire to make corrections in the Investigator's timekeepers, and on this occasion a somewhat longer stay was made. The ship arrived on April 2nd, and did not leave again till the 7th.

Very few aboriginals were seen upon the shores of the two gulfs, and these only through a telescope. At Port Lincoln some blacks were known to be in the neighbourhood, but the expedition did not succeed in getting into contact with them. Flinders scrupulously observed the policy of doing nothing to alarm them; and his remarks in this relation are characterised by as much good sense as humane feeling. Writing of a small party of natives who were heard calling but did not show themselves, probably having hidden in thick shrub to observe the boat's crew, he said:

No attempt was made to follow them, for I had always found the natives of this country to avoid those who seemed anxious for communication; whereas, when left entirely alone, they would usually come down after having watched us for a few days. Nor does this conduct seem to be unnatural; for what, in such case, would be the conduct of any people, ourselves for instance, were we living in a state of nature, frequently at war with our neighbours, and ignorant of the existence of any other nation? On the arrival of strangers so different in complexion and appearance to ourselves, having power to transplant themselves over, and even living upon, an element which to us was impossible, the first sensation would probably be terror, and the first movement flight. We should watch these extraordinary people from our retreats in the woods and rocks, and if we found ourselves sought and pursued by them, should conclude their designs to be inimical; but if, on the contrary, we saw them quietly employed in occupations which had no reference to us, curiosity would get the better of fear, and after observing them more closely, we should ourselves risk a communication. Such seemed to have been the conduct of these Australians; and I am persuaded that their appearance on the morning when the tents were struck was a prelude to their coming down; and that, had we remained a few days longer, a friendly communication would have ensued. The way was, however, prepared for the next ship which may visit this port, as it was to us in King George's Sound by Captain Vancouver and the ship Elligood; to whose previous visits and peaceable conduct we were most probably indebted for our early intercourse with the inhabitants of that place. So far as could be perceived with a glass, the natives of this port were the same in personal appearance as those of King George's Sound and Port Jackson. In the hope of conciliating their goodwill to succeeding visitors, some hatchets and various other articles were left in their paths, fastened to stumps of trees which had been cut down near our watering pits.

More wildlife was seen at Kangaroo Island than in the gulf region. Thirty emus were observed on one day; Kangaroos, as has been remarked, were plentiful; and a large colony of pelicans caused the name of Pelican Lagoon to be given to a feature of the island's eastern lobe. The marsupial, the seal, the emu, and the bag-billed bird that nature built in one of her whimsical moods, had held unchallenged possession for tens of thousands of years, probably never visited by any ships, nor even preyed upon by blacks. The reflections of Flinders upon Pelican Lagoon have a tinting of poetic feeling which we do not often find in his solid pages:

> Flocks of the old birds were sitting upon the beaches of the lagoon, and it appeared that the islands were their breeding places: not only so, but from the number of skeletons and bones there scattered it should seem that they had for ages been selected for the closing scene of their existence. Certainly none more likely to be free from disturbance of every kind could have been chosen, than these inlets in a hidden lagoon of an uninhabited island, situated upon an unknown coast near the antipodes of Europe; nor can anything be more consonant to the feelings, if pelicans have any, than quietly to resign their breath whilst surrounded by their progeny, and in the same spot where they first drew it. Alas, for the pelicans! their golden age is past; but it has much exceeded in duration that of man.

The picture of the zoological interests of Kangaroo Island is heightened by Flinders' account of the seals and marsupials. "Never perhaps has the dominion possessed here by the kangaroo been invaded before this time. The seal shared with it upon the shores, but they seemed to dwell amicably together. It not unfrequently happened that the report of a gun fired at a kangaroo, near the beach, brought out two or three bellowing seals from under bushes considerably further from the water side. The seal, indeed, seemed to be much the more discerning animal of the two; for its actions bespoke a knowledge of our not being kangaroos, whereas the kangaroo not unfrequently appeared to consider us to be seals." In the quotation, it may be as well to add, the usual spelling of "kangaroo" is followed, but Flinders invariably spelt it "kanguroo." The orthography of the word was not settled in his time; Cook wrote "kangooroo" and "kanguru," but Hawkesworth, who edited his voyages, made it "kangaroo."

The quantity of fallen timber lying upon the island prompted the curiosity of Flinders. Trunks of trees lay about in all directions "and were nearly of the same size and in the same progress towards decay; from whence it would seem that they had not fallen from age nor yet been thrown down in a gale of wind. Some general conflagration, and there were marks apparently of fire on many of them, is perhaps the sole cause which can be reasonably assigned; but whence came the woods on fire? There were no inhabitants upon the island, and that the natives of the continent did not visit it was demonstrated, if not by the want of all signs of such visits, yet by the tameness of he kangaroo, an animal which, on the continent, resembles the wild deer in timidity. Perhaps lightning might have been the cause, or possibly the friction of two dead trees in a strong wind; but it would be somewhat extraordinary that the same thing should have happened at Thistle's Island, Boston Island, and at this place, and apparently about the same time. Can this pary of Terra Australis have been visited before, unknown to the world? The French navigator, Laperouse, was ordered to explore it, but there seems little probability that he ever passed Torres Strait.

Some judgment may be formed of the epoch when these conflagrations happened, from the magnitude of the growing trees; for they must have sprung up since that period. They were a species of eucalyptus, and being less than the fallen tree, had most probably not arrived at maturity: but the wood is hard and solid, and it may thence be supposed to grow slowly. With these considerations, I should be inclined to fix the period at not less than ten, nor more than twenty years before our arrival. This brings us back to Laperouse. He was in Botany Bay in the beginning of 1788, and, if he did pass through Torres Strait, and come round to this coast, as was his intention, it would probably be about the middle or latter end of that year, or between thirteen and fourteen years before the Investigator. My opinion is not favourable to this conjecture; but I have furnished all the data to enable the reader to form his own opinion upon the cause which might have prostrated the woods of these islands.

The passage is worth quoting, if only for the interesting allusion to Laperouse, whose fate was, at the time when Flinders sailed and wrote, an unsolved mystery of the sea. Captain Dillon's discovery of relics at Vanikoro, in 1826, twelve years after the death of Flinders, informed the world that the illustrious French navigator did not pass through Torres Strait, but was wrecked in the Santa Cruz group. The fire, so many signs of which were observed on Kangaroo Island, was in all probability caused naturally in the heat of a dry summer.

CHAPTER 8

IN A CUBAN CAVE

By Julius A. Palmer

Julius A. Palmer, courtesy of the
New York Public Library.

Between the Morro Casle at Santiago and Cape Maisi, or the eastern point of the island of Cuba, lie a number of remarkable defiles cut by the sea this precipitous coast. There is port Escondido, or the Hidden port, with an entrance of, say one hundred feet, yet by the peculiar contour of the adjacent land a ship may sail close to the mouth of the channel without observing the harbor.

Not twelve hours' sail from Santiago, in the direction of Escondido, may be found that wondrous cave, often mentioned by tourists, which has not been explored because of the belief that no boat which has entered its mouth has been known to return. An adventure of my younger days indicates that there may be more truth than superstition in the tradition.

My sister Bertina and I, being thoroughly acquainted with the regular alternation of land-and sea-breezes on that coast, were able to enjoy together many delightful sails in the course of the years when our parents were residing at Santiago. With the farewell sighing of the morning's land-breeze, we sailed our little skiff down the channel, and gained an offing. We then laid our course alongshore close to the wind with the first puffs of the change, and came back to port with the final breathings of the sea-breeze,

Bertina had suggested from time to time that we should explore the nameless cave.

I shook my head at first, thinking it was a passing whim; but she came back to the proposal day after day.

The result of these entreaties was, that on one of the national holidays of the year 1853 it was agreed that our sail should be to the mouth of the mysterious cave. We passed the frowning bastions of the Morro with a fresh land-breezes that came when we were opposite the cavern. Into its mouth we shot our boat and unshipped the mast, though this seemed an unnecessary precaution. A delicious coolness welcomed us into the shade.

The inward draught of the breeze made a perceptible current from the mouth of the cavern to its dark background. I had taken the precaution to bring a bull's-eye lantern, and lighting it, we took in the grapnel, and allowed the boat to drift slowly into the unknown recesses, the bull's-eye pointing ahead like a locomotive light, insuring us against collision with any projection of the rock. There was no sign of danger, however. Though the altitude of the roof grew less as we advanced, its height, for the whole distance before us illuminated by the lantern, exceeded that of the tallest man. The width perceptibly enlarged.

"It is all perfectly fascinating!" cried Bertina, in a rapture.

The waters were dark, smooth and still; I had just spoken of their apparently great depth, when a slight concussion shook our boat.

"We're touching bottom," said Bertina. I at once thrust my paddle down its full length into the water, touching nothing.

"How queer!" said my sister, looking a little grave.

After advancing a few yards farther, another tremor jarred the boat. It was a very peculiar motion, similar to that of a swiftly moving craft when it slips over a bar of soft ooze. Then came a third shock, this time under the stern of the skiff, so that the boat shot ahead as though propelled by a shove or kick. I turned the light of the lantern astern, but saw nothing, though it seemed strange that so light a craft should leave a track so disturbed.

The next vibration and impetus from astern was still more violent. Turning instantly, I brought the rays of the bull's-eye to bear on the wake, and plainly saw, moving here and there on the surface of the water the fin which rises from the back of the shark.

Not one only, but two three, four—I could not tell how many, since they constantly appeared and disappeared. The fearful truth flashed upon me that we were in one of those sheltered localities on the Caribbean Sea which are selected by sharks for the home of their young. Our boat had disturbed them. It was useless to make any attempt to turn the boat and retreat from the cave. The sharks were now breaking the water in every direction, and with the sweeping of their powerful tails they made such a cession of whirlpools and currents that they made the light boat almost unmanageable.

The sharks were evidently attempting to upset. From the gentle nudge, which first had startled, the shocks had become so heavy that they seemed like the bumping of a yacht when she passes over a short reach of shoal water with headway enough to enable her to clear one after another of the obstructions. The single chance for us was that the cavern might have an outlet at the farther end.

Bertina was not nervous or alarmed; she did not realize our danger. I availed myself of this coolness on her part. The boat was moving, carried forward apparently by a slight current.

"Lie down flat, forward, as near the bow as you can get," I said, and she obeyed promptly. I took a position astern, with my hand on the tiller. By means of this arrangement I had the boat well trimmed, and although the motion imparted by the sharks was like that given by a short, choppy sea, their striking was not so likely to make her overturn.

Soon, however, a new peril was evident; the channel perceptibly narrowed, and what was still more ominous, the height of the roof quickly lessened. I glanced toward the bow, wondering if it were not best to tell Bertina our danger, when I perceived a faint ray of light. If there were any exit ahead, I thought it might conduct us into a basin where young sharks are nourished, prior to their venture into the deep sea.

There are species of these creatures, the young of which are enclosed at the earliest stage of their existence in small sacks. There are left by the female shark in protected localities until the growth of the infant fish allows it to break the confinement, after which it takes care of itself.

The prow of our boat now grated on the irregularities of the rocky roof. We were still pursed by our foes, who continued to thrust themselves with more or less of energy against the bottom of the boat.

The lantern was eclipsed by something very like sunlight ahead, when the projecting stem of the boat met with an obstruction. For one awful moment I thought that the sharks and the current would swing the boat broadside on to the narrow aperture, which seemed to open into lighted chamber.

"Put your hand upon the rock, and press the boat downward," I cried to Bertina.

My brave sister saw that this was the critical moment, and without rising stretched upward her hands, and by her skilful pressure guided the prow so that in a few seconds we were moved out into an open lake, the sun beating down upon the glassy water, and the mountains towering above our heads. The side seemed steep and abrupt, and the basin to have been hewn out of solid rock.

Our enemies did not accompany us farther. With sharp turns and quick flashes, which revealed their ugly under-jaws and long, white bellies, they disappeared under the rocks, leaving, by the swing of their powerful tails, a succession of eddies which soon disappeared. We had escaped the sharks, but seemed imprisoned in the lagoon. Soon, however, I saw that by abandoning our boat we might ascend a portion of the cliffs and probably find our way back to Santiago down the farther slope. Some natural steps to the summit were soon found. They had evidently been used by others, ignorant that the lake communicated with the cavern.

By means of these rocky projections we reached the hilltop, and from thence once more looked forth on the fertile valleys, wooded hill-sides and smiling plains of beautiful Cuba. By good fortune the heat of the day had moderated, and we arrived safely at our house before sunset.

A cave in the Topes de Collantes reservation in Cuba.

CHAPTER 9

HUNTING MUSK-OXEN NEAR THE POLE

By Lieutenant R. E. Peary, USN

Peary in naval uniform circa 1911.

O n the fifteenth of May, 1895, the storm ceased which had held Lee, Hensen and myself prisoners for two days upon the Independence Bay moraine, the northern shore of the "Great Ice," more than four thousand feet above the level of the sea. Then, in a very short time, I completed all the preparations for a trip down over the land in search of the musk-oxen which would be our salvation. Matt and all the dogs were to accompany me.

I took the little "Chopsie" sledge, our rifles, four days' supply of tea, biscuits and oil—we had had no meat for several days—and the remainder of the dog-food, which was a lump of frozen walrus meat somewhat larger than a man's head. Lee was to remain at the tent during our absence.

The almost total lack of snow on this northern land was a surprise as well as an annoyance to me, since it threatened to damage my sledges seriously. But by keeping well ahead of the dogs, I was able to pick out a fairly good though circuitous path along the numerous snow drifts which lay on the leeward side of the hills and mountains.

After some twelve hours of steady marching, we were close to Musk-Ox Valley, where, three years before, Astrup and myself had first seen and killed some of these animals.

Leaving Matt with the sledge and dogs, I took my rifle and entered the valley, hoping to find them there again. So far we had not seen the slightest indication of musk-oxen though we had followed the same route, where, on my previous visit, their traces had been visible on almost every square rod of ground.

In the valley I found no trace of their presence, and I returned to the sledge in a gloomy mood. Could it be that the musk-oxen of this region were migratory? Did they retreat southward along the east coast in the autumn, and return in early summer, and were we too early for them? Or had the sight and smell of us and our dogs, and the sound of our guns and the sight of carcasses of the oxen we had slain three years before, terrified the others so that they had deserted this region completely?

These questions disturbed me deeply. We had now been marching for a long time; we were tired with the unaccustomed work of climbing up and down hills, and were weak and hungry from our long and scant diet of tea and biscuits.

Our hunger was partially appeased by the dog-food. True, this was a frozen mixture of walrus meat, blubber, hair, sand, and various other foreign substances, but we had to eat something, and the fact that the meat was "high" and the blubber more or less rancid did not deter us. Yet we dared not satisfy ourselves, even with dog-food, as we were dependent on the dogs, and they were more in need of food than we.

A few miles beyond Musk-Ox Valley I saw a fresh hare-track leading in the same direction in which we were going; and within five minutes I saw the hare itself squatting among the rocks a few paces distant. I called to Matt, who was some little distance back, to stop the dogs and come up with his rifle.

He was so affected by the prospect of a good dinner that his first and second bullets missed the mark, although usually he was a good marksman. But at the third shot the beautiful, spotless little animal collapsed into a shapeless mass, and on the instant gaunt hunger took from us the power of further endurance. We must stop at once and cook the hare.

Near us was a little pond surrounded by high banks. This offered the advantages of ice, from which to melt water for cooking purposes. So here we camped, lit our lamp, and cooked and ate the entire hare. It was the first full meal we had had for nearly six weeks—the first meal furnishing sufficient substance and nourishment for the doing of a heavy day's work.

Ease from hunger and pleasure in the process of digestion made us drowsy. Lying down as we were, upon the snow-covered shore of the little pond, without tent or sleeping-bag or anything except the clothes we wore, we slept the sleep of tired children in their cosy beds, though the snowflakes were falling thickly upon us.

The next morning we pushed on for a valley near Navy Cliff, where Astrup and myself had seen numerous musk-ox tracks. At the entrance of this valley I came upon a track, so indistinct that it might have been made the previous autumn. Following it a short distance, I saw the accompanying tracks of a calf, showing at once that the tracks were of this season; and a little farther on there were traces but a few days old.

Fastening our dogs securely to a rock and muzzling them so that they could neither gnaw themselves loose or make a noise to disturb the musk-oxen, we passed rapidly down the valley, Winchesters in hand, with our eyes fixed eagerly upon the tracks. Soon we reached the feeding-ground of the herd on the preceding day, and knew by their tracks and the places where they had dug away the snow in search of grass and moss that there was quite a herd of them.

We circled the feeding-ground as rapidly as we could, and at length found the tracks of the herd leading out of the labyrinth and up the slopes of the surrounding mountains. Following these, our eyes were soon gladdened by sight of a group of black spots on a little terrace just below the crest of the mountain.

Looking through the field-glass, we saw that some of the animals were lying down. Evidently the herd was beginning its midday snooze. We moved cautiously up to the edge of the terrace to leeward of the animals and sought shelter behind a big boulder. The musk-oxen were about two hundred yards distant and numbered twenty-two.

I wonder if one of my readers knows what hunger is. Hensen and I were worn to the bone with scant rations and hard work, which had left little on our bones except lean, tense muscles and wires of sinew. The supper from the hare—that meal of fresh, hot, luscious meat—the first adequate meal in nearly six hundred miles of snow-shoeing, had wakened every merciless hunger-fang that during the previous weeks had been gradually dulled into insensibility.

Gazing on the big black animals before us, we saw not game, but meat; and every nerve and fibre in my gaunt body was vibrating with a furious and savage hunger for that meat—meat that should be soft and warm; meat into which the teeth could sink and tear and rend; meat that would not blister the lips and tongue with its frost, nor ring like rock against the teeth.

Panting and quivering with excitement we lay for a few moments. We could not risk a shot at that distance.

"Do you think they will come for us?" said Matt.

"God knows I hope so, boy, for then we are sure of some of them. Are you ready?"

"Yes, sir."

"Come on, then."

Rising one of us one side of the boulder, the other on the other side, we dashed across the rocks and snow straight toward them.

There was a snort and stamp from the big bull guarding the herd, and the next instant every animal was on his feet, facing us, thank God! The next moment they were in close line, with lowered heads and horns. I could have yelled for joy if I had had the breath to spare.

Everyone one of us has read thrilling stories of deer chased by hungry wolves, and it is in the nature of man to sympathise with the creatures that are trying to escape. But did any of us ever stop to think how those other poor creatures, the wolves, were feeling? I know now just what their feelings are, and I cannot help sympathising with them. I was no better than a wolf myself at that moment.

We were within less than fifty yards of the herd when the big bull with a quick motion lowered his horns still more. Instinct, Providence—call it what you will—told me it was the signal for the herd to charge. Without slackening my pace, I pulled my Winchester to my shoulder and sent a bullet at the back of his neck over the white, impervious shield of the great horns.

Heart and soul and brain and eyes went with that singing bullet. I felt that I was strong enough, and hungry enough, and wild enough so that, had the bull been alone, I could have sprung upon him barehanded and somehow made meat of him. But against the entire herd we should have been powerless; once the black avalanche had gained momentum, we should have been crushed by it like the crunching snow crystals under our feet.

As the bull fell upon his knees the herd wavered. A cow half turned and, as Matt's rifle cracked, fell with a bullet back of her fore-shoulder. Without raising my rifle above my hips another one dropped. Then another, for Matt; then the herd broke, and we hurried in pursuit.

A wounded cow wheeled and, with lowered head, was about to charge me; again Matt's rifle cracked, and she fell. As I rushed past her he shouted, "That was my last cartridge!"

A short distance beyond, the remainder of the herd faced about again and I put a bullet into the breast of another bull, but it did not stop him, and the herd broke again and disappeared over a sharp ridge. I had neither wind nor strength to follow.

Suddenly the back of one of the animals appeared above the ridge. I whirled and fired. I did not see the sights—I think I scarcely saw my rifle, but felt my aim as I would with harpoon or stone. I heard the thud of the bullet. I knew the beast was hit behind the fore-shoulder. As the animal disappeared I sank down on the snow, quite unable to go farther.

But after a little rest I was able to move. Matt came up. We instantly set about bleeding the last beast I had killed. How delicious that tender, raw, warm meat was—a mouthful here and a mouthful there, cut from the animal as we skinned it! It seems dreadful and loathsome to have made such a meal. But I wish those who stay at home at ease to realise what hunger drives men to. This was the barbarism out of which our race has risen. Matt and I were savages for the time. I ate till I dared eat no more, although still unsatisfied.

Then Matt went back to bring up the dogs and sledge, while I began removing the skins from our game. With Matt's return came the supremest luxury of all! That was to toss great lumps of meat to the gaunt shadows which we called dogs, till they, too, could eat no more, and lay gorged and quiet upon the rocks.

The removal of the great shaggy, black pelts of the musk-oxen was neither an easy nor a rapid job. By the time it was completed it was midnight; the sun was low over the mountains in the north, and a biting wind whistled about our airy location.

We were glad to drag the skins to a central place, construct a wind guard with the assistance of the sledge, a few stones and a couple of the skins, and make a bed of the other on the lee side of it.

We built up a little stone shelter for our cooking lamp, and then, stretched upon our luxurious, thick, soft, warm couch, we were, for the first time, able to spare the time to make ourselves some tea, and cook some of the delicious musk-ox meat.

Then, with the savage, sombre northern land lying like a map below us—the barren rocks, mottled here and there with eternal snowdrifts; with the summits of the distant mountains disappearing in a mist of driving snow; with the biting breath of the "Great Ice" following us even here and drifting the fine snow over and about our shelter, we slept again as tired children—nay as tired savages—sleep.

SECTION TWO

SURVIVING WAR

CHAPTER 10

THE BATTLE OF PALO ALTO, THE BATTLE OF RESACA DE LA PALMA, MOVEMENT ON CAMARAGO

by Ulysses S. Grant

While General Taylor was away with the bulk of his army, the little garrison up the river was besieged [May 3]. As we lay in our tents upon the sea-shore, the artillery at the fort on the Rio Grande could be distinctly heard.

The war had begun.

There were no possible means of obtaining news from the garrison, and information from outside could not be otherwise than unfavorable. What General Taylor's feelings were during this suspense I do not know; but for myself, a young second-lieutenant who had never heard a hostile gun before, I felt sorry that I had enlisted. A great many men, when they smell battle afar off, chafe to get into the fray. When they say so themselves they generally fail to convince their hearers that they are as anxious as they would like to make believe, and as they approach danger they become more subdued. This rule is not universal, for I have known a few men who were always aching for a fight when there was no enemy near, who were as good as their word when the battle did come. But the number of such men is small.

On the 7th of March [May] the wagons were all loaded and General Taylor started on his return, with his army reinforced at Point Isabel, but still less than three thousand strong [2,200], to relieve the garrison on the Rio Grande. The road from Point Isabel to Matamoras is over an open, rolling, treeless prairie, until the timber that borders the bank of the Rio Grande is reached. This river, like the Mississippi, flows through a rich alluvial valley in the most meandering manner, running towards all points of the compass at times within a few miles. Formerly the river ran by Resaca de la Palma, some four or five miles east of the present channel. The old bed of the river at Resaca had become filled at places, leaving a succession of little lakes. The timber that had formerly grown upon both banks, and for a considerable distance out, was still standing. This timber was struck six or eight miles out from the besieged garrison, at a point known as Palo Alto—'Tall trees' or 'woods.'

Early in the forenoon of the 8th of May as Palo Alto was approached, an army [estimated at 6,000], certainly outnumbering our little force, was seen, drawn up in line of battle just in front of the timber. Their bayonets and spear-heads glistened in the sunlight formidably. The force was composed largely of cavalry armed with lances. Where we were the grass was tall, reaching nearly to the shoulders of the men, very stiff, and each stalk was pointed at the top, and hard and almost as sharp as a darning-needle. General Taylor halted his army before the head of column came in range of the artillery of the Mexicans. He then formed a line of battle, facing the enemy. His artillery, two batteries and two eighteen-pounder iron guns, drawn by oxen, were placed in position at intervals along the line. A battalion was thrown to the rear, commanded by Lieutenant-Colonel [Thomas] Childs, of the artillery, as reserves. These preparations completed, orders were given for a platoon of each company to stack arms and go to a stream off to the right of the command, to fill their canteens and also those of the rest of their respective companies. When the men were all back in their places in line, the command to advance was given. As I looked down that long line of about three thousand armed men, advancing towards a larger force also armed, I thought what a fearful responsibility General Taylor must feel, commanding such a host and so far away from friends. The Mexicans immediately opened fire upon us, first with artillery and then with infantry. At first their shots did not reach us, and the advance was continued. As we got nearer, the cannon balls commenced going through the ranks. They hurt no one, however, during this advance, because they would strike the ground long before they reached our line, and ricochetted through the tall grass so slowly that the men would see them and open ranks and let them pass. When we got to a point where the artillery could be used with effect, a halt was called, and the battle opened on both sides.

The infantry under General Taylor was armed with flint-lock muskets, and paper cartridges charged with powder, buck-shot and ball. At the distance of a few hundred yards a man might fire at you all day without your finding it out. The artillery was generally six-pounder brass guns throwing only solid shot; but General Taylor had with him three or four twelve-pounder howitzers throwing shells, besides his eighteen-pounders before spoken of, that had a long range. This made a powerful armament. The Mexicans were armed about as we were so far as their infantry was concerned, but their artillery only fired solid shot. We had greatly the advantage in this arm.

The artillery was advanced a rod or two in front of the line, and opened fire. The infantry stood at order arms as spectators, watching the effect of our shots upon the enemy, and watching his shots so as to step out of their way. It could be seen that the eighteen-pounders and the howitzers did a great deal of execution. On our side there was little or no loss while we occupied this position. During the battle Major [Samuel] Ringgold, an accomplished and brave artillery officer, was mortally wounded, and Lieutenant Luther, also of the artillery, was struck. During the day several advances were made, and just at dusk it became evident that the Mexicans were falling back. We again advanced, and occupied at the close of the battle substantially the ground held by the enemy at the beginning. In this last move there was a brisk fire upon our troops, and some execution was done. One cannon ball passed through our ranks, not far from me. It took off the head of an enlisted man, and the under jaw of Captain [John] Page of my regiment, while the splinters from the musket of the killed soldier, and his brains and bones, knocked down two or three others, including one officer, Lieutenant [Henry D.] Wallen—hurting them more or less. Our casualties for the day were nine killed and forty-seven wounded.

At the break of day on the 9th, the army under Taylor was ready to renew the battle; but an advance showed that the enemy had entirely left our front during the night. The chaparral before us was impenetrable except where there were roads or trails, with occasionally clear or bare spots of small dimensions. A body of men penetrating it might easily be ambushed. It was better to have a few men caught in this way than the whole army, yet it was necessary that the garrison at the river should be relieved. To get to them the chaparral had to be passed. Thus I assume General Taylor reasoned. He halted the army not far in advance of the ground occupied by the Mexicans the day before, and selected Captain C. F. Smith, of the artillery, and Captain McCall, of my company, to take one hundred and fifty picked men each and find where the enemy had gone. This left me in command of the company, an honor and responsibility I thought very great.

Smith and McCall found no obstruction in the way of their advance until they came up to the succession of ponds, before described, at Resaca. The Mexicans had passed them and formed their lines on the opposite bank. This position they had strengthened a little by throwing up dead trees and brush in their front, and by placing artillery to cover the approaches and open places. Smith and McCall deployed on each side of the road as well as they could, and engaged the enemy at long range. Word was sent back, and the advance of the whole army was at once commenced. As we came up we were deployed in like manner. I was with the right wing, and led my company through the thicket wherever a penetrable place could be found, taking advantage of any clear spot that would carry me towards the enemy. At last I got pretty close up without knowing it. The balls commenced to whistle very thick overhead, cutting the limbs of the chaparral right and left. We could not see the enemy, so I ordered my men to lie down, an order that did not have to be enforced. We kept our position until it became evident that the enemy were not firing at us, and then withdrew to find better ground to advance upon.

By this time some progress had been made on our left. A section of artillery had been captured by the cavalry, and some prisoners had been taken. The Mexicans were giving way all along the line, and many of them had, no doubt, left early. I at last found a clear space separating two ponds. There seemed to be a few men in front and I charged upon them with my company. There was no resistance, and we captured a Mexican colonel, who had been wounded, and a few men. Just as I was sending them to the rear with a guard of two or three men, a private came from the front bringing back one of our officers, who had been badly wounded in advance of where I was. The ground had been charged over before. My exploit was equal to that of the soldier who boasted that he had cut off the leg of one of the enemy. When asked why he did not cut off his head, he replied: 'Some one had done that before.' This left no doubt in my mind but that the battle of Resaca de la Palma would have been won, just as it was, if I had not been there.

There was no further resistance. The evening of the 9th the army was encamped on its old ground near the Fort, and the garrison was relieved. The siege had lasted a number of days, but the casualties were few in number. Major Jacob Brown, of the 7th infantry, the commanding officer, had been killed, and in his honor the fort was named. Since then a town of considerable importance had sprung up on the ground occupied by the fort and troops, which has also taken his name.

The battles of Palo Alto and Resaca de la Palma seemed to us engaged, as pretty important affairs; but we had only a faint conception of their magnitude until they were fought over in the North by the Press and the reports came back to us. At the same time, or about the same time, we learned that war existed between the United States and Mexico, by the acts of the latter country. On learning this fact General Taylor transferred our camps to the south or west bank of the river, and Matamoras was occupied [May 18]. We then became the 'Army of Invasion.'

Up to this time Taylor had none but regular troops in his command; but now that invasion had already taken place, volunteers for one year commenced

The Battle of Palo Alto by Aldolphe Jean-Baptiste Bayote, circa 1851.

arriving. The army remained at Matamoras until sufficiently reinforced to warrant a movement into the interior.

General Taylor was not an officer to trouble the administration much with his demands, but was inclined to do the best he could with the means given him. He felt his responsibility was going no further. If he had thought that he was sent to perform an impossibility with the means given him, he would probably have informed the authorities of his opinion and left them to determine what should be done. If the judgment was against him he would have gone on and done the best he could with the means at hand without parading his grievance before the public. No soldier could face either danger or responsibility more calmly than he. These are qualities more rarely found than genius or physical courage.

General Taylor never made any great show or parade, either of uniform or retinue. In dress he was possibly too plain, rarely wearing anything in the field to indicate his rank, or even that he was an officer; but he was known to every soldier in his army, and was respected by all. I can call to mind only one instance when I saw him in uniform, and one other when I heard of his wearing it. On both occasions he was unfortunate. The first was at Corpus

Christi. He had concluded to review his army before starting on the march
and gave orders accordingly. Colonel Twiggs was then second in rank with the
army, and to him was given the command of the review. Colonel and Brevet
Brigadier-General [William J.] Worth, a far different soldier from Taylor in
the use of the uniform, was next to Twiggs in rank, and claimed superiority
by virtue of his brevet rank when the accidents of service threw them where
one or the other had to command. Worth declined to attend the review as
subordinate to Twiggs until the question was settled by the highest authority.
This broke up the review, and the question was referred to Washington for
final decision.

General Taylor was himself only a colonel, in real rank, at that time,
and a brigadier-general by brevet. He was assigned to duty, however, by the
President, with the rank which his brevet gave him. Worth was not so assigned, but by virtue of commanding a division he must, under the army regulations of that day, have drawn the pay of his brevet rank. The question was
submitted to Washington, and no response was received until after the army
had reached the Rio Grande. It was decided against General Worth, who at
once tendered his resignation and left the army, going north, no doubt, by
the same vessel that carried it. This kept him out of the battles of Palo Alto
and Resaca de la Palma. Either the resignation was not accepted, or General
Worth withdrew it before action had been taken.

At all events he returned to the army in time to command his division in
the battle of Monterey, and served with it to the end of the war.

The second occasion on which General Taylor was said to have donned
his uniform, was in order to receive a visit from the Flag Officer [David Con-
ner] of the naval squadron off the mouth of the Rio Grande. While the army
was on that river the Flag Officer sent word that he would call on the General to pay his respects on a certain day. General Taylor, knowing that naval
officers habitually wore all the uniform the 'law allowed' on all occasions of
ceremony, thought it would be only civil to receive his guest in the same style.
His uniform was therefore got out, brushed up, and put on, in advance of the
visit. The Flag Officer, knowing General Taylor's aversion to the wearing of

the uniform, and feeling that it would be regarded as a compliment should he meet him in civilian's dress, left off his uniform for this occasion. The meeting was said to have been embarrassing to both, and the conversation was principally apologetic.

The time was whiled away pleasantly enough at Matamoras, while we were waiting for volunteers. It is probable that all the most important people of the territory occupied by our army left their homes before we got there, but with those remaining the best of relations apparently existed. It was the policy of the Commanding General to allow no pillaging, no taking of private property for public or individual use without satisfactory compensation, so that a better market was afforded than the people had ever known before.

Among the troops that joined us at Matamoras was an Ohio regiment, of which Thomas L. Hamer, the Member of Congress who had given me my appointment to West Point, was major. He told me then that he could have had the colonelcy, but that as he knew he was to be appointed a brigadier-general, he preferred at first to take the lower grade. I have said before that Hamer was one of the ablest men Ohio ever produced. At that time he was in the prime of life, being less than fifty years of age, and possessed an admirable physique, promising long life. But he was taken sick before Monterey, and died within a few days. I have always believed that had his life been spared, he would have been President of the United States during the term filled by President Pierce. Had Hamer filled that office his partiality for me was such, there is but little doubt I should have been appointed to one of the staff corps of the army—the Pay Department probably—and would therefore now be preparing to retire.

Neither of these speculations is unreasonable, and they are mentioned to show how little men control their own destiny.

Reinforcements having arrived, in the month of August the movement commenced from Matamoras to Camargo, the head of navigation on the Rio Grande. The line of the Rio Grande was all that was necessary to hold, unless it was intended to invade Mexico from the North. In that case the most natural route to take was the one which General Taylor selected. It entered a pass in the Sierra Madre Mountains, at Monterey [now Monterrey], through which the main road runs to the City of Mexico. Monterey itself was a good point to hold, even if the line of the Rio Grande covered all the territory we desired to occupy at that time. It is built on a plain two thousand feet above tide water, where the air is bracing and the situation healthy.

On the 19th of August the army started for Monterey, leaving a small garrison at Matamoras. The troops, with the exception of the artillery, cavalry, and the brigade to which I belonged, were moved up the river to Camargo on steamers. As there were but two or three of these, the boats had to make a number of trips before the last of the troops were up. Those who marched did so by the south side of the river. Lieutenant-Colonel Garland, of the 4th infantry, was the brigade commander, and on this occasion commanded the entire marching force. One day out convinced him that marching by day in that latitude, in the month of August, was not a beneficial sanitary measure, particularly for Northern men. The order of marching was changed and night marches were substituted with the best results.

When Camargo was reached, we found a city of tents outside the Mexican hamlet. I was detailed to act as quartermaster and commissary to the regiment. The teams that had proven abundantly sufficient to transport all supplies from Corpus Christi to the Rio Grande over the level prairies of Texas, were entirely inadequate to the needs of the reinforced army in a mountainous country. To obviate the deficiency, pack mules were hired, with Mexicans to pack and drive them. I had charge of the few wagons allotted to the 4th infantry and of the pack train to supplement them. There were not men enough in the army to manage that train without the help of Mexicans who had learned how. As it was the difficulty was great enough. The troops would take up their march at an early hour each day. After they had started, the tents and cooking utensils had to be made into packages, so that they could be lashed to the backs of the mules. Sheet-iron kettles, tent-poles and mess chests were inconvenient articles to transport in that way. It took several hours to get ready to start each morning, and by the time we were ready some of the mules first loaded would be tired of standing so long with their loads on their backs. Sometimes one would start to run, bowing his back and kicking up until he scattered his load; others would lie down and try to disarrange their loads by attempting to get on the top of them by rolling on them; other with tent-poles for part of their loads would manage to run a tent-pole on one side of a sapling while they would take the other. I am not aware of ever having used a profane expletive in my life; but I would have the charity of a train of Mexican pack mules at the time.

A monument to the Battle of Palo Alto at West Point.

CHAPTER 11

THE *KEARSARGE* SINKS THE *ALABAMA*

by Lt. Arthur Sinclair, C. S. A.

The Battle between the *Kearsarge* and the *Alabama,* as depicted by
Édouard Manet, circa 1861.

Sunday morning, June 19, 1864, preparations for the fight are made early in the day. At breakfast the officers are advised of the last communication with the shore, and to make their arrangements accordingly. Soon after breakfast the yacht *Deerhound*, which we had observed to be getting up steam, moved out of the port, passing quite near us. The party on her were watching us with glasses, though no demonstration occurred, even from the ladies. At this time it was unknown to us that the departure was for the purpose of taking up a position of vantage to observe the engagement. We had no communication with the yacht or her people, and did not know but that her owner was continuing his pleasure cruise. She passed from sight, and the French ironclad frigate *Couronne* weighed anchor and stood out of the harbor. We could readily surmise that her purpose was to police the channel at the three-mile limit and overlook the fight. She never moved from the league distance during the entire period of the engagement, nor did she offer any assistance at the termination. The neutrality of the Couronne was of the positive, unmistakable kind. It would have occupied a court but a short time to consider and pass upon it.

Between ten and eleven o'clock we got underway, and stood out of the harbor, passing the French liner *Napoleon* quite near. We were surprised and gratified as she manned the rigging and gave us three rousing cheers, her band at the same time playing a Confederate national air. It must have been an enthusiasm of local birth, a sort of private turn-out of their own. It was much appreciated by us, and no doubt stirred our brave lads to the centre.

Sailors are generous fellows, and always take sides, when allowed, with the little fellow underneath. The scene from the deck of the *Alabama* is one never to be effaced from memory. We are passing out of the harbor through the dense shipping, the bulwarks of all of them crowded with heads watching our exit, and the shores and mole a moving mass of humanity. The day is perfect, scarcely a breath of air stirring, and with but a light cloud here and there in the sky. We soon clear the mole, and shape our course for the offing, to testify by blows and blood the sincerity of our faith in the justice of our cause, and to win, if possible, a crowning triumph for our brave commander.

Our ship as she steams offshore for her antagonist, hull down in the distance and waiting for us, presents a brave appearance. The decks and brass-work shine in the bright morning sunlight from recent holystoning and polishing. The crew are all in muster uniform, as though just awaiting Sunday inspection. They are ordered to lie down at their quarters for rest while we approach the enemy. A beautiful sight—the divisions stripped to the waist, and with bare arms and breasts looking the athletes they are. The decks have been sanded down, tubs of water placed along the spar-deck, and all is ready for the fray. The pipe of the boatswain and mates at length summons all hands aft; and Semmes, mounting a gun-carriage, delivers a stirring address:

"Officers and Seamen of the *Alabama*: You have at length another opportunity of meeting the enemy—the first that has been presented to you since you sunk the *Hatteras*. In the meantime, you have been all over the world; and it is not too much to say that you have destroyed, and driven for protection under neutral flags, one-half of the enemy's commerce, which at the beginning of the war covered every sea. This is an achievement of which you may well be proud; and a grateful country will not be unmindful of it. The name of your ship has become a household word wherever civilization extends. Shall that name be tarnished by defeat? The thing is impossible. Remember that you are in the English Channel,—the theatre of so much of the naval glory of our race,—and that the eyes of all Europe are at this moment upon you. The flag that floats over you is that of a young republic, who bids defiance to her enemies whenever and wherever found. Show the world that you know how to uphold it. Go to your quarters."

Again at quarters, and resting "at will." It is the hour of prayer in old England; and many a petition is now going up to the God of battle and of mercy for these brave fellows, many of them now about to embrace their watery winding-sheets. We are soon up with the cavalcade and leave the *Couronne*, the yacht still steaming seaward, and evidently bent upon witnessing the engagement. She is about two miles distant at the time we "open the ball." The *Kearsarge* suddenly turns her head inshore and steams towards us, both ships being at this time about seven or eight miles from the shore. When at about one mile distant from us, she seems from her sheer-off with helm to have chosen this distance for her attack. We had not yet perceived that the *Kearsarge* had the speed of us. We open the engagement with our entire starboard battery, the writer's thirty-two pounder of the port side having been shifted to the spare port, giving us six guns in broadside; and the shift caused the ship to list to starboard about two feet, by the way, quite an advantage, exposing so much less surface to the enemy, but somewhat retarding our speed. The *Kearsarge* had pivoted to starboard also; and both ships with helms a-port fought out the engagement, circling around a common centre, and gradually approaching each other. The enemy replied soon after our opening; but at the distance her pivot shell-guns were at a disadvantage, not having the long range of our pivot-guns, and hence requiring judgment in guessing the distance and determining the proper elevation. Our pivots could easily reach by ricochet, indeed by point-blank firing, so at this stage of the action, and with a smooth sea, we had the advantage.

The battle is now on in earnest; and after about fifteen minutes' fighting, we lodge a hundred-pound percussion-shell in her quarter near her screw; but it fails to explode, though causing some temporary excitement and anxiety on board the enemy, most likely by the concussion of the blow. We find her soon after seeking closer quarters (which she is fully able to do, having discovered her superiority in speed), finding it judicious to close so that her eleven-inch pivots could do full duty at point-blank range. We now ourselves noted the advantage in speed possessed by our enemy; and Semmes felt her pulse, as to whether very close quarters would be agreeable, by sheering towards her to close the distance; but she had evidently reached the point wished for to fight out the remainder of the action, and demonstrated it by sheering off and resuming a parallel to us. Semmes would have chosen to bring about yard-arm quarters, fouling, and boarding, relying upon the superior physique of his crew to overbalance the superiority of numbers; but this was frustrated, though several times attempted, the desire on our part being quite apparent. We had therefore to accept the situation, and make the best of it we could, to this end directing our fire to the midship section of the enemy, and alternating our battery with solid shot and shell, the former to pierce, if possible, the cable chain-armor, the latter for general execution.

Up to the time of shortening the first distance assumed, our ship received no damage of any account, and the enemy none that we could discover, the shot in the quarter working no serious harm to the *Kearsarge*. At the distance we were now fighting (point-blank range), the effects of the eleven-inch guns were severely felt, and the little hurt done the enemy clearly proved the un-serviceableness of our powder, observed at the commencement of the action.

The boarding tactics of Semmes having been frustrated, and we unable to pierce the enemy's hull with our fire, nothing can place victory with us but some unforeseen and lucky turn. At this period of the action our spanker-gaff is shot away, bringing our colors to the deck; but apparently this is not ob-served by the *Kearsarge,* as her fire does not halt at all. We can see the splinters flying off from the armor covering of the enemy; but no penetration occurs, the shot or shell rebounding from her side. Our colors are immediately hoist-ed to the mizzenmast-head. The enemy having now the range, and being able with her superior speed to hold it at ease, has us well in hand, and the fire from her is deliberate and hot. Our bulwarks are soon shot away in sec-tions; and the after pivot-gun is disabled on its port side, losing, in killed and wounded, all but the compresser-man. The quarter-deck thirty-two pounder of this division is now secured, and the crew sent to man the pivot-gun. The spar-deck is by this time being rapidly torn up by shell bursting on the between-decks, interfering with working our battery; and the compartments below have all been knocked into one. The *Alabama* is making water fast, showing severe punishment; but still the report comes from the engine-room that the ship is being kept free to the safety-point. She also has now become dull in response to her helm, and the sail-trimmers are ordered out to loose the head-sails to pay her head off. We are making a desperate but forlorn resistance, which is soon culminated by the deathblow. An eleven-inch shell enters us at the water-line, in the wake of the writer's gun, and passing on, explodes in the engine-room, in its passage throwing a volume of water on board, hiding for a moment the guns of this division. Our ship trembles from stem to stern from the blow. Semmes at once sends for the engineer on watch, who reports the fires out, and water beyond the control of the pumps. We had previously been aware our ship was whipped, and fore-and-aft sail was set in endeavor to reach the French coast; the enemy then moved in shore of us, but did not attempt to close any nearer, simply steaming to secure the shore-side and await events.

It being now apparent that the *Alabama* could not float longer, the colors are hauled down, and the pipe given, "All hands save yourselves." Our waist-boats had been shot to pieces, leaving us but two quarter-boats, and one of them much damaged. The wounded are despatched in one of them to the enemy in charge of an officer, and this done we await developments. The *Kearsarge* evidently failed to discover at once our surrender, for she continued her fire after our colors were struck. Perhaps from the difficulty of noting the absence of a flag with so much white in it, in the powder smoke. But, be the reason what it may, a naval officer, a gentleman by birth and education, would certainly not be guilty of firing on a surrendered foe; hence we may dismiss the matter as an undoubted accident.

The *Kearsarge* is at this time about three hundred yards from us, screw still and vessel motionless, awaiting our boat with the wounded. The yacht is steaming full power towards us both. In the meantime, the two vessels are slowly parting, the *Alabama* drifting with her fore-and-aft sails set to the light air. The inaction of the *Kearsarge* from the time of the surrender until the last man was picked up by the boats of the two vessels will ever remain a mystery to all who were present, and with whom the writer has since conversed. The fact is, the *Kearsarge* was increasing her distance slowly and surely all the time. Whether the drift of our ship under the sail that was set was accomplishing this alone I am not prepared to say. But both Capt. Jones and Mr. Lancaster noted it, and were under the impression that the fact entitled the yacht to the greater credit in saving life. There really seemed to be more method and judgment displayed by the crews from the yacht than those from the *Kearsarge*. Capt. Jones and Mr. Lancaster both expressed themselves in their communications to the press, that in their opinions but few of the *Alabama*'s men would have been saved but for their presence, so little enterprise was shown by our enemy in looking out for us in the water.

The *Deerhound* approaches the *Kearsarge*, and is requested by Capt. Winslow to assist in saving life; and then, scarcely coming to a full stop, turns to us, at the same time lowering all her boats, the *Kearsarge* doing the same. The officers and crew of our ship are now leaving at will, discipline and rule being temporarily at an end. The ship is settling to her spar-deck, and her wounded spars are staggering in the "steps," held only by the rigging. The decks present a woful appearance, torn up in innumerable holes, and air-bubbles rising and bursting, producing a sound as though the boat was in agony. Just before she settled, it was a desolate sight for the three or four men left on her deck.

Engineer O'Brien and self were standing by the forward pivot port, a man from his department near, as his companion for the coming swim, a man from my gun-division to act in the same capacity with me; namely, mutual aid and assistance. We comprised all remaining on board of the late buoyant and self-confident band. The ship had settled by the stern, almost submerging it, and bringing the forward part of the hull, consequently, out of water. We were all stripped for the swim, and watching with catlike intensity the rise of air-bubbles from the hatches, indicating that the ship would yet float. From the wake of the *Alabama*, and far astern, a long, distinct line of wreckage could be seen winding with the tide like a snake, with here and there a human head appearing amongst it. The boats were actively at work, saving first those who were without such assistance.

It has frequently been asked me, and in a recent conversation with engineer O'Brien I found the question had been put to him often, "Why did you remain so long on board?" We both seem to have been actuated by the same motive and impulse, first to avoid the confusion and struggle going on in the efforts to reach the wreckage; but the paramount feeling with me was inability to grasp the fact that the *Alabama* was gone! Our home! around which clustered memories as dear and cherished as attended that first childhood one, and the faculties utterly refused to have the stubborn fact thus ruthlessly thrust upon them. They are rude wrenches these, that scatter shipmate from shipmate in a twinkling, some to death, as in our case, and bury out of sight forever the ship which had come to be the material embodiment of a cause dear almost as life. A happier ship-hold it would be difficult to realize or picture, a sympathetic heart encountered at each turn of mess-room or quarter-deck, and this for two long years. O'Brien broke into the revery or day-dream by unceremoniously pushing the writer overboard, and following in his wake. It need scarcely be added that the bath cooled effectually the heated and disturbed brain, and turned the thoughts of all four of us to the practical question of the moment,—how expert a swimmer are you?

The *Alabama's* final plunge was a remarkable freak, and witnessed by O'Brien and self about one hundred yards off. She shot up out of the water bow first, and descended on the same line, carrying away with her plunge two of her masts, and making a whirlpool of considerable size and strength.

The *Kearsarge* mounted two eleven-inch Dahlgren shell guns, four thirty-two pounders, and one rifled twenty-eight pounder. The *Alabama* mounted more guns; but the difference in the bore of the pivot-guns of the two ships gave the *Kearsarge* much more weight of metal at a broadside, and made the disparity very great. The complement of the *Kearsarge* was one hundred and sixty five all told, officers and men. The action lasted one hour and a half.

A great deal has been said as to the merits of the fight; and no little feeling has been displayed on both sides, each championing its own, and seeking to evolve from the result so much of credit and praise as the circumstances permit. With the floods of light thrown on the event from time to time by the actors on both sides, assisted by the testimony of reliable and impartial outside lookers on, the reader should without a fear of erring be able to judge for himself the amount of credit to be apportioned to each of the combatants, and also to satisfy himself whether or no Semmes is under all the circumstances to be censured for offering battle, and if blamed at all, to what extent, and in what particulars. Winslow, for protecting his ship with chain-armor, should, in the humble judgment of the writer, submitted with diffidence, be accounted as simply using proper prudence in the direct line of duty. He had not given, accepted, or declined a challenge. But it was his duty to fight if he could, and to win. Semmes knew all about it, and could have adopted the same scheme. It was not his election to do so. Winslow took every means at his disposal to destroy a vessel which had been a scourge to United States commerce, and most likely banished from his thoughts all sentiment of chivalry as out of place.

The writer has already suggested from his own standpoint the motives for seeking the fight which may have moved Semmes; but after all they are mere speculations, simply the sum-up of his own thoughts. No one will know just why he fought, and the reader has as good a right at a guess as any one. Semmes took the chances with the odds against him, and lost all but honor. He could have stayed in port, refitted, and been in good trim to meet any boat of the *Kearsarge* class. But we can look farther, and see that in this case no fight with her would have been probable. The chances are by the time the *Alabama* was ready for sea a fleet of American cruisers would have been off Cherbourg to blockade her. So looking at it, surely it was best to take the bull by the horns, and fight while there was some sort of a chance. Semmes fought his ship with all the skill possible under the circumstances, and displayed throughout the coolness and nerve you would look for from a man who had guided the *Alabama* to such marked success. The career of the ship under him is perhaps the most conspicuous object-lesson of judicious management and forethought in the annals of any navy, and the fact of defeat should weigh not at all against his judgment when we consider the fickle chances of battle.

The courage of the man needs no telling; but the incident of his wounding, and the manner in which he bore it, may be of interest to the reader. He was on the horse-block at the time, and where he remained during the battle; and upon finding his right arm totally disabled by a fragment of shell, he simply called the quartermaster, and having him bind and sling the wounded arm, kept his position, and directed the steering and fighting of his ship up to the surrender. Kell was a devoted friend to him from the moment of his (Semmes's) personal misfortune, sticking close by him, entering the water with him, and having the satisfaction of getting with him, safe from all harm, on the deck of the *Deerhound*. In the state of Semmes's health at this time, considering his age and the wearing cruise he had just wound up, it was fortunate for him that such a strong, athletic fellow as Kell kept near him all the while; and who knows how much Semmes may owe to Kell for that companionship?

The writer had the deck just before getting under way, prior to being relieved, as customary, by the first lieutenant. The commander came up from his breakfast, saluted the deck, and received the usual touch of the hat in return; then he said, "If the bright, beautiful day is shining for our benefit, we should be happy at the omen; "and remarked how well the deck appeared, and that the crew (casting his eye forward) seemed "to enter into the spirit of the fight with bright faces." Finally, he put the direct question, "How do you think it will turn out to-day, Mr. Sinclair?" I was surprised that he should care to have my opinion, or that of any one else; for he rarely addressed any of us off duty, and never asked advice or opinion of his subordinates on weighty matters; at least, not to my knowledge. My reply was necessarily vague: "I cannot answer the question, sir, but can assure you the crew will do their full duty, and follow you to the death."—"Yes," he answered; "that is true." And leaving me, he resumed his usual pacing of the quarter-deck. Most gratifying to Semmes must have been the sympathy and attention of the gallant, generous souls on the yacht; and no doubt it contributed much to ease his sufferings of body and mind.

In England he was warmly received on all sides; and a number of his naval admirers united in a testimonial, which assumed the form of a handsome regulation gold-mounted sword, presented, it was stated, "To replace the one so gallantly worn, defended, and lost."

* * *

SOME INCIDENTS OF THE FIGHT

When the order was passed to lower the colors, and the pipe "All hands save yourselves" was given by boatswain Mecaskey and mates, there was at once a rush of men from the gun divisions to protest against surrender. The excitement was great; the men failing to realize that their ship was whipped beyond a shadow of doubt, and able to float but little longer. They demanded to have the honor of sinking with the colors at the peak (or rather at the mizzen-mast-head; for the spanker-gaff had long since been shot away). But a few positive words from Semmes and Kell quieted them. The *Kearsarge* was by this time on our quarter, in position for a raking fire, and we were altogether helpless. It was time to stop the useless slaughter, though the lowering of our colors was not apparently seen on the *Kearsarge* for a time, since she did not at once cease firing. No one was hurt on board of us after the act of surrender.

The sad fate of assistant-surgeon Llewellyn has elsewhere been recorded. Late in the fight the writer went below to get a bottle of brandy to sustain Wright of his division, who had been seriously wounded, and came upon Llewellyn, standing deep in water, attending to the injured. "Why, Pills!" I cried, "you had better get yourself and wounded out of this, or you'll soon be drowned!" His reply was, "I must wait for orders, you know." But just then a gang of men came below, and he was enabled to get his injured men off the operating table, and to the deck. The wounded were immediately placed in the boat, for transfer to the *Kearsarge*. Why Llewellyn did not accompany them it is impossible to say. It is quite likely he did not know the custom in such cases, and he may have waited for orders. The boat with the wounded, under the command of Lieut. Wilson, marine-officer Howell and master's mate Fulham each taking an oar, was at once cleared from the side. It soon becoming known that Llewellyn could not swim, a couple of empty shell-boxes were procured, and secured on his person, one under each arm, to serve as an improvised life-preserver. He took the water with this arrangement, and when last seen from the ship was making good weather of it, the sea being as calm as a dish. I learned later, on the yacht, that Llewellyn's death was brought about by the shifting of the floats upon his person, which seems most probable. Had he taken a moment's thought for himself, and let it be known that he could not swim earlier, he might easily have been saved. But he was the last man to think of himself in a time of general danger.

Lieutenant of marines Howell was known to be no swimmer, and was allowed to take an oar in the boat with the wounded. After the transfer, his dress, or rather undress, not being recognized, and Wilson having gone up the side of the *Kearsarge*, and formally surrendered, he was requested by Capt. Winslow to return with the rest of the boat's crew to the wreckage, and do all he could to save life. It is hardly necessary to say that the request was cheerfully obeyed, or that the boat took all the men it saved to the *Deerhound*.

During this time I made a second visit between decks. The scene was one of complete wreck. The shot and shell of the enemy had knocked all the compartments into one; and a flush view could be had fore and aft, the water waist-deep, and air-bubbles rising and breaking with a mournful gurgle at the surface. It was a picture to be dwelt upon in memory, but not too long in the reality. I returned hastily to the spar-deck. By this time most of the officers and men had left for the water. The battery was disarranged, some guns run out and secured, some not. The spars were wounded wofully, some of them toppling, and others only held by the wire rigging. The smoke-stack was full of holes, the decks torn up by the bursting of shell, and lumbered with the wreckage of woodwork and rigging and empty shell-boxes. Some sail was set; and the vessel slowly forged ahead, leaving a line of wreckage astern, with the heads of swimmers bobbing up and down amongst it. Toward this the boats from the yacht were rapidly pulling. The *Kearsarge* lay a few hundred yards on our starboard quarter, with her boats apparently free from the davits, and pivot-gun ports not yet closed, nor her guns secured.

I went forward, and with a sailor of my division commenced to strip for the swim, the deep settling of the ship warning us that she was about to go. I was ready first, and sat with my legs dangling in the water, which was now almost flush with the spar-deck, trying to secure a handkerchief containing a lot of English sovereigns about my neck while I waited for my companion. At this moment O'Brien suddenly appeared in our rear, and with a hasty "What are you loafing round here for? Don't you see the ship is settling for a plunge? Over you go!" suited the action to the word, and shoved us both into the sea.

He immediately followed us, and struck out sharply for the boats. But O'Brien's hurry cost me my gold; for it was torn from my neck with the plunge, and went down to enrich the bottom of the Channel. However, we had got away none too soon; for we had hardly cleared her when her bow made a wild leap into the air, and she plunged down on an inclined plane to her grave beneath the waves. As she leaped upward there was a crash, her

main-topmast going by the board; and the fore gave way in turn as she took
her downward slide. The suction where we were was terribly strong, carrying
us all down to a very uncomfortable depth. So deep, indeed, that with my
eyes open in perfectly clear water, I found myself in the darkness of midnight.
But our struggles soon popped us to the surface, which was by this time quite
a luxury; and we kept there very contentedly, swimming in an easy, take-your-
time style until picked up. Being rescued, we were deposited, like caught fish,
under the thwarts. But my sailor-companion soon discovered that it was a
boat from the Kearsarge which had done us this favor; and promptly consulting, we arranged to give it the slip, which was successfully accomplished in
the confusion, taking again to the sea. The next time we were picked up, it
was by a boat from the *Deerhound*.

It was an incident of note in the fight that nearly all the killed were
allotted to Joe Wilson's division. I can recollect of but one in Armstrong's,
and in my division we had only one man wounded; and yet the bulk of the
enemy's fire was concentrated at the midships of the *Alabama*, and the death-
wound was given at the third division, in the wake of the engine-hatch.

Nothing could exceed the cool and thorough attention to details of our
first lieutenant on this eventful day. From point to point of the spar-deck in
his rapid movement he was directing here, or advising there; now seeing to
the transfer of shot, shell, or cartridge; giving his orders to this and that man
or officer, as though on dress-muster; occasionally in earnest conversation
with Semmes, who occupied the horse-block, glasses in hand, and leaning on
the hammock-rail; at times watching earnestly the enemy, and then casting
his eye about our ship, as though keeping a careful reckoning of the damage
given and received. Nothing seemed to escape his active mind or eye, his
commanding figure at all times towering over the heads of those around.
How it must have touched him to see the wreck of our gallant boat, of which
he was so proud, and which had been for two years his heart's chiefest care!
One must be in actual touch with such a life as ours to feel the inspiration.

In the latter part of the engagement Semmes, from the vantage-ground
of the horse-block, had observed that the *Alabama* was not answering to her

helm promptly, and sent for engineer O'Brien, to ascertain the condition of the water in the lower hold. O'Brien reported it as almost flush with the furnace-fires, and rapidly rising; also that the ship could not possibly float much longer. He was ordered to return to duty. Reaching the engine-room, engineer Pundt interviewed him; and upon learning that the ship's condition was known to Semmes, and the only reply to this statement was, "Return to your duty!" exclaimed excitedly, "Well, I suppose ' Old Beeswax' has made up his mind to drown us like a lot of rats! Here, Matt! take off my boots"; and suiting the action to the word, each assisted the other in removing the wet and soggy boots. But Semmes had made up his mind, from the report of his engineer, to give the order, "All hands save yourselves!" The furnace-fires were soon after flooded, and all hands on duty below ordered to the spar-deck. Nor was the order given any too soon.

Said engineer O'Brien, after the landing of the rescued party at Southampton, "I think for Spartan coolness and nerve these two German messmates of ours (Meulnier and Schroeder) surpass anything in my observation and reading. I was on duty close to them, a few yards only separating us. They had command of the shot-and-shell passing division, and were stationed at the shell-room hatch, tending the 'whip-tackle.' A shell entered, and brought up a few yards from them. It must have been a five-second fuse, from the distance of the *Kearsarge* from us at this stage of the action, for it exploded almost immediately. I protected myself as well as I could from the fragments. So soon as the smoke and dust cleared away, I looked, intending to go to their assistance, expecting to find them wounded, or perhaps dead; when, to my amazement, there they stood hauling on the tackle as though attending an exercise drill. They were the calmest men I ever saw; the most phlegmatic lot it was ever my privilege to fight alongside of."

A most remarkable case of desperate wounding and after-tenacity of life was noted by the writer in the latter part of the fight. It was imperative to get the ship's head off if possible, the vessel not answering to her helm as quickly as desired, and the danger imminent. The *Kearsarge* would soon be in a position to rake us; and though the wind was light, and the manoeuvre not likely to be of much practical benefit, a sail-trimmer and forecastle-man, John Roberts, was ordered out by Kell to loose the jib. He had executed the order, and was returning, when he was struck by a solid shot or shell, which completely disembowelled him. Roberts in this desperate plight clung to the jib-boom, and working along the foot-rope, reached the top-gallant-forecastle, thence climbed down the ladder to the spar-deck, and with shrieks of agony, and his hands over his head, beating the air convulsively, reached the port gangway, where he fell and expired. He was a man of commanding stature, five or six and twenty years of age, of unusual physical strength, an able seaman, and as well behaved at all times as would be expected of an officer. An Englishman by birth, and a typical English man-of-war's man.

It was a touching scene, the transfer of our wounded men as prisoners to the *Kearsarge*, in our only boat left seaworthy at the davits. Among them was James King 2d, an Irishman, and a man of powerful frame. He had been made quite a "butt" by all our crew, quizzed on all occasions, not being an educated "sailor-man," but what we designated on shipboard a "landsman."

Sinking of the CSS Alabama, by Xanthus Smith, 1922. Courtesy of the Franklin D. Roosevelt Library, Hyde Park, N.Y. U.S. Navy photo.

"Connemara" was the nickname attached to him, suggested by the county in which he was born. King, who was of a hot, quick temper, had constantly resented the practical jokes of the men at his expense, causing the vexed first lieutenant to wonder if it was practical to keep Connemara out of the "brig." He was for all this a generous, open-hearted Irishman; and his attachment was strong for officers and ship. He was mortally wounded; and just as his comrades were about to lift him into the boat destined for the Kearsarge, he sent for Kell, and stretching out his feeble hand to him, remarked, "I have sent for you, Mr. Kell, to ask your forgiveness for all the trouble I've caused you since my enlistment on the ship. Please forgive poor Connemara now he is going to his long home." Kell, kneeling by his side, supporting and stroking his head, said, "My poor, dear boy, I have nothing to forgive; nothing against you, my brave lad; and I trust you will be in better trim soon."—"No," was the reply; "Connemara is going fast. Good-by, Mr. Kell. God bless you, Mr. Kell!" He died on the *Kearsarge*.

Michael Mars was another son of Erin, a splendid type of the English man-of-war's man, and appropriately named. He was in many ways the most remarkable figure among our crew, and trustworthy to the uttermost. Still, strange to say, constantly in the "brig" for minor offences, such as playing practical jokes on his messmates, and even at times including the younger officers, if the field was clear for the exercise of his pranks. Nothing vicious or of serious moment happened among his offences, making it therefore a worry to Kell to report and Semmes to punish him. An admirable part of his composition was his indifference to rum. Mars distinguished himself in this memorable fight. He was compresser-man of the after pivot-gun, commanded by Lieut. Joseph D. Wilson, manned by twenty-two men, ten on each side, and two captains, first and second, in the rear. The gun, a very heavy one, eight-inch solid shot or shell weapon, had just been loaded and run out to fire, and Mars had stooped on his knees to compress (to retard recoil), when an eleven-inch shell from the enemy struck full in the middle of the first man on the port side of the gun, passing through the entire lot, killing or wounding them, and piling up on the deck a mass of human fragments. Such a ghastly sight the writer never saw before, and hopes never to see again. Mars at once rose to his feet uninjured, seized a shovel from the bulwarks, and soon had the mass of flesh overboard, and the deck resanded. To have observed the man, you would have supposed him engaged in the ordinary morning-watch cleaning of decks. The pivot -gun had a picked crew, selected principally from the coal-heavers and firemen, they being heavy, powerful men. At this stage the quarter-deck thirty-two pounder of Wilson's division, and commanded in person by Midshipman Anderson, was "secured," and the crew sent to man the more important gun, depleted of half its crew. Later in the action, when the *Alabama* had settled with her spardeck flush with the water, and all hope was abandoned, the order was given, "All hands save yourselves!" through the boatswain and his mates. Semmes, who, with Kell, was stripping for the swim, seated on the quarter-deck, sent for Mars and Freemantle, and telling them that he (Semmes) was unable to save his diary and ship-papers, his right arm being wounded by a fragment of shell, asked if they could take care of them. The seamen accepted the trust; and Bartelli, wading into the cabin, returned with them. Easing themselves down in the sea, Mars swam with one arm to the boat of the *Deerhound*, holding the documents above the water, and Freemantle to a French boat. Semmes and Kell followed suit; and the former had the gratification of knowing his notes were safe and once more in his possession. Mars would deliver the precious papers to none other on the yacht, though told Semmes was safe in the cabin. He wished to deliver them in person, and succeeded. This latter fact was learned by the writer from Capt. Jones of the *Deerhound*.

We were soon steaming in the yacht to Southampton, which port we reached without further adventure. Here Mars left us, sailor-like, for another cruise. As the years roll by the writer often thinks of Mars, and wonders what is his fate; whether he who did such gallant deeds was at last swallowed by insatiable old ocean, or whether we shall meet again, and tell each other of our later pilgrimage through life. If toiling here yet, may God, as in the past, keep watch and ward over the jovial, generous, and brave Irishman!

Capt. Jones narrates a pleasing instance of noble self-sacrifice on the part of our captain of the forecastle. In coming up to a number of men struggling in the water, he observed an old gray-haired seaman swimming along content-edly, and while engaged pulling some others into his boat, called out to the old fellow, "Come this way, and get on board." To which the old fellow re-plied, "Oh, I can keep up for a while longer! Save those other lads; they need your services more than I do. Your boat can't carry all of us."

CHAPTER 12

BLOWING UP A TRAIN

by T. E. Lawrence

Lieutenant Colonel Thomas Edward Lawrence, based on a photograph by Lowell Thomas, circa 1919.

B lowing up trains was an exact science when done deliberately, by a sufficient party, with machine-guns in position. If scrambled at it might become dangerous. The difficulty this time was that the available gunners were Indians; who, though good men fed, were only half-men in cold and hunger. I did not propose to drag them off without rations on an adventure which might take a week. There was no cruelty in starving Arabs; they would not die of a few days' fasting, and would fight as well as ever on empty stomachs; while, if things got too difficult, there were the riding camels to kill and eat; but the Indians, though Moslems, refused camel-flesh on principle.

I explained these delicacies of diet. Ali at once said that it would be enough for me to blow up the train, leaving him and the Arabs with him to do their best to carry its wreck without machine-gun support. As, in this unsuspecting district, we might well happen on a supply train, with civilians or only a small guard of reservists aboard, I agreed to risk it. The decision having been applauded, we sat down in a cloaked circle, to finish our remaining food in a very late and cold supper (the rain had sodden the fuel and made fire not possible), our hearts somewhat comforted by the chance of another effort.

At dawn, with the unfit of the Arabs, the Indians moved away for Azrak miserably. They had started up country with me in hope of a really military enterprise and first had seen the muddled bridge and now were losing this prospective train. It was hard on them; and to soften the blow with honour I asked Wood to accompany them. He agreed, after argument, for their sakes; but it proved a wise move for himself, as a sickness which had been troubling him began to show the early signs of pneumonia.

The balance of us, some sixty men, turned back towards the railway. None of them knew the country so I led them to Minifir, where, with Zaal, we had made havoc in the spring. The re-curved hill-top was an excellent observation-post, camp, grazing ground and way of retreat, and we sat there in our old place till sunset, shivering and staring out over the immense plain which stretched map-like to the clouded peaks of Jebel Druse, with Um el Jemal and her sister-villages like ink-smudges through the rain.

In the first dusk we walked down to lay the mine. The rebuilt culvert of kilometre 172 seemed still the fittest place. While we stood by it there came a rumbling and through the gathering darkness and mist a train suddenly appeared round the northern curve, only two hundred yards away. We scurried under the long arch and heard it roll overhead. This was annoying; but when the course was clear again, we fell to burying the charge. The evening was bitterly cold with drifts of rain blowing down the valley.

The arch was solid masonry, of four metres span, and stood over a shingle water-bed which took its rise on our hill-top. The winter rains had cut this into a channel four feet deep, narrow and winding, which served us as an admirable approach till within three hundred yards of the line. There the gully widened out and ran straight towards the culvert, open to the sight of anyone upon the rails.

We hid the explosive carefully on the crown of the arch, deeper than usual, beneath a tie, so that the patrols could not feel its jelly softness under their feet. The wires were taken down the bank into the shingle bed of the watercourse, where concealment was quick; and up it as far as they could reach. Unfortunately, this was only sixty yards, for there had been difficulty in Egypt over insulated cable and no more had been available when our expedition started.

Sixty yards was plenty for the bridge, but little for a train: however, the ends happened to coincide with a little bush about ten inches high, on the edge of the watercourse, and we buried them beside this very convenient mark. It was impossible to leave them joined up to the exploder in the proper way, since the spot was evident to the permanent way-patrols as they made their rounds.

Owing to the mud the job took longer than usual, and it was very nearly dawn before we finished. I waited under the draughty arch till day broke, wet and dismal, and then I went over the whole area of disturbance, spending another half-hour in effacing its every mark, scattering leaves and dead grass over it, and watering down the broken mud from a shallow rain-pool near. Then they waved to me that the first patrol was coming and I went up to join the others.

Before I had reached them they came tearing down into their prearranged places, lining the watercourse and spurs each side. A train was coming from the north. Hamud, Feisal's long slave, had the exploder; but before he reached me a short train of closed box-wagons rushed by at speed. The rainstorms on the plain and the thick morning had hidden it from the eyes of our watchman until too late. This second failure saddened us further and Ali began to say that nothing would come right this trip. Such a statement held risks as prelude of the discovery of an evil eye present; so, to divert attention, I suggested new watching posts be sent far out, one to the ruins on the north, one to the great cairn of the southern crest.

The rest, having no breakfast, were to pretend not to be hungry. They all enjoyed doing this and for a while we sat cheerfully in the rain huddled against one another for warmth behind a breastwork of our streaming camels. The moisture made the animals' hair curl up like a fleece so that they looked queerly dishevelled. When the rain paused, which it did frequently, a cold moaning wind searched out the unprotected parts of us very thoroughly. After a time we found our wetted shirts clammy and comfortless things. We had nothing to eat, nothing to do and nowhere to sit except on wet rock, wet grass or mud. However, this persistent weather kept reminding me that it would delay Allenby's advance on Jerusalem and rob him of his great possibility. So large a misfortune to our lion was a half-encouragement for the mice. We would be partners into next year.

In the best circumstances, waiting for action was hard. Today it was beastly. Even enemy patrols stumbled along without care, perfunctorily, against the rain. At last near noon, in a snatch of fine weather, the watchmen on the south peak flagged their cloaks wildly in signal of a train. We reached our positions in an instant, for we had squatted the late hours on our heels in a streaming ditch near the line so as not to miss another chance. The Arabs took cover properly. I looked back at their ambush from my firing point and saw nothing but the grey hillsides.

I could not hear the train coming but trusted, and knelt ready for perhaps half an hour when the suspense became intolerable, and I signalled to know what was up. They sent down to say it was coming very slowly and was an enormously long train. Our appetites stiffened. The longer it was the more would be the loot. Then came word that it had stopped. It moved again.

Finally, near one o'clock, I heard it panting. The locomotive was evidently defective, (all these wood-fired trains were bad), and the heavy load on the upgradient was proving too much for its capacity. I crouched behind

my bush while it crawled slowly into view past the south cutting and along
the bank above my head towards the culvert. The first ten trucks were open
trucks, crowded with troops. However, once again it was too late to choose,
so when the engine was squarely over the mine I pushed down the handle of
the exploder. Nothing happened. I sawed it up and down four times.

Still nothing happened; and I realised that it had gone out of order and
that I was kneeling on a naked bank, with a Turkish troop train crawling past
fifty yards away. The bush, which had seemed a foot high, shrank smaller
than a figleaf; and I felt myself the most distinct object in the countryside.
Behind me was an open valley for two hundred yards to the cover where my
Arabs were waiting, and wondering what I was at. It was impossible to make a
bolt for it or the Turks would step off the train and finish us. If I sat still, there
might be just a hope of my being ignored as a casual Bedouin.

So there I sat, counting for sheer life, while eighteen open trucks, three
box-wagons, and three officers' coaches dragged by. The engine panted slower and slower and I thought every moment that it would break down. The
troops took no great notice of me but the officers were interested, and they
came out to the little platforms at the ends of their carriages, pointing and
staring. I waved back at them, grinning nervously and feeling an improbable
shepherd in my Meccan dress with its twisted golden circlet about my head.
Perhaps the mud-stains, the wet and their ignorance made me accepted. The
end of the brake van slowly disappeared into the cutting on the north.

As it went, I jumped up, buried my wires, snatched hold of the wretched
exploder, and went like a rabbit uphill into safety. There I took breath and
looked back to see that the train had finally stuck. It waited, about five hundred yards beyond the mine, for nearly an hour to get up a head of steam,
while an officers' patrol came back and searched, very carefully, the ground
where I had been seen sitting. However the wires were properly hidden: they
found nothing: the engine plucked up heart again and away they went.

Mifleh was past tears, thinking I had intentionally let the train through;
and when the Serahin had been told the real cause they said "bad luck is with
us." Historically they were right; but they meant it for a prophecy so I made

sarcastic reference to their courage at the bridge the week before, hinting
that it might be a tribal preference to sit on camel guard. At once there was
uproar, the Serahin attacking more furiously, the Beni Sakhr defending. Ali
heard the trouble and came running.

When we had made it up the original despondency was half forgotten.
Ali backed me nobly, though the wretched boy was blue with cold and shivering in an attack of fever. He gasped that their ancestor the Prophet had
given to Sherifs the faculty of "sight," and by it he knew that our luck was
turning. This was comfort for them: my first instalment of good fortune
came when in the wet, without other tool than my dagger, I got the box of
the exploder open and persuaded its electrical gear to work properly once
more.

We returned to our vigil by the wires, but nothing happened, and evening drew down with more squalls and beastliness, everybody full of grum-
bles. There was no train; it was too wet to light a cooking fire; our only
potential food was camel. Raw meat did not tempt anyone that night and so
our beasts survived to the morrow.

Ali lay down on his belly, which position lessened the hunger-ache, trying to sleep off his fever. Khazen, Ali's servant, lent him his cloak for extra
covering. For a spell I took Khazen under mine, but soon found it becoming
crowded. So I left it to him and went downhill to connect up the exploder. Afterwards I spent the night there alone by the singing telegraph wires,
hardly wishing to sleep, so painful was the cold. Nothing came all the long
hours, and dawn, which broke wet looked even uglier than usual. We were
sick to death of Minifir, of railways, of train watching and wrecking, by now.
I climbed up to the main body while the early patrol searched the railway.
Then the day cleared a little. Ali awoke much refreshed and his new spirit
cheered up. Hamud, the slave, produced some sticks which he had kept under his clothes by his skin all night. They were nearly dry. We shaved down
some blasting gelatine and with its hot flame got a fire going while the Sukhar
hurriedly killed a mangy camel, the best spared of our riding-beasts, and began with entrenching tools to hack it into handy joints.

The Desert of Wadi Rum, where Lawrence passed through during the Arab Revolt.

Just at that moment the watchman on the north cried, "A train." We left the fire and made a breathless race of the six hundred yards downhill to our old position. Round the bend, whistling its loudest, came the train, a splendid two-engined thing of twelve passenger coaches travelling at top speed on the favouring grade. I touched off under the first driving wheel of the first locomotive, and the explosion was terrific. The ground spouted blackly into my face and I was sent spinning, to sit up with the shirt torn to my shoulder and the blood dripping from long, ragged scratches on my left arm. Between my knees lay the exploder, crushed under a twisted sheet of sooty iron. In front of me was the scalded and smoking upper half of a man. When I peered through the dust and steam of the explosion the whole boiler of the first engine seemed to be missing.

I dully felt that it was time to get away to support but when I moved, I learnt that there was a great pain in my right foot because of which I could only limp along with my head swinging from the shock. Movement began to clear away this confusion as I hobbled towards the upper valley, whence the Arabs were now shooting fast into the crowded coaches. Dizzily I cheered myself by repeating aloud in English, "Oh, I wish this hadn't happened."

When the enemy began to return our fire, I found myself much between the two. Ali saw me fall and, thinking that I was hard hit, ran out with Turki and about twenty men of his servants and the Beni Sakhr to help me. The Turks found their range and got seven of them in a few seconds. The others, in a rush, were about me—fit models, after their activity, for a sculptor. Their full white cotton drawers drawn in, belllike, round their slender waists and ankles; their hairless brown bodies, and the love-locks plaited tightly over each temple in long horns; made them look like Russians dancers.

We scrambled back into cover together and there, secretly, I felt myself over, to find I had not once been really hurt; though besides the bruises and cuts of the boiler-plate and a broken toe, I had five different bullet-grazes on me (some of them uncomfortably deep) and my clothes ripped to pieces.

From the watercourse we could look about. The explosion had destroyed the arched head of the culvert and the frame of the first engine was lying beyond it at the near foot of the embankment down which it had rolled. The second locomotive had toppled into the gap and was lying across the ruined tender of the first. Its bed was twisted. I judged them both beyond repair. The second tender had disappeared over the further side and the first three wagons had telescoped and were smashed in pieces.

The rest of the train was badly derailed, with the listing coaches butted end to end at all angles zigzagged along the track. One of them was a saloon decorated with flags. In it had been Mehmed Jemal Pasha, commanding the Eighth Army Corps, hurrying down to defend Jerusalem against Allenby.

His chargers had been in the first wagon; his motor-car was on the end of the train and we shot it up. Of his staff we noticed a fat ecclesiastic, whom we thought to be Assad Shukair, Imam to Ahmed Jemal Pasha and a notorious pro-Turk pimp. So we blazed at him till he dropped.

It was all long bowls. We could see that our chance of carrying the wreck was slight. There had been some four hundred men on board and the survivors, now recovered from the shock, were under shelter and shooting hard at us. At the first moment our party on the north spur had closed and nearly won the game. Mifleh on his mare chased the officers from the saloon into the lower ditch. He was too excited to stop and shoot and so they got away scathless. The Arabs following him had turned to pick up some of the rifles and medals littering the ground and then to drag bags and boxes from the train. If we had had a machine-gun posted to cover the far side, according to my mining practice, not a Turk would have escaped.

Mifleh and Adhub rejoined us on the hill and asked after Fahad. One of the Serahin told how he had led the first rush, while I lay knocked out beside the exploder, and had been killed near it. They showed his belt and rifle as proof that he was dead and that they had tried to save him. Adhub said not a word but leaped out of the gully and raced downhill. We caught our breaths till our lungs hurt us watching him, but the Turks seemed not to see. A minute later he was dragging a body behind the left-hand bank.

Mifleh went back to his mare, mounted, and took her down behind a spur. Together they lifted the inert figure on to the pommel and returned. A bullet had passed through Fahad's face, knocking out four teeth and gashing the tongue. He had fallen unconscious but had revived just before Adhub reached him and was trying on hands and knees, blinded with blood, to crawl away. He now recovered poise enough to cling to a saddle. So they changed him to the first camel they found and led him off at once.

The Turks, seeing us so quiet, began to advance up the slope. We let them come half-way and then poured in volleys which killed some twenty and drove the others back. The ground about the train was strewn with dead, and the broken coaches had been crowded but they were fighting under the eye of their Corps Commander and, undaunted began to work round the spurs to outflank us.

We were now only about forty left and obviously could do no good against them. So we ran in batches up the little stream-bed, turning at each sheltered angle to delay them by pot-shots. Little Turki much distinguished himself by quick coolness, though his straight-stocked Turkish cavalry carbine made him so exposed that he got four bullets through his head-cloth. Ali was angry with me for retiring slowly. In reality my raw hurts crippled me but to hide from him this real reason I pretended to be easy, interested in and studying the Turks. Such successive rest while I gained courage for a new run kept him and Turki far behind the rest.

At last we reached the hill-top. Each man there jumped on the nearest camel and made away at full speed eastward into the desert for an hour. Then in safety we sorted our animals. The excellent Rahail, despite the ruling excitement, had brought off with him, tied to his saddle-girth, a huge haunch of the camel slaughtered just as the train arrived. He gave us the motive for a proper halt, five miles farther on, as a little party of four camels appeared marching in the same direction. It was our companion, Matar, coming back from his home village to Azrak with loads of raisins and peasant delicacies.

So we stopped at once, under a large rock in Wadi Dhuleil, where there was a barren fig-tree, and cooked our first meal for three days. There, also, we bandaged up Fahad, who was sleepy with the lassitude of his severe hurt. Adhub, seeing this, took one of Matar's new carpets and, doubling it across the camel-saddle, stitched the ends into great pockets. In one they laid Fahad while Adhub crawled into the other as makeweight and the camel was led off southward towards their tribal tents.

The other wounded men were seen to at the same time. Mifleh brought up the youngest lads of the party and had them spray the wounds with their piss as a rude antiseptic. Meanwhile we whole ones refreshed ourselves. I bought another mangy camel for extra meat, paid rewards, compensated the relatives of the killed and gave prize-money for the sixty or seventy rifles we had taken. It was small booty but not to be despised. Some Serahin, who had gone into the action without rifles able only to throw unavailing stones, had now two guns apiece. Next day we moved into Azrak, having a great welcome and boasting—God forgive us—that we were victors.

SECTION THREE

SURVIVING THE ELEMENTS

CHAPTER 13

THE END

by Robert Falcon Scott

Photograph of Robert Scott, by
John Thomson, circa 1911.

ight, 15 January. It is wonderful to think that two long marches would land us at the Pole. We left our depot today with nine days' provisions, so that it ought to be a certain thing now, and the only appalling possibility the sight of the Norwegian flag forestalling ours. Little Bowers continues his indefatigable efforts to get good sights, and it is wonderful how he works them up in his sleeping-bag in our congested tent. (Minimum for night –27.5°.) Only 27 miles from the Pole. We ought to do it now.

Tuesday, 16 January Camp 68. Height 9,760. T –23.5°. The worst has happened, or nearly the worst. We marched well in the morning and covered 7 1/2 miles. Noon sight showed us in Lat. 89° 42′S, and we started off in high spirits in the afternoon, feeling that tomorrow would see us at our destination. About the second hour of the march Bowers' sharp eyes detected what he thought was a cairn; he was uneasy about it, but argued that it must be a sastrugus. Half an hour later he detected a black speck ahead. Soon we knew that this could not be a natural snow feature. We marched on, found that it was a black flag tied to a sledge bearer; near by the remains of a camp; sledge tracks and ski tracks going and coming and the clear trace of dogs' paws—many dogs. This told us the whole story. The Norwegians have forestalled us and are first at the Pole. It is a terrible disappointment, and I am very sorry for my loyal companions. Many thoughts come and much discussion have we had. Tomorrow we must march on to the Pole and then hasten home with all the speed we can compass. All the day-dreams must go; it will be a wearisome return. Certainly we are descending in altitude—certainly also the Norwegians found an easy way up.

Wednesday, 17 January Camp 69. T –22° at start. Night –21°. The Pole. Yes, but under very different circumstances from those expected. We have had a horrible day—add to our disappointment a head wind 4 to 5,* with a temperature –22 °, and companions labouring on with cold feet and hands.

We started at 7.30, none of us having slept much after the shock of our discovery. We followed the Norwegian sledge tracks for some way; as far as we make out there are only two men. In about three miles we passed two small cairns. Then the weather overcast, and the tracks being increasingly drifted up and obviously going too far to the west, we decided to make straight for the Pole according to our calculations. At 12.30 Evans had such cold hands we camped for lunch—an excellent 'weekend' one. We had marched 7.4 miles. Lat. sight gave 89° 53′ 37″. We started out and did 6 1/2 miles due

---

*Half a gale. The velocity of wind is denoted by numbers (1–10).

south. Tonight little Bowers is laying himself out to get sights in terrible diffi-cult circumstances; the wind is blowing hard, T–21°, and there is that curious damp, cold feeling in the air which chills one to the bone in no time. We have been descending again, I think, but there looks to be a rise ahead; otherwise there is very little that is different from the awful monotony of past days. Great God! this is an awful place and terrible enough for us to have laboured to it without the reward of priority. Well, it is something to have got here, and the wind may be our friend tomorrow. We have had a fat Polar hoosh in spite of our chagrin, and feel comfortable inside—added a small stick of chocolate and the queer taste of a cigarette brought by Wilson. Now for the run home and a desperate struggle. I wonder if we can do it.

Thursday morning, 18 January Decided after summing up all observations that we were 3.5 miles away from the Pole—one mile beyond it and 3 to the right. More or less in this direction Bowers saw a cairn or tent.

We have just arrived at this tent, 2 miles from our camp, therefore about 1 1/2 miles from the Pole. In the tent we find a record of five Norwegians having been here, as follows:

Roald Amundsen
Olav Olavson Bjaaland
Hilmer Hanssen
Sverre H. Hassel
Oscar Wisting.   16 Dec. 1911

The tent is fine—a small compact affair supported by a single bamboo. A note from Amundsen, which I keep, asks me to forward a letter to King Haakon!

The following articles have been left in the tent: 3 half bags of reindeer containing a miscellaneous assortment of mits and sleeping socks, very vari-ous in description, a sextant, a Norwegian artificial horizon and a hypsometer without boiling-point thermometers, a sextant and hypsometer of English make.

Left a note to say I had visited the tent with companions; Bowers photographing and Wilson sketching. Since lunch we have marched 6.2 miles SSE by compass (i.e. northwards). Sights at lunch gave us a mile from the Pole, so we call it the Pole Camp. (Temp. Lunch–21°.) We built a cairn, put up our poor slighted Union Jack, and photographed ourselves—mighty cold work all of it—less than 1/2 a mile south we saw stuck up an old underrunner of a sledge. This we commandeered as a yard for a floorcloth sail. I imagine it was intended to mark the exact spot of the Pole as near as the Norwegians could fix it. (Height 9,500.) A note attached talked of the tent as being 2 miles from the Pole. Wilson keeps the note. There is no doubt that our predecessors have made thoroughly sure of their mark and fully carried out their programme. I think the Pole is about 9,500 feet in height; this is remarkable, considering that in Lat. 88 we were about 10,500.

We carried the Union Jack about a mile north with us and left it on a piece of stick as near as we could fix it. I fancy the Norwegians arrived at the pole on the 15th Dec. and left on the 17th, ahead of a date quoted by me in London as ideal, viz. Dec. 22. It looks as though the Norwegian party expected

The *Terra Nova*, Scott's vessel on his Antarctic journey.

colder weather on the summit than they got; it could scarcely be otherwise from Shackleton's account. Well, we have turned our back now on the goal of our ambition and must face our 800 miles of solid dragging—and good-bye to most of the day-dreams!

Tuesday, 6 February Lunch 7,900; Supper 7,210. Temp–15° [R. 20]. We've had a horrid day and not covered good mileage. On turning out found sky overcast; a beastly position amidst crevasses. Luckily it cleared just before we started. We went straight for Mt Darwin, but in half an hour found ourselves amongst huge open chasms, unbridged, but not very deep, I think. We turned to the north between two, but to our chagrin they converged into chaotic disturbance. We had to retrace our steps for a mile or so, then struck to the west and got on to a confused sea of sastrugi, pulling very hard; we put up the sail, Evans's nose suffered, Wilson very cold, everything horrid. Camped for lunch in the sastrugi; the only comfort, things looked clearer to the west and we were obviously going downhill. In the afternoon we struggled on, got out of sastrugi and turned over on glazed surface, crossing many crevasses—very easy work on ski. Towards the end of the march we realised the certainty of maintaining a more or less straight course to the depot, and estimate distance 10 to 15 miles.

Food is low and weather uncertain, so that many hours of the day were anxious; but this evening, though we are not as far advanced as I expected, the outlook is much more promising. Evans is the chief anxiety now; his cuts and wounds suppurate, his nose looks very bad, and altogether he shows considerable signs of being played out. Things may mend for him on the glacier, and his wounds get some respite under warmer conditions. I am indeed glad to think we shall so soon have done with plateau conditions. It took us 27 days to reach the Pole and 21 days back—in all 48 days—nearly 7 weeks in low temperature with almost incessant wind.

Sunday, 11 February R. 25. Lunch Temp. +6.5°; Supper + 3.5°. The worst day we have had during the trip and greatly owing to our own fault. We started on a wretched surface with light SW wind, sail set, and pulling on ski—in a horrible light, which made everything look fantastic. As we went on the light got worse, and suddenly we found ourselves in pressure. Then came the fatal decision to steer east. We went on for 6 hours, hoping to do a good distance, which in fact I suppose we did, but for the last hour or two we pressed on into a regular trap. Getting on to a good surface we did not reduce our lunch meal, and thought all going well, but half an hour after lunch we got into the worst ice mess I have ever been in. For three hours we plunged on on ski, first thinking we were too much to the right, then too much to the left; meanwhile the disturbance got worse and my spirits received a very rude shock. There were times when it seemed almost impossible to find a way out of the awful turmoil in which we found ourselves. At length, arguing that there must be a way on our left, we plunged in that direction. It got worse, harder, more icy and crevassed. We could not manage our ski and pulled on foot, falling into crevasses every minute—most luckily with no bad accident. At length we saw a smoother slope towards the land, pushed for it, but knew it was a woefully long way from us. The turmoil changed in character, irregular crevassed surface giving way to huge chasms, closely packed and most difficult to cross. It was very heavy work, but we had grown desperate. We won through at 10 p.m. and I write after 12 hours on the march. I think we are on or about the right track now, but we are still a good number of miles from the depot, so we reduced rations tonight. We had three pemmican meals left and decided to make them into four. Tomorrow's lunch must serve for two if we do not make big progress. It was a test of our endurance on the march and our fitness with small supper. We have come through well. A good wind has come down the glacier which is clearing the sky and surface. Pray God the wind holds tomorrow.

Wednesday, 14 February There is no getting away from the fact that we are not pulling strong: probably none of us. Wilson's leg still troubles him and he doesn't like to trust himself on ski; but the worst case is Evans, who is giving us serious anxiety. This morning he suddenly disclosed a huge blister on his foot. It delayed us on the march, when he had to have his crampon readjusted.

Sometimes I fear he is going from bad to worse, but I trust he will pick up again when we come to steady work on ski like this afternoon. He is hungry and so is Wilson. We can't risk opening out our food again, and as cook at present I am serving something under full allowance. We are inclined to get slack and slow with our camping arrangements, and small delays increase. I have talked of the matter tonight and hope for improvement. We cannot do distance without the hours. The next depot some 30 miles away and nearly 3 days' food in hand.

Saturday, 17 February A very terrible day. Evans looked a little better after a good sleep, and declared, as he always did, that he was quite well. He started in his place on the traces, but half an hour later worked his ski shoes adrift, and had to leave the sledge. The surface was awful, the soft recently fallen snow clogging the ski and runners at every step, the sledge groaning, the sky overcast, and the land hazy. We stopped after about one hour, and Evans came up again, but very slowly. Half an hour later he dropped out again on the same plea. He asked Bowers to lend him a piece of string. I cautioned him to come on as quickly as he could, and he answered cheerfully as I thought. We had to push on, and the remainder of us were forced to pull very hard, sweating heavily. Abreast the Monument Rock we stopped, and seeing Evans a long way astern, I camped for lunch. There was no alarm at first, and we prepared tea and our own meal, consuming the latter. After lunch, and Evans still not appearing, we looked out, to see him still afar off. By this time we were alarmed, and all four started back on ski. I was first to reach the poor man and shocked at his appearance; he was on his knees with clothing disarranged, hands uncovered and frostbitten, and a wild look in his eyes. Asked what was the matter, he replied with a slow speech that he didn't know, but thought he must have fainted. We got him on his feet, but after two or three steps he sank down again. He showed every sign of complete collapse. Wilson, Bowers and I went back for the sledge, whilst Oates remained with him. When we returned he was practically unconscious, and when we got him into the tent quite comatose. He died quietly at 12.30 a.m. On discussing the symptoms we think he began to get weaker just before we reached the Pole, and that his downward path was accelerated first by the shock of his frostbitten fingers, and later by falls during rough travelling on the glacier, further by his loss of all confidence in himself. Wilson thinks it certain he must have injured his brain by a fall. It is a terrible thing to lose a companion in this way, but calm reflection shows that there could not have been a better ending to the terrible anxieties of the past week. Discussion of the situation at lunch yesterday shows us what a desperate pass we were in with a sick man on our hands so far from home . . .

Friday, 2 March Lunch. Misfortunes rarely come singly. We marched to the [Middle Barrier] depot fairly easily yesterday afternoon, and since that have suffered three distinct blows which have placed us in a bad position. First we found a shortage of oil; with most rigid economy it can scarce carry us to the next depot on this surface [71 miles away]. Second, Titus Oates disclosed his feet, the toes showing very bad indeed, evidently bitten by the late temperatures. The third blow came in the night, when the wind, which we had hailed with some joy, brought dark overcast weather. It fell below −40° in the night, and this morning it took 1 1/2 hours to get our foot-gear on, but we got away before eight. We lost cairn and tracks together and made as steady as we could N by W, but have seen nothing. Worse was to come—the surface is simply awful. In spite of strong wind and full sail we have only done 5 miles. We are in a *very* queer street, since there is no doubt we cannot do the extra marches and feel the cold horribly.

Monday, 5 March Lunch. Regret to say going from bad to worse. We got a slant of wind yesterday afternoon, and going on 5 hours we converted our wretched morning run of 3 1/2 miles into something over 9. We went to bed on a cup of cocoa and pemmican solid with the chill off. (R. 47.) The result is telling on all, but mainly on Oates, whose feet are in a wretched condition. One swelled up tremendously last night and he is very lame this morning. We started march on tea and pemmican as last night—we pretend to prefer the pemmican this way. Marched for 5 hours this morning over a slightly better surface covered with high moundy sastrugi. Sledge capsized twice; we pulled on foot, covering about 5 miles. We are two pony marches and 4 miles about from our depot. Our fuel dreadfully low and the poor soldier nearly done. It is pathetic enough because we can do nothing for him; more hot food might do a little, but only a little, I fear. We none of us expected these terribly low temperatures, and of the rest of us Wilson is feeling them most; mainly, I fear, from his self-sacrificing devotion in doctoring Oates's feet. We cannot help each other, each has enough to do to take care of himself. We get cold on the march when the trudging is heavy, and the wind pierces our worn garments. The others, all of them, are unendingly cheerful when in the tent. We mean to see the game through with a proper spirit, but it's tough work to be pulling harder than we ever pulled in our lives for long hours, and to feel that the progress is so slow. One can only say 'God help us!' and plod on our weary way, cold and very miserable, though outwardly cheerful. We talk of all sorts of subjects in the tent, not much of food now, since we decided to take the risk of running a full ration. We simply couldn't go hungry at this time.

Saturday, 10 March Things steadily downhill. Oates's foot worse. He has rare pluck and must know that he can never get through. He asked Wilson if he had a chance this morning, and of course Bill had to say he didn't know. In point of fact he has none. Apart from him, if he went under now, I doubt whether we could get through. With great care we might have a dog's chance, but no more. The weather conditions are awful, and our gear gets steadily more icy and difficult to manage. At the same time, of course, poor Titus is the greatest handicap. He keeps us waiting in the morning until we have partly lost the warming effect of our good breakfast, when the only wise policy is to be up and away at once; again at lunch. Poor chap! it is too pathetic to watch him; one cannot but try to cheer him up.

Yesterday we marched up the depot, Mt Hooper. Cold comfort. Shortage on our allowance all round . . .

Sunday, 11 March Titus Oates is very near the end, one feels. What we or he will do, God only knows. We discussed the matter after breakfast; he is a brave fine fellow and understands the situation, but he practically asked for advice. Nothing could be said but to urge him to march as long as he could. One satisfactory result to the discussion; I practically ordered Wilson to hand over the means of ending our troubles to us, so that any one of us may know how to do so. Wilson had no choice between doing so and our ransacking the medicine case. We have 30 opium tabloids apiece and he is left with a tube of morphine. So far the tragical side of our story.

The sky was completely overcast when we started this morning. We could see nothing, lost the tracks, and doubtless have been swaying a good deal since—3.1 miles for the forenoon—terribly heavy dragging—expected it. Know that 6 miles is about the limit of our endurance now, if we get no help from wind or surfaces. We have 7 days' food and should be about 55 miles from One Ton Camp tonight, 6 x 7 = 42, leaving us 13 miles short of our distance, even if things get no worse. Meanwhile the season rapidly advances . . .

Wednesday, 14 March No doubt about the going downhill, but everything going wrong for us. Yesterday we woke to a strong northerly wind with temp. –37°. Couldn't face it, so remained in camp till 2, then did 50 miles. Wanted to march later, but party feeling the cold badly as the breeze (N) never took off entirely, and as the sun sank the temp. fell. Long time getting supper in dark.

This morning started with southerly breeze, set sail and passed another cairn at good speed; halfway, however, the wind shifted to W by S or WSW, blew through our wind clothes and into our mits. Poor Wilson horribly cold, could [not] get off ski for some time. Bowers and I practically made camp, and when we got into the tent at last we were all deadly cold. Then temp. now midday down –43° and the wind strong. We must go on, but now the making of every camp must be more difficult and dangerous. It must be near the end, but a pretty merciful end. Poor Oates got it again in the foot. I shudder to think what it will be like tomorrow. It is only with greatest pains rest of us keep off frostbites. No idea there could be temperatures like this at this time of year with such winds. Truly awful outside the tent. Must fight it out to the last biscuit, but can't reduce rations.

Friday, 16 March, or Saturday 17 Lost track of dates, but think the last correct. Tragedy all along the line. At lunch, the day before yesterday, poor Titus Oates said he couldn't go on; he proposed we should leave him in his sleeping-bag. That we could not do, and we induced him to come on, on the afternoon march. In spite of its awful nature for him he struggled on and we made a few miles. At night he was worse and we knew the end had come.

Should this be found I want these facts recorded. Oates's last thoughts were of his mother, but immediately before he took pride in thinking that his regiment would be pleased with the bold way in which he met his death. We can testify to his bravery. He has borne intense suffering for weeks without complaint, and to the very last was able and willing to discuss outside subjects. He did not—would not—give up hope till the very end. He was a brave soul. This was the end. He slept through the night before last, hoping not to wake; but he woke in the morning—yesterday. It was blowing a blizzard. He said, 'I am just going outside and may be some time.' He went out into the blizzard and we have not seen him since.

I take this opportunity of saying that we have stuck to our sick companions to the last. In case of Edgar Evans, when absolutely out of food and he lay insensible, the safety of the remainder seemed to demand his abandonment, but Providence mercifully removed him at this critical moment. He died a natural death, and we did not leave him till two hours after his death. We knew that poor Oates was walking to his death, but though we tried to dissuade him, we knew it was the act of a brave man and an English gentleman. We all hope to meet the end with a similar spirit, and assuredly the end is not far.

I can only write at lunch and then only occasionally. The cold is intense, –40° at midday. My companions are unendingly cheerful, but we are all on the verge of serious frostbites, and though we constantly talk of fetching through, I don't think any one of us believes it in his heart.

We are cold on the march now, and at all times except meals. Yesterday we had to lie up for a blizzard and today we move dreadfully slowly. We are at No. 14 pony camp, only two pony marches from One Ton Depot. We leave here our theodolite, a camera, and Oates's sleeping-bags. Diaries, etc., and geological specimens carried at Wilson's special request, will be found with us or on our sledge.

Sunday, 18 March Today, lunch, we are 21 miles from the depot. Ill fortune presses, but better may come. We have had more wind and drift from ahead yesterday; had to stop marching; wind NW, force 4, temp. −35°. No human being could face it, and we are worn out nearly.

My right foot has gone, nearly all the toes—two days ago I was proud possessor of best feet. These are the steps of my downfall. Like an ass I mixed a small spoonful of curry powder with my melted pemmican—it gave me violent indigestion. I lay awake and in pain all night; woke and felt done on the march; foot went and I didn't know it. A very small measure of neglect and I have a foot which is not pleasant to contemplate. Bowers takes first place in condition, but there is not much to choose after all. The others are still confident of getting through—or pretend to be—I don't know! We have the last *half* fill of oil in our primus and a very small quantity of spirit—this alone between us and thirst. The wind is fair for the moment, and that is perhaps a fact to help. The mileage would have seemed ridiculously small on our outward journey.

Monday, 19 March Lunch. We camped with difficulty last night and were dreadfully cold till after our supper of cold pemmican and biscuit and a half a pannikin of cocoa cooked over the spirit. Then, contrary to expectation, we got warm and all slept well. Today we started in the usual dragging manner. Sledge dreadfully heavy. We are 15 miles from the depot and ought to get there in three days. What progress! We have two days' food, but barely a day's fuel. All our feet are getting bad—Wilson's best, my right foot worse, left all right. There is no chance to nurse one's feet till we can get hot food into us. Amputation is the least I can hope for now, but will the trouble spread? That is the serious question. The weather doesn't give us a chance—the wind from N to NW and −40° temp today.

Wednesday, 21 March Got within 11 miles of depot Monday night; had to lie up all yesterday in severe blizzard. Today forlorn hope, Wilson and Bowers going to depot for fuel.

22 and 23 Blizzard bad as ever—Wilson and Bowers unable to start—tomorrow last chance—no fuel and only one or two [rations] of food left—must be near the end. Have decided it shall be natural—we shall march for the depot with or without our effects and die in our tracks.

Thursday, 29 March Since the 21st we have had a continuous gale from WSW and SW. We had fuel to make two cups of tea apiece and bare food for two days on the 20th. Every day we have been ready to start for our depot 11 miles away, but outside the door of the tent it remains a scene of whirling drift. I do not think we can hope for any better things now. We shall stick it out to the end, but we are getting weaker, of course, and the end cannot be far.

It seems a pity, but I do not think I can write more.

R. Scott

Last entry.
For God's sake look after our people.

The Observation Hill Cross, erected in 1913 near McMurdo Station as a memorial to Robert Scott and his crew.

CHAPTER 14

88 DEGREES SOUTH

by Ernest Shackleton

A formal portrait of Sir Ernest Shackleton,
from the State Library of Victoria.

29 December Yesterday I wrote that we hoped to do fifteen miles today; but such is the variable character of this surface that one cannot prophesy with any certainty an hour ahead. A strong southerly wind, with from 44° to 49° of frost, combined with the effect of short rations, made our distance 12 miles 600 yards instead. We have reached an altitude of 10,310 ft, and an uphill gradient gave us one of the most severe pulls for ten hours that would be possible. It looks serious, for we must increase the food if we are to get on at all, and we must risk a depot at seventy miles off the Pole and dash for it then. Our sledge is badly strained, and on the abominably bad surface of soft snow is dreadfully hard to move. I have been suffering from a bad headache all day; and Adams also was worried by the cold. I think that these headaches are a form of mountain sickness, due to our high altitude. The others have bled from the nose, and that must relieve them. Physical effort is always trying at a high altitude, and we are straining at the harness all day, sometimes slipping in the soft snow that overlies the hard sastrugi. My head is very bad. The sensation is as though the nerves were being twisted up with a corkscrew and then pulled out. Marshall took our temperature tonight, and we are all at about 94°, but in spite of this we are getting south. We are only 198 miles off our goal now. If the rise would stop the cold would not matter, but it is hard to know what is man's limit. We have only 150 lb per man to pull, but it is more severe work than the 250 lb per man up the glacier was. The Pole is hard to get.

30 December We only did 4 miles 100 yards today. We started at 7 a.m., but had to camp at 11 a.m., a blizzard springing up from the south. It is more than annoying. I cannot express my feelings. We were pulling at last on a level surface, but very soft snow, when at about 10 a.m. the south wind and drift commenced to increase, and at 11 a.m. it was so bad that we had to camp. And here all day we have been lying in our sleeping-bags trying to keep warm and listening to the threshing drift on the tent-side. I am in the cooking-tent, and the wind comes through, it is so thin. Our precious food is going and the time also, and it is so important to us to get on. We lie here and think of how to make things better, but we cannot reduce food now, and the only thing will be to rush all possible at the end. We will do and are doing all humanly possible. It is with Providence to help us.

31 December The last day of the old year, and the hardest day we have had almost, pushing through soft snow uphill with a strong head wind and drift all day. The temperature is minus 7° Fahr., and our altitude is 10,477 ft above sea-level. The altitude is trying. My head has been very bad all day, and we are all feeling the short food, but still we are getting south. We are in latitude 86° 54' South tonight, but we have only three weeks' food and two weeks' biscuit to do nearly 500 geographical miles. We can only do our best. Too tired to write more tonight. We all get iced-up about our faces, and are on the verge of frostbite all the time. Please God the weather will be fine during the next fourteen days. Then all will be well. The distance today was eleven miles.

NOTE If we had only known that we were going to get such cold weather as we were at this time experiencing, we would have kept a pair of scissors to trim our beards. The moisture from the condensation of one's breath accumulated on the beard and trickled down on to the Burberry blouse. Then it froze into a sheet of ice inside, and it became very painful to pull the Burberry off in camp. Little troubles of this sort would have seemed less serious to us if we had been able to get a decent feed at the end of the day's work, but we were very hungry. We thought of food most of the time. The chocolate certainly seemed better than the cheese, because the two spoonfuls of cheese per man allowed under our scale of diet would not last as long as the two sticks of chocolate. We did not have both at the same meal. We had the bad luck at this time to strike a tin in which the biscuits were thin and overbaked. Under ordinary circumstances they would probably have tasted rather better than the other biscuits, but we wanted bulk. We soaked them in our tea so that they would swell up and appear larger, but if one soaked a biscuit too much, the sensation of biting something was lost, and the food seemed to disappear much too easily.

1 January 1909 Head too bad to write much. We did 11 miles 900 yards (statute) today, and the latitude at 6 p.m. was 87° 6W South, so we have beaten North and South records. Struggling uphill all day in very soft snow. Everyone done up and weak from want of food. When we camped at 6 p.m. fine warm weather, thank God. Only 172 1/2 miles from the Pole. The height above sea-level, now 10,755 ft, makes all work difficult. Surface seems to be better ahead. I do trust it will be so tomorrow.

The *Nimrod,* from the Archive of Alfred Wegener Institute for Polar and Marine Research, 1908.

2 January Terribly hard work today. We started at 6.45 a.m. with a fairly good surface, which soon became very soft. We were sinking in over our ankles, and our broken sledge, by running sideways, added to the drag. We have been going uphill all day, and tonight are 11,034 ft above sea-level. It has taken us all day to do 10 miles 450 yards, though the weights are fairly light. A cold wind, with a temperature of minus 14° Fahr., goes right through us now, as we are weakening from want of food, and the high altitude makes every movement an effort, especially if we stumble on the march. My head is giving me trouble all the time. Wild seems the most fit of us. God knows we are doing all we can, but the outlook is serious if this surface continues and the plateau gets higher, for we are not travelling fast enough to make our food spin out and get back to our depot in time. I cannot think of failure yet. I must look at the matter sensibly and consider the lives of those who are with me. I feel that if we go on too far it will be impossible to get back over this surface, and then all the results will be lost to the world. We can now definitely locate the South Pole on the highest plateau in the world, and our geological work and meteorology will be of the greatest use to science; but all this is not the Pole. Man can only do his best, and we have arrayed against us the strongest forces of nature. This cutting south wind with drift plays the mischief with us, and after ten hours of struggling against it one pannikin of food with two biscuits and a cup of cocoa does not warm one up much. I must think over the situation carefully tomorrow, for time is going on and food is going also.

3 January Started at 6.55 a.m., cloudy but fairly warm. The temperature was minus 8 Fahr. at noon. We had a terrible surface all the morning, and did only 5 miles 100 yards. A meridian altitude gave us latitude 87° 22' South at noon. The surface was better in the afternoon, and we did six geographical miles. The temperature at 6 p.m. was minus 11 Fahr. It was an uphill pull towards the evening, and we camped at 6.20 p.m., the altitude being 11,220 ft above the sea. Tomorrow we must risk making a depot on the plateau, and make a dash for it, but even then, if this surface continues, we will be two weeks in carrying it through.

4 January The end is in sight. We can only go for three more days at the most, for we are weakening rapidly. Short food and a blizzard wind from the south, with driving drift, at a temperature of 47° of frost, have plainly told us today that we are reaching our limit, for we were so done up at noon with cold that the clinical thermometer failed to register the temperature of three of us at 94°. We started at 7.40 a.m., leaving a depot on this great wide plateau, a risk that only this case justified, and one that my comrades agreed to, as they have to every one so far, with the same cheerfulness and regardlessness of self that have been the means of our getting as far as we have done so far. Pathetically small looked the bamboo, one of the tent poles, with a bit of bag sewn on as a flag, to mark our stock of provisions, which has to take us back to our depot, one hundred and fifty miles north. We lost sight of it in half an hour, and are now trusting to our foot-prints in the snow to guide us back to each bamboo until we pick up the depot again. I trust that the weather will keep clear. Today we have done 12 1/2 geographical miles, and with only 70 lb per man to pull it is as hard, even harder, work than the 100 odd lb was yesterday, and far harder than the 250 lb were three weeks ago, when we were climbing the glacier. This, I consider, is a clear indication of our failing strength. The main thing against us is the altitude of 11,200 ft and the biting wind. Our faces are cut, and our feet and hands are always on the verge of frostbite. Our fingers, indeed, often go, but we get them round more or less. I have great trouble with two fingers on my left hand. They had been badly jammed when we were getting the motor up over the ice face at winter quarters, and the circulation is not good. Our boots now are pretty well worn out, and we have to halt at times to pick the snow out of the soles. Our stock of sennegrass is nearly exhausted, so we have to use the same frozen stuff day after day. Another trouble is that the lamp-wick with which we tie the finnesko is chafed through, and we have to tie knots in it. These knots catch the snow under our feet, making a lump that has to be cleared every now and then. I am of the opinion that to sledge even in the height of summer on this plateau, we should have at least forty ounces of food a day per man, and we are on short rations of the ordinary allowance of thirty-two ounces. We depoted our extra underclothing to save weight about three weeks ago, and are now in the same clothes night and day. One suit of underclothing, shirt and guernsey, and our thin Burberries, now all patched. When we get up in the morning, out of the wet bag, our Burberries become like a coat of mail at once, and our heads and beards get iced-up with the moisture when breathing on the march. There is half a gale blowing dead in our teeth all the time. We hope to reach within 100 geographical miles of the Pole; under the circumstances we can expect to do very little more. I am confident that the Pole lies on the great plateau we have discovered, miles and miles from any outstanding land. The temperature tonight is minus 24° Fahr.

5 January Today head wind and drift again, with 50° of frost, and a terrible surface. We have been marching through 8 in of snow, covering sharp sastrugi, which plays havoc with our feet, but we have done 13 1/3 geographical miles, for we increased our food, seeing that it was absolutely necessary to do this to enable us to accomplish anything. I realise that the food we have been having has not been sufficient to keep up our strength, let alone supply the wastage caused by exertion, and now we must try to keep warmth in us, though our strength is being used up. Our temperatures at 5 a.m. were 24° Fahr. We got away at 7 a.m. sharp and marched till noon, then from 1 p.m. sharp till 6 p.m. All being in one tent makes our campwork slower, for we are so cramped for room, and we get up at 4.40 a.m. so as to get away by 7 a.m. Two of us have to stand outside the tent at night until things are squared up inside, and we find it cold work. Hunger grips us hard, and the food supply is very small. My head still gives me great trouble. I began by wishing that my worst enemy had it instead of myself, but now I don't wish even my worst enemy to have such a headache; still, it is no use talking about it. Self is a subject that most of us are fluent on. We find the utmost difficulty in carrying through the day, and we can only go for two or three more days. Never once had the temperature been above zero since we got on to the plateau, though this is the height of summer. We have done our best, and we thank God for having allowed us to get so far.

6 January This must be our last outward march with the sledge and camp equipment. Tomorrow we must leave camp with some food, and push as far south as possible, and then plant the flag. Today's story is 57° of frost, with a strong blizzard and high drift; yet we marched 13 geographical miles through soft snow, being helped by extra food. This does not mean full rations, but a bigger ration than we have been having lately. The pony maize is all finished. The most trying day we have yet spent, our fingers and faces being frost-bitten continually. Tomorrow we will rush south with the flag. We are at 88° 7' South tonight. It is our last outward march. Blowing hard tonight. I would fail to explain my feelings if I tried to write them down, now that the end has come. There is only one thing that lightens the disappointment, and that is the feeling that we have done all we could. It is the forces of nature that have prevented us from going right through. I cannot write more.

7 January A blinding, shrieking blizzard all day, with the temperature ranging from 60° to 70° of frost. It has been impossible to leave the tent, which is snowed up on the lee side. We have been lying in our bags all day, only warm at food time, with fine snow making through the walls of the worn tent and covering our bags. We are greatly cramped. Adams is suffering from cramp every now and then. We are eating our valuable food without marching. The wind has been blowing eighty to ninety miles an hour. We can hardly sleep. Tomorrow I trust this will be over. Directly the wind drops we march as far south as possible, then plant the flag, and turn homeward. Our chief anxiety is lest our tracks may drift up, for to them we must trust mainly to find our depot; we have no land bearings in this great plain of snow. It is a serious risk that we have taken, but we had to play the game to the utmost, and Providence will look after us.

8 January Again all day in our bags, suffering considerably physically from cold hands and feet, and from hunger, but more mentally, for we cannot get on south, and we simply lie here shivering. Every now and then one of our party's feet go, and the unfortunate beggar has to take his leg out of the sleeping-bag and have his frozen foot nursed into life again by placing it inside the shirt, against the skin of his almost equally unfortunate neighbour. We must do something more to the south, even though the food is going, and we weaken lying in the cold, for with 72° of frost the wind cuts through our thin tent, and even the drift is finding its way in and on to our bags, which are wet enough as it is. Cramp is not uncommon every now and then, and the drift all round the tent has made it so small that there is hardly room for us at all. The wind has been blowing hard all day; some of the gusts must be over seventy or eighty miles an hour. This evening it seems as though it were going to ease down, and directly it does we shall be up and away south for a rush. I feel that this march must be our limit. We are so short of food, and at this high altitude, 11,600 ft, it is hard to keep any warmth in our bodies between the scanty meals. We have nothing to read now, having depoted our little books to save weight, and it is dreary work lying in the tent with nothing to read and too cold to write much in the diary.

9 January Our last day outwards. We have shot our bolt, and the tale is latitude 88° 23' South, longitude 162° East. The wind eased down at 1 a.m., and at 2 a.m. we were up and had breakfast. At 4 a.m. started south, with the Queen's Union Jack, a brass cylinder containing stamps and documents to place at the furthest south point, camera, glasses, and compass. At 9 a.m. we were in 88° 23' South, half running and half walking over a surface much hardened by the recent blizzard. It was strange for us to go along without the nightmare of a sledge dragging behind us. We hoisted Her Majesty's flag and the other Union Jack afterwards, and took possession of the plateau in the name of His Majesty. While the Union Jack blew out stiffly in the icy gale that cut us to the bone, we looked south with our powerful glasses, but could see nothing but the dead white snow plain. There was no break in the plateau as it extended towards the Pole, and we feel sure that the goal we have failed to reach lies on this plain. We stayed only a few minutes, and then, taking the Queen's flag and eating our scanty meal as we went, we hurried back and reached our camp about 3 p.m. We were so dead tired that we only did two hours' march in the afternoon and camped at 5.30 p.m. The temperature was minus 19° Fahr. Fortunately for us, our tracks were not obliterated by the blizzard; indeed, they stood up, making a trail easily followed. Homeward bound at last. Whatever regrets may be, we have done our best.

Four years later, Shackleton returned to Antarctica and led an epic of survival when his boat Endurance *was crushed in the ice.*

Photograph from the *Nimrod* Expedition, circa 1907; from Archive of Alfred Wegener Institute for Polar and Marine Research.

CHAPTER 15

DOG DAYS

by A. J. Barrington

Mining for gold in New Zealand, circa late nineteenth century.

21 April Very heavy rain has now set in and every appearance of its continuing. This is the heaviest rain I have seen since I left Victoria. The lake has risen four feet today, and the rivers are at a fearful height. Nothing to eat since a small snack this morning. There is nothing at all that we can find here eatable—no fern root, no spear-grass, no annis, or any vegetable whatever; nothing but stones, timber and water. I am certain we can get payable gold here if we can only get to work. It continued to rain at a fearful rate during the four following days, and flooded the lake and river, entirely precluding any work. Obtained just sufficient game to keep life in us, only after great hardships and difficulties.

Present day Jackson's Bay, New Zealand.

26 April Foggy morning; cleared up about 12; put our blankets out to dry. One of the boys started early this morning to look after some game, but returned without any. Have but about 4lbs oatmeal now, and are 80 miles from the Wakatip in a straight line, but it will take us twice 80 to get there. My two mates made up their minds to start back again the first fine day we get, but I do not fancy going back the same route. I have tried all I know to induce them to continue east with me, as we cannot be more than 30 miles from the west river running into Lake Hawea, which lies NE from the Wanaka Lake, and which I believe to be the centre of the golden line of country, as the farther we get eastward the better we find the gold, and it is not half the distance that it is to the Wakatip. They however refused, and I then said I should go alone, which I was afterwards sorry I did not do, as I believe we had got almost to the end of the chain of mountains which runs north to Jackson's Bay from the Wakatip. If I had had a dog nothing should have prevented me from going alone, as I know it cannot be a worse road than we have had coming here.

27 April Turned out early and tore up one of my blankets to make shirts, as my clothes were worn out in the bush. The river and creeks so high that we cannot cross any of them; the smallest stream a few days since is now impassable.

28 April Rained till night, when it cleared up. Made a good fire and dried our clothes, ready for a start back in the morning, should it be fine. We are all very weak for the want of sufficient food. If we could travel we could always get sufficient food, but it is having to camp in wet weather that kills us.

29 April Packed up a few things which we cannot do well without, leaving behind picks, shovels, tin dishes, gimlets, nails, spoke-shave, chisels, and several other things, which made our swags much lighter, but they felt just as heavy, on account of our weak state. We got a few miles up the river south, and had a good feed on some paradise ducks that we shot, turned in and felt much refreshed. The place we left this morning is situated about half a mile east of the river, lies due south from Jackson's Bay, and 30 miles east of the coast.

30 April Continued on our course up the river—a very bushy sideling of a steep mountain gorge, with the white foam of the river some hundreds of feet below us—jumping from one precipice to another, which under any other circumstances would have looked pretty. We did not, however, stop long to admire it, as then it looked hideous. Toiled away till night, when we had a hard matter to find a piece of ground 6ft square on which to pitch the tent, and harder still to light a fire and cook four magpies we had shot on the road.

1 May Got up the river a few miles and came to a precipice and a very large and deep waterfall. It took us a long time to ascend, but we succeeded after many difficulties and dangers, our lives many times depending on a few blades of grass, which grow out of the face of the rocks. After a few miles further we came to a nice flat, where we could see there was any amount of game. Camped here the following day, hunting.

3 May Crossed the river and up the saddle, which leads up the side of a large burnt mountain; in gaining the top of which we had a few hours of fearful danger. The stones are so soft or rotten that we could not tell the moment our feet would give way and down we should go several hundred feet. At

one time we were two hours getting twenty yards. Reached the top at 1 p.m. Ran it along south, which way our course lay, till near dark, then camped at the side of a little creek rumbling down the side of the mountain higher up. There are three small lakes on this mountain nearly of the same size, with a few ducks on them.

4 May Made an early start, but it commenced raining about 10 a.m. and continued so all day. I lost the run of my mates all of a sudden, I having kept a little lower down on the side of the mountain. I thought nothing of it at the time, as we had often parted and met together again, but this time I cooeyed and got no answer. Thinking they were ahead I hurried on, but left them behind. Cooeyed all the way as I went, but got no answer. Could see the river down under me in the flat; got down, waited for an hour, but no sign of them; fired two guns hoping they would hear them, but no answer; so I gave them up, thinking that they had crossed along the side and over the mountain more to the eastward. I proceeded to follow up the river all the afternoon and shot one blue mountain duck, which I may say is all the provisions I have.

I am very badly fitted for the road before me, having no dog and every appearance of a week or two's rain, as at every change of the moon we have had a week's rain lately, sometimes more. I have about three-quarters of a pound of oatmeal and a long weary road to travel. Travelled all the afternoon up the river; saw several creeks coming in, with quartz reefs showing and quartz boulders, and every indication of gold, but did not stop, as I had nothing to try a bit of dirt with. Still continued walking. Camped.

5 May I am camped on the side of a mountain by the side of a foaming creek, the rain coming down in torrents; cannot light a fire. Got two little ducks, but cannot cook them; had raw oatmeal for breakfast; have had nothing since yesterday morning, and walked all day, then pitched the tent and turned in with wet clothes and blankets. Got a fire at night, cooked one of my little ducks and ate it.

6 May Still raining, with snow mixed. I am certain this is snow on the mountains; if so I shall have a hard matter to get over. Very cold; could not sleep last night, my teeth cracking together all night with cold, and cramp in my legs. I do not feel at all well. The rats stole my little duck, which I intended for this day's food. This is the first day I have been heartily sick of the country. Nothing to eat; cannot light a fire; all my clothes and blankets wet. I am indeed miserable.

7 May Turned out and had a look; any amount of snow on the surrounding hills, and still snowing fast and freezing. Turned in again; slept all day, or rather stopped in bed.

8 May Still snowing and no sign of a change; no food.

9 May Turned out early; any amount of snow in the night. I do not know what to do now. I intended to have started this morning, wet or dry, snow or rain, but I am completely jammed in. I cannot move; snow falling thick and fast. Whether to go back and follow the river round to Plenty Lake, or to try and get over the mountains to Mineral Creek is a consideration which I cannot decide on. Night coming on again; nothing to eat, and fearfully cold.

10 May Turned out early; wrung the tent and clothes as well as I could, packed up and tried to go right up the mountain to the eastward, in hopes of seeing a smoke from my mates' fire, knowing they cannot be far off; but after toiling hard for half a day and falling in the snow head-first some hundreds of times, found it impossible to get up. Had to start away for the river again, and try and get up to its head and over the saddle. I have not eaten anything now for several days. There is a little spear-grass here; if I could get a fire to boil, or rather roast it, I think I could pass a day or two, but even that is forbidden. It is now snowing; two feet six inches solid snow by my tent, and I believe there is a deal more on the mountain. Turned into my wet blankets again for another night's misery.

11 May Could not sleep a minute all night; had to keep my legs and feet constantly in motion to keep the blood in circulation, and if I stopped a minute my feet felt dead with cold, and I should have the cramp in my legs. My clothes are still wet; there can be very little heat in me, or my clothes would dry sleeping in them all night; I must try and get a fire before I leave here if possible, to dry my blankets and flannels or another night like last will cook me. Rain, snow, and sleet, very heavy all day. Tried hard to get a fire, but could not; turned in again to my wet blankets.

12 May Rain and sleet very heavy; looks very bad; cannot get out of the tent; I do not know what is to be done, so turn into my wet blankets again to keep me warm, for it is fearful cold, thinking of Edward Dunmore and the 'Maori Hen'. If I have to stop here a few days more I shall be just as bad. (By the bye, I forgot to mention that I made every enquiry possible about the 'Maori Hen', but could not hear whether he got to Fox's or not.) I have had one little duck to eat for the last six days, yet strange to say I do not feel hungry. This will not do much longer, but on the side of a mountain covered with three or four feet of snow it is a hard matter to get food of any description. Went out in the afternoon to try and shoot something, but could not see anything to shoot—not even a robin. Found a root of spear-grass, ate some of it but could not enjoy it raw; then turned in for another night's rocking about.

13 May Turned out this morning with the intention of making a start, but the weather is so bad I am afraid to stir, it is raining heavily and the snow is thawing a little.

14 May Turned out early; wrung the tent and other things, which were very wet, packed up once more, and made a start. Got on very well for about half a mile, when my legs began to fail me, and I found I could not get more than twenty yards at a spell. Toiled away till I saw by the sun it was nearly noon, and I had not got one mile away from the timber where I was camped, and was completely done, so there was nothing for it but desert my swag or die here. The former idea I carried into effect. I threw away everything but my blankets, gun, and a little powder and shot, which was my only dependence. Amongst the things I abandoned was a couple of specimens which we got in the Little River, and a small parcel of gold, which we found in prospecting, with maps, books, etc., all of which I have before mentioned. After throwing away my swag I had a very hard task to get up the hill, as there was over two feet snow and very soft. I kept slipping and falling, till at length I arrived at the top of the saddle and saw a creek at the other side, and a grassy flat about a mile long and half a mile wide. I got to the river by sundown, and was going to the west end of the flat to camp, and try to get a duck or something to eat; but on looking up the creek I saw a smoke, which I went to and found my mates camped there. They were surprised to see me. I was greatly reduced since they saw me, and was very weak—just able to put one foot before another. I asked them if they had anything to eat; they said they had had nothing that day, but they started hunting, and got two Maori hens which they gave me, and with the heat of the fire I was much refreshed.

15 May Rained all day till noon. Miserable living; we are just alive and very weak.

16 May Turned out and started up the creek with nothing to eat; walked all day up right-hand branch of Wild Dog Creek; shot two magpies at noon and ate them raw, which refreshed us much at the time. We reached a long way up by night and camped under an overhanging rock, just under the snow. Nothing to eat but a little grass root: fearfully cold.

17 May Started early to try and get over the snow and down the other side. Had a fearful hard day's toil. Here is about a mile long of pure ice, as clear as crystal; you can see down into it several fathoms, just like looking down into the blue ocean, and no such thing as walking on it. We had to go round several times to where there was a little fresh snow lying on it, to be able to get along. At length made the foot of the saddle, and then we had some climbing to do to get up the mountain, which was covered with frost and snow, at an angle of 75 degrees. I was so weak that I thought I must give in, but I ate plenty of the little snowberries which grow under the snow. They helped us on a good deal, and we reached the top about 2 p.m. What a sight then met our eyes! Nothing but mountains of snow as far as we could see, in every direction but west. We got down by powerful exertion. At one time Simonin was behind me; I heard him sing out 'Look out', I turned round and he was corning down the snow at a fearful rate, head first, on his back. He held the gun in one hand, but had to let it go, when both he and the gun passed me at the rate of a swallow, and did not stop till they reached a little flat about two miles down, with a fall of 1,000 feet. I thought he was killed, but he was all right, with the exception of being a little frightened. We got down to the head of the flat and camped. Such a day I hope never to see again.

18 May Snow and sleet all day. Tried to get away, but had to camp again about six miles down the gorge. Had to camp under a rock, in a foot of snow. No fire, wet clothes, and nothing to eat. Hard times.

19 May Turned out early and started down the gorge, which took us all day. Snow and rain all day. Reached the flat at dark and camped in the bush with two feet of snow. Had a fearful job to light a fire. Fearfully cold night; our feet frostbitten and very sore.

20 May Rain and snow. Could not stir out before the evening, when it turned out fine and we went hunting. Night very cold; snowing hard again and freezing.

21 May Travelled down a large flat and entered into the heaviest and steepest gorge* I ever saw. Here we were very near losing Farrell. He volunteered to be lowered down by a flax rope on to a rock about 14ft over the water, and thus pass our swags across; but when he got halfway down the rope broke and away he went into a fearful boiling eddy in the creek. I looked but could not see him anywhere for over a minute and a half, when I saw him rise just at the top of the precipice and seize at another rock, which he succeeded in catching hold of and getting upon. If he had gone 4ft farther, he would have been dashed down a precipice 200ft so that he would never have been seen any more. Camped that night on the bare stones by the side of the creek. Nothing for a bed and nothing to eat. Very cold.

22 May Made a start early. Saw the Plenty Lake. Could not make out where we were till we got near the flat; then could see the Wild Dog River, and knew we were about halfway between the two lakes. Just able to walk, but very weak. Caught two kakapo and two magpies, and had a better supper than we had had for many a day.

23 May Went out early to shoot something for breakfast, but could get nothing. Kept close to the left-hand range, going down towards Poverty Lake.

24 May Kept on down the side of the range, hunting as we went along.

---

*The gorge of the Olivine River, into which Forgotten River flows.

25 May Turned out before daylight to try and shoot some kakas, which were over us in the high trees, as the pine is an immense height; these birds come here to roost at night, and fly away to the mountains at daylight. Could not see them; got to our old camp on Poverty Lake by sundown. Camped and had a good supper. Feel much refreshed but our feet are very sore; all our toes are covered with running sores; Simonin's feet are not bad; I believe mine are far the worst. I do hope we shall get a few days fine weather, so as to enable us to get into the Wakatip once more.

26 May Another change in the weather. Rain again. Cannot get out of the tent. Nothing to eat all day.

27 May Rain again all day. We shall be worse off than ever if this weather continues. We are very weak and no chance of any fish or game here as we are now on an island, on account of the lake rising all round us and running back into the lagoons. Got a little fern root.

28 May Rain in torrents again. I do not know what we shall do. This is the third day again and nothing to eat but a bit of fern root. We cannot get out of the tent; the water is rising slowly but surely.

29 May This is the most miserable day of my existence. We had to turn out last night at 10 o'clock, and the water rose so fast that we could not get anything away but our blankets. Had to wade to the side of the range up to our middles in water. We tied the powder and guns and a few other things up to the ridge pole, afraid to carry them away in case of getting them wet. The night was very dark and before [we rea]ched the hill I got up to my arms in water. [I thought] I should never get across, but we reached the land safe about a quarter of a mile distant. Had to walk up and down all night, the rain still pouring down. If this night does not kill us we shall never die. Daylight broke upon us, each looking for the other and wondering that we are all alive. Got a fire this morning: kept it going all day, but could not get back to our tent, as there is ten feet of water to go through, so we shall have another night, which I hope will be fine or we shall perish.

30 May Fine morning. Did not rain much all night. I cut my blanket in two, to make a tent of one half of it, and slept by the fire very comfortably, considering our situation. Farrell crossed to the tent up to his middle in water this morning, and brought the two guns and some powder, and shot a duck, which came up swimming in the lake. We also shot a little kaka, which we boiled with some fern root, for the first meal we have had in four days.

31 May Whilst in the act of packing up, I saw a rat which the dog had killed in the night. I never picked up a nugget of gold during the last ten years with more satisfaction than I picked him up, put him in the fire, and roasted him just as he was, then cut him in three parts, which we pronounced the sweetest bit of meat we ever ate. Proceeded up the side of the range, very weak and tired, and the bush wet. Camped about one-third of the way up the range with clothes wet. Could not get a fire.

1 June Started early, to try and get over today. Camped about two miles from the saddle. Raining, very weak, and our feet awfully painful.

2 June Got over the saddle through the snow and down to Kakapo Flat, where we expected to stop a day or two and get plenty of game; but the flat was covered with snow, and consequently the birds do not come down out of the range at night, but stop under the rocks and in the timber in the warmest place. Caught one kakapo and one Maori hen, which we cooked for supper under a rock, where we camped about 10 o'clock. It rained all the remainder of the day. Went hunting, but the dog would not work, as he had had a bird that morning and eaten it.

3 June Continued on our road (feet getting worse) through the snow up the creek. Crossed over the flat and down to our old camp at the head of Mineral

Creek. Caught one Maori hen and cooked it for supper, or rather for thirty-six hours' food for three men. Went to bed very weak and bad.

4 June Continued our course down the creek, made the old camp at the west foot of the dividing range, so tired that we would give all the world to be at the other side of it. Weather likely to be wet. Got three Maori hens, which is indeed a treat. Went to bed in good spirits, hoping we shall have good weather to get over the range, as that is all that troubles us. We know if we were over the divide we can get to the Wakatip if we do not get anything more to eat, as it is all downhill afterwards.

5 June Got down to the edge of the bush, when it commenced raining, with a heavy thick fog on the mountain. We consulted as to whether we should go on or not, the weather looking so bad. Camped. Rained all day. Caught one kakapo; very poor store to carry us over the divide. My feet are in an awful mess, and nothing to put on them but Maori hen fat. I do not think we shall be able to get over; we are three skeletons just alive.

6 June Packed up once more to cross the divide if possible. If we cannot cross, we shall have to follow the creek down to the Awarua River, from thence to the Kakapo Lake, down to the sea, and stop there all the winter if possible. We are now six days coming from Poverty Lake, which I have done in one day before now. Got up to the head of the timber by night, and camped under a rock.

7 June Raining very heavy this morning. This is the worst of all to be caught here, where we cannot get anything to eat. Commenced to snow at noon, and has every appearance of a heavy fall; so we must start. Did not get up a mile when we were up to our knees in soft snow; the higher we ascended the deeper it got, and we could scarcely see each other ten yards off. However we managed it after a long time, and when we got on top the snow was first-rate to walk on—just hard enough to keep us up, and down this side was beautiful, till we came within a mile of the bottom, when the snow became very soft, and we were till eight o'clock at night before we got down to our old camp, where we camped on three feet of snow. Our blankets and clothes all wet.

8 June Snowed all night. Made a start down the creek, tumbling and rolling over rocks and stones, sometimes wholly disappearing in the snow, till we got down a few miles. Saw some kakas in a tree; my gun was too wet to be used, so Simonin got one of his barrels in the humour and shot seven of them, which saved our dog, as we had agreed to kill and eat him this afternoon. Still snowing. We here camped and cooked six of them. Had a good dinner and dried our clothes a little. Commenced to rain very hard again.

9 June Rained heavily all day. Cooked our remaining bird. I went up the creek in the afternoon but could not see anything. Our feet are breaking out in fresh places, and are very sore.

10 June Rain again. I wonder if we shall ever reach the Wakatip—only two and a half days' tramp even in our state, and yet we cannot get a fine day, or anything to eat. If fasting and praying is of any value to sinners, we ought soon to become saints, for we have had enough of it lately. Cleared up about noon, when we made a start and got down a few miles further to our old camp.

11 June Got nearly to the Dart and in sight of the Wakatip, which was indeed a welcome sight to us. We caught plenty of Maori hens and had a good feast—happy once more, even under our circumstances. Nearly skeletons, and can scarcely put one foot before the other.

12 June Turned out in good spirits, hoping this will be the last day of our hardships. Started down the Dart. Feet bad, and the gravel hurt them very much. Got down to the Island and heard some person shooting; crossed over to see who it was, and found the captain of Mr Rees's yacht and his mate, who were up pigeon shooting. We asked them to send a boat across to the other side of the Dart to fetch us when they returned, as they would be down before we should. They said they would either send a boat for us or come and fetch us themselves. We arrived at the Lake just at sundown; made a fire and commenced firing guns, which were answered from the township. In the course of an hour five of the boys came across for us in Mr Barrett's whale boat. We were invited by Mr Reid, at the station, to come up and stop there for a while till we got better. From thence we went to Frankton Hospital where, with the constant care and attention we receive, we hope to be soon recovered.

CHAPTER 16

ACROSS THE GREAT DIVIDE

by Meriwether Lewis and William Clark

Meriwether Lewis and William
Clark.

[Lewis] *Monday, 26 August 1805* [Shoshone Indian camp, Rocky Moun-
tains] I found it a folly to think of attemp[t]ing to decend this river [the
Snake] in canoes and therefore determined to commence the purchase of
horses in the morning from the indians in order to carry into execution the
design we had formed of passing the Rocky Mountains. I now informed
Cameahwait of my intended expedition overland to the great river which lay

in the plains beyond the mountains and told him that I wished to purchase 20 horses of himself and his people to convey our baggage. He observed that the Minnetares had stolen a great number of their horses this spring but hoped his people would spear me the number I wished. I also asked a guide, he observed that he had no doubt but the old man who was with Capt. C. would accompany us if we wished him and that he was better informed of the country than any of them. Matters being thus far arranged I directed the fiddle to be played and the party danced very merily much to the amusement and gratification of the natives, though I must confess that the state of my own mind at this moment did not well accord with the prevailing mirth as I somewhat feared that the caprice of the indians might suddenly induce them to withhold their horses from us without which my hopes of prosicuting my voyage to advantage was lost; however I determined to keep the indians in a good humour if possible, and to loose no time in obtaining the necessary number of horses. I directed the hunters to turn out early in the morning and indeavor to obtain some meat. I had nothing but a little parched corn to eat this evening.

[Clark] *Thursday, 29 August 1805* I left our baggage in possession of 2 men and proceeded on up to join Capt. Lewis at the upper Village of Snake Indians where I arrived at 1o'Clock found him much engaged in Councelling and attempting to purchase a fiew more horses. I spoke to the Indians on various Subjects endeavoring to impress on theire minds the advantage it would be to them for to sell us horses and expedite the [our] journey the nearest and best way possibly that we might return as soon as possible and winter with them at Some place where there was plenty of buffalow, our wish is to get a horse for each man to carry our baggage and for Some of the men to ride occasionally, The horses are handsom and much acustomed to be changed as to their Parsture, we cannot calculate on their carrying large loads & feed on the Grass which we may calculate on finding in the Mountain thro' which we may expect to pass on our rout.

[Clark] *Friday, 30 August 1805* finding that we Could purchase no more horse[s] than we had for our goods &c. (and those not a Sufficient number for each of our Party to have one which is our wish) I Gave my Fuzee to one of the men & Sold his musket for a horse which Completed us to 29 total horses, we Purchased pack cords Made Saddles & Set out on our rout down the [Lemhi] river by land guided by my old guide [and] one other who joined him, the old gu[i]de's 3 Sons followed him, before we Set out our hunters killed three Deer proceeded on 12 Miles and encamped on the river South Side.

at the time we Set out from the Indian Camps the greater Part of the Band Set out over to the waters of the Missouri. we had great attention paid to the horses, as they were nearly all Sore Backs, and Several pore, & young Those horses are indifferent, maney Sore backs and others not acustomed to pack, and as we cannot put large loads on them are Compelled to purchase as maney as we can to take our Small proportion of baggage of the Parties, (& Eate if necessary) Proceeded on 12 Miles to day.

[Clark] *Monday, 2 September 1805* proceeded on up the Creek, proceded on thro' thickets in which we were obliged to Cut a road, over rockey hill Sides where our horses were in [per]peteal danger of Slipping to their certain distruction & up & Down Steep hills, where Several horses fell, Some turned over, and others Sliped down Steep hill Sides, one horse Crippeled & 2 gave out.

[Clark] *Tuesday, 3 September 1805* hills high & rockey on each Side, in the after part of the day the high mountains closed the Creek on each Side and obliged us to take on the Steep Sides of those Mountains, So Steep that the horses Could Scur[ce]ly keep from Slipping down, Several sliped & Injured themselves verry much, with great dificuelty we made [blank space in MS.] miles & Encamped on a branch of the Creek we assended after crossing Several Steep points & one mountain, but little to eate

The mouintains to the East Covered with Snow. we met with a great misfortune, in haveing our last Th[er]mometer broken, by accident. This day we passed over emence hils and Some of the worst roads that ever horses passed, our horses frequently fell Snow about 2 inches deep when it began to rain which terminated in a Sleet [storm].

Tuesday, 3 September 1805

N. 25.° W. 2½	Miles to a Small fork on the left Hilley and thick assending
N. 15.° W. 2	miles to a fork on the right assending
N. 22.° W. 2½	miles to a fork on the left passing one on the left Several Spring runs on the right Stoney hills & much falling timber
N. l8.° E. 2	miles passing over Steep points & winding ridges to a high Point passed a run on the right
N. 32.° E. 2	miles to the top of a high hill passed 2 runs from the left, passing on the Side of a Steep ridge. no road
N.40.° W3 14	miles leaveing the waters of the Creek to the right & passing over a high pine Mountn. o the head of a Drean running to the left

[Clark] *Wednesday, 4 September 1805* a verry cold morning every thing wet and frosed, Groun[d] covered with Snow, we assended a mountain & took a Divideing ridge* which we kept for Several Miles & fell on the head of a Creek which appeared to run the Course we wished to go

prosued our Course down the Creek to the forks about 5 miles where we met a part[y] of the Tushepau nation, of 33 Lodges about 80 men 400 Total and at least 500 horses, those people rec[e]ved us friendly, threw white robes over our Sholders & Smoked in the pipes of peace, we Encamped with them & found them friendly but nothing but berries to eate a part of which they gave us, those Indians are well dressed with Skin shirts & robes, they [are] Stout & light complected more So than Common for Indians, The Chief harangued untill late at night, Smoked in our pipe and appeared Satisfied. I was the first white man who ever wer on the waters of this river.

---

* Lost Trail Pass into Montana on the west slope of the Continental Divide.

[Clark] *Thursday, 5 September 1805* we assembled the Chiefs & warriers and Spoke to them (with much dificuel[t]y as what we Said had to pass through Several languages before it got into theirs, which is a gugling kind of language Spoken much thro the throught [throat]) we informed them who we were, where we came from, where bound and for what purpose &c. &c. and requested to purchase & exchange a fiew horses with them, in the Course of the day I purchased 11 horses & exchanged 7 for which we gave a fiew articles of merchendize, those people possess ellegant horses.

[Clark] *Friday, 6 September 1805* took a Vocabelary of the language listened our loads & packed up, rained contd. untill 12 oClock

all our horses purchased of the flat heads (oote-lash-shutes) we Secured well for fear of their leaveing of us, and Watched them all night for fear of their leaving us or the Indians prosuing & Steeling them.

[Lewis] *Monday, 9 September 1805* two of our hunters have arrived, one of them brought with him a redheaded woodpecker of the large kind common to the U States. this is the first of the kind I have seen since I left the Illinois. just as we were seting out Drewyer arrived with two deer. we continued our rout down the valley about 4 miles and crossed the river; it is hear a handsome stream about 100 yards wide and affords a considerable quantity of very clear water, the banks are low and it's bed entirely gravel the stream appears navigabk but from the circumstance of their being no sammon in it I believe that there must be a considerable fall in it below. our guide could not inform us where this river* discharged itself into the columbia river, he informed us that it continues it's course along the mountains to the N as far as he knew it and that not very distant from where we then were it formed a junction with a stream nearly as large as itself which took it's rise in the mountains near the Missouri to the East of us and passed through an extensive valley generally open prarie which forms

---

*Bitterroot River, originally named Clark's River by the explorers.

an excellent pass to the missouri. the point of the Missouri where this Indian pass intersects it, is about 30 miles above the *gates of the rocky mountain*, or the place where the valley of the Missouri first widens into an extensive plain after entering the rockey Mountains. the guide informed us that a man might pass to the Missouri from hence by that rout in four days.

we continued our rout down the W. side of the river about 5 miles further and encamped on a large creek which falls in on the West. as our guide inform[ed] me that we should leave the river at this place and the weather appearing settled and fair I determined to halt the next day rest our horses and take some scelestial Observations. we called this Creek *Travellers rest*.

[Clark] *Wednesday, 11 September 1805* proceeded on up the *Travellers rest Creek* accompanied by the Flat head Indian about 7 miles our guide tels us a fine large roade passes up this river to the Missouri. The loss of 2 of our horses detained us unl. 3 oClock P.M. our *Flat head* Indian being restless thought proper to leave us and proceed on alone, Sent out the hunters to hunt in advance as usial. (we have Selected 4 of the best hunters to go in advance to hunt for the party. This arrangement has been made long since)

Encamped at Some old Indian Lodges, nothing killed this evening hills on the right high & ruged, the mountains on the left high & Covered with Snow. The day Verry worm.

[Clark] *Thursday, 12 September 1805* The road through this hilley Countrey is verry bad passing over hills & thro' Steep hollows, over falling timber &c. &c. continued on & passed Some most intolerable road on the Sides of the Steep Stoney mountains, which might be avoided by keeping up the Creek which is thickly covered with under groth & falling timber, Crossed a Mountain 8 miles with out water & encamped on a hill Side on the Creek after Decending a long Steep mountain, Some of our Party did not get up untill 10 oClock P.M.

[Clark] *Thursday (Saturday), 14 September 1805* a verry high Steep mountain for 9 miles to a large fork from the left which appears to head in the Snow toped mountains we Encamped opposit a Small Island at the mouth of a branch on the right side of the river which is at this place 80 yards wide, Swift and Stoney, here we were compelled to kill a Colt for our men & Selves to eat for the want of meat & we named the South fork Colt killed Creek, and this river we call *Flat head* River; the flat head name is Koos koos ke The Mountains which we passed to day much worst than yesterday the last excessively bad & thickly Strowed with falling timber & Pine Spruce fur Hackmatak & Tamerack, Steep & Stoney our men and horses much fatigued.

[Clark] *Wednesday (Sunday), 15 September 1805* Several horses Sliped and roled down Steep hills which hurt them verry much the one which Carried my desk & Small trunk Turned over & roled down a mountain for 40 yards & lodged against a tree, broke the Desk the horse escaped and appeared but little hurt Some others very much hurt, from this point I observed a range of high mountains Covered with Snow from SE to SW with their tops bald or void of timber,

after two hours delay we proceeded on up the mountain Steep & ruged as usial, more timber near the top, when we arrived at the top As we Conceved, we could find no water and Concluded to Camp and make use of the Snow we found on the top to cook the remns. of our Colt & make our Supe, evening verry cold and cloudy. Two of our horses gave out, pore and too much hurt to proceed on and left in the rear. nothing killed to day except 2 Phests.

From this mountain I could observe high ruged mountains in every direction as far as I could see. with the greatest exertion we could only make 12 miles up this mountain.

[Clark] *Saturday (Monday), 16 September 1805* began to Snow about 3 hours before Day and continued all day the Snow in the morning 4 inches deep on the old Snow, and by night we found it from 6 to 8 inches deep, I walked in front to keep the road and found great dificuelty in keeping it as in maney places the Snow had entirely filled up the track, and obliged me to hunt Several minits for the track, at 12 oClock we halted on the top of the mountain to worm & dry our Selves a little as well as to let our horses rest and graze a little on Some long grass which I observed, (on) The (South) Knobs Steep hill Sides & falling timber Continue to day, and a thickly timbered Countrey of 8 different kinds of pine, which are so covered with Snow, that in passing thro' them we are continually covered with Snow.

I have been wet and as cold in every part as I ever was in my life, indeed I was at one time fearfull my feet would freeze in the thin Mockirsons which I wore, after a Short Delay in the middle of the Day, I took one man and proceeded on as fast as I could about 6 miles to a Small branch passing to the right, halted and built fires for the party agains[t] their arrival which was at Dusk, verry cold and much fatigued, we Encamped at this Branch in a thickly timbered bottom which was scurcely large enough for us to lie leavil, men all wet cold and hungary. Killed a Second Colt which we all Suped hartily on and thought it fine meat.

[Lewis] *Wednesday, 18 September 1805* Cap Clark set out this morning to go a head with six hunters. there being no game in these mountains we concluded it would be better for one of us to take the hunters and hurry on to the leavel country a head and there hunt and provide some provisions while the other remained with and brought on the party. the latter of these was my part; accordingly I directed the horses to be gotten up early being deter-mined to force my march as much as the abilities of our horses would permit.

this morning we finished the remainder of our last coult. we dined & suped on a skant proportion of portable soupe, a few canesters of which, a lit-tle bears oil and about 20 lbs of candles form our stock of provision, the only resources being our guns & packhorses. the first is but a poor dependance in our present situ-ation where there is nothing upon earth ex[c]ept ourselves and a few small pheasants, small grey Squirrels, and a blue bird of the vulter kind about the size of a turtle dove or jay bird.

[Clark] *Monday (Wednesday), 18 September 1805* I proceeded on in advance with Six hunters to try and find deer or Something to kill.

[Lewis] *Thursday, 19 September 1805* Fraziers horse fell from this road in the evening, and roled with his load near a hundred yards into the Creek. we all expected that the horse was killed but to our astonishment when the load was taken off him he arose to his feet & appeared to be but little injured, in 20 minutes he proceeded with his load. this was the most wonderfull escape I ever witnessed, the hill down which he roled was almost perpendicu-lar and broken by large irregular and broken rocks.

we took a small quantity of portable soup, and retired to rest much fatigued. several of the men are unwell of the disentary. brakings out, or irruptions of the Skin, have also been common with us for some time.

[Clark] *Tuesday (Thursday), 19 September 1805* Set our early proceeded on up the [*Hungry*] Creek passing through a Small glade at 6 miles at which place we found a horse. I derected him killed and hung up for the party after take-ing a brackfast off for our Selves which we thought fine.

[Lewis] *Friday, 20 September 1805* This morning my attention was called to a species of bird which I had never seen before. It was reather larger than a robbin, tho' much it's form and action. the colours were a blueish brown on the back the wings and tale black, as wass a stripe above the croop 3/4 of an inch wide in front of the neck, and two others of the same colour passed from it's eyes back along the sides of the head. the top of the head, neck brest and belly and butts of the wing were of a fine yellowish brick reed [red]. it was feeding on the buries of a species of shoe-make or ash which grows com-mon in [this] country & which I first observed on 2d. of this month. I have also observed two birds of a blue colour both of which I believe to be of the haulk or vulter kind. the one of a blue shining colour with a very high tuft of feathers on the head a long tale, it feeds on flesh the beak and feet black. it's note is cháàh, cháàh. it is about the size of a pigeon, and in shape and action resembles the jay bird.

Three species of Pheasants, a large black species, with some white feath-ers irregularly scattered on the brest neck and belley—a smaller kind of a dark uniform colour with a red stripe above the eye, and a brown and yellow species that a gooddeel resem-bles the phesant common to the Atlantic States.

we were detained this morning untill ten oclock in consequence of not being enabled to collect our horses. we had proceeded about 2 Miles when we found the greater part of a horse which Capt. Clark had met with and killed for us. he informed me by note that he should proceed as fast as possible to the leavel country which lay to the SW of us, which we discovered from the heights of the mountains on the 19th there he intended to hunt until our arrival. at one oclock we halted on a small branch runing to the left and made a hearty meal on our horse beef much to the comfort of our hungry stomachs. here I learnt that one of the Packhorses with his load was missing and immediately dispatched Baptiest Lapage who had charge of him, to surch for him. he returned at 3 OC. without the horse. The load of the horse was of considerable value consisting of merchandize and all my stock of winter cloathing. I therefore dispatched two of my best woodsmen in surch of him, and proceeded with the party.

our road was much obstructed by fallen timber particularly in the evening. we encamped on a ridge where ther was but little grass for our horses, and at a distance from water. however we obtained as much as served our culinary pur-poses and suped on our beef. the soil as you leave the heights of the mountains becomes gradually more fertile. the land through which we passed this evening is of an excellent quality tho' very broken, it is a dark grey soil. a grey free stone appearing in large masses above the earth in many places. saw the hucklebury, honeysuckle, and alder common to the Atlantic states, also a kind of honey-suckle which bears a white bury and rises about 4 feet high not common but to the western side of the rockey mountains. a growth which resembles the choke cherry bears a black bury with a single stone of sweetish taste, it rises to the hight of 8 or 10 feet and grows in thick clumps. the Arborvita is also common and grows to an immence size, being from 2 to 6 feet in diameter.

[Clark] *Wednesday (Friday), 20 September 1805* I set out early and proceeded on through a Countrey as ruged as usial at 12 miles decended the mountain to a level pine Countrey proceeded on through a butifull Countrey for three miles to a Small Plain in which I found maney Indian lodges,* a man Came out to meet me, & Conducted me to a large Spacious Lodge which he told me (by Signs) was the Lodge of his great Chief who had Set out 3 days previous with all the Warriers of the nation to war on a South West derection & would return in 15 or 18 days. the fiew men that were left in the Village and great numbers of women geathered around me with much apparent signs of fear, and apr. pleased they those people gave us a Small piece of Buffalow meat, Some dried Salmon beries & roots in different States, Some round and much like an onion which they call Pas she co [*quamash. the Bread or Cake is called Pas-shi-co*] Sweet, of this they make bread & Supe they also gave us, the bread made of this root all of which we eate hartily) I gave them a fiew Small articles as preasents, and proceeded on with a Chief to his Village 2 miles in the Same Plain, where we were treated kindly in their way and continued with them all night Those two Villages consist of about 30 double lodges, but fiew men a number of women & children, they call themselves *Cho pun-nish* or *Pierced nosest*+ Their diolect appears verry different from the flat heads, [*Tushapaws*], altho origineally the Same people.

Emence quantity of the [*quawmash or*] *Pas-shi-co* root gathered & in piles about the plain, those roots grow much like an onion in marshey places the seed are in triangular Shells, on the Stalk. they sweat them in the following manner i.e. dig a large hole 3 feet deep, cover the bottom with Split wood on the top of which they lay Small Stones of about 3 or 4 Inches thick, a Second layer of

Splited wood & Set the whole on fire which heats the Stones, after the fire is extinguished they lay grass & mud mixed on the Stones, on that dry grass which Supports the Pásh-shi-co root a thin Coat of the Same grass is laid on the top, a Small fire is kept when necessary in the Center of the kill &c.

I find myself verry unwell all the evening from eateing the fish & roots too freely Sent out hunters they killed nothing.

---

*· At Weippe, Idaho.
+ The Chopunnish, or Nez Perces, were located on the Salmon and Snake rivers.

[Lewis] *Saturday, 21 September 1805* we killed a few Pheasants, and I killed a prarie woolf which together with the ballance of our horse beef and some crawfish which we obtained in the creek enabled us to make one more hearty meal, not knowing where the next was to be found.

the Arborvita increases in quantity and size. I saw several sticks today large enough to form eligant perogues of at least 45 feet in length. I find myself growing weak for the want of food and most of the men complain of a similar deficiency, and have fallen off very much.

[Clark] *Thursday (Saturday), 21 September 1805* A fine Morning Sent out all the hunters in different directions to hunt deer, I my self delayed with the Chief to prevent Suspission and to Collect by Signs as much information as possible about the accord[ingly] we purchased all we could, Such as roots dried, in bread, & in their raw State, Berries of red Haws & *Fish*.

Capt. Lewis & 2 men Verry Sick this evening, my hip Verry Painfull, the men trade a few old tin Canisters for dressed Elk Skin to make themselves Shirts. At dark a hard wind from the SW accompanied with rain which lasted half an hour. The *twisted hare* envited Capt. Lewis & myself to his lodge which was nothin[g] more than Pine bushes & bark, and gave us Some broiled dried *Salmon* to eate, great numbers about us all night. at this village

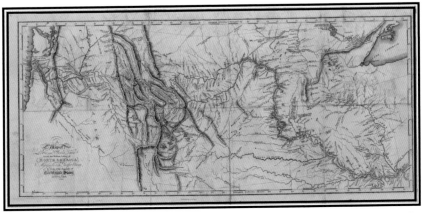

A map of Lewis and Clark's travels across North America, circa 1814. Courtesy of the Library of Congress.

the women were busily employed in gathering and drying the *Pas-she-co* root of which they had great quantities dug in piles.

[Clark] *Sunday (Tuesday), 24 September 1805* despatched J. Colter back to hunt the horses lost in the mountains & bring up Some Shot left behind, and at 10 oClock we all Set out for the river and proceeded on by the Same rout I had previously traveled, and at Sunset we arrived at the Island on which I found the *Twisted hare*, and formed a Camp on a large Island a little below, Capt. Lewis scercely able to ride on a jentle horse which was furnished by the Chief, Several men So unwell that they were Compelled to lie on the Side of the road for Some time others obliged to be put on horses. I gave rushes Pills to the Sick this evening. Several Indians follow us.

[Clark] *Monday (Wednesday), 25 September 1805* I Set out early with the Chief and 2 young men to hunt Some trees Calculated to build Canoes, as we had previously deturmined to proceed on by water, I was furnished with a horse and we proceeded on down the river Passed down on the N side of the river to a fork from the North we halted about an hour, one of the young men took his guig and killed 6 fine Salmon two of them were roasted and we eate, I Saw fine timber for Canoes.

[Clark] *Tuesday (Thursday), 26 September 1805* I had the axes distributed and handled and men apotned. [apportioned] ready to commence building canoes on tomorrow, our axes are Small & badly calculated to build Canoes of the large Pine, Capt Lewis Still very unwell, Several men taken Sick on the way down, I administered *Salts* Pils Galip, [jalap] Tarter emetic &c. I feel unwell this evening, two Chiefs & their families follow us and encamp near us, they have great numbers of horses. This day proved verry hot, we purchase fresh Salmon of the Indians.

[Clark] *Thursday (Saturday), 28 September 1805* Our men nearly all Complaining of their bowels, a heaviness at the Stomach & Lax, Some of those taken first getting better, a had one of the other Canoes unloaded & with the assistance of our Small Canoe and one Indian Canoe took out every thing & toed the empty Canoe on Shore.

[Clark] *Wednesday, 9 October 1805* at Dark we were informed that our old guide & his son had left us and had been Seen running up the river Several miles above, we could not account for the cause of his leaveing us at this time, without receiving his pay for the services he had rendered us, or letting us know anything of his intention.

we requested the Chief to Send a horseman after our old guide to come back and receive his pay &c. which he advised us not to do as his nation would take his things from him before he passed their camps. The Indians and our party were verry mery this after noon a woman faind madness &c. &c. Singular acts of this woman in giveing in small po[r]tions all she had & if they were not received She would Scarrify her self in a horid manner &c. Capt Lewis recovering fast.

[Clark] *Wednesday (Thursday), 10 October* passed 2 Islands and two bad rapids at 3 miles lower passed a Creek on the Lard. with wide cotton willow bottoms we arrived at the heade of a verry bad riffle at which place we landed near 8 Lodges of Indians after viewg. this riffle two Canoes were taken over verry well; the third stuck on a rock which took us an hour to get her off which was effected without her receiving a greater injurey than a Small Split in her Side which was repaired in a Short time, we purchased fish & dogs of those people, dined and proceeded on. here we met with an Indian from the ·falls at which place he Sais he saw white people, and expressed an inclination to accompany us, we passed a few miles above this riffle 2 Lodges and an Indian batheing in a hot bath made by hot stones thrown into a pon[d] of water. at five miles lower and Sixty miles below the forks arived at a large southerly fork which is the one we were on with the *Snake* or *So-So-nee* nation (haveing passed 5 rapids). This South fork or number of Indians about us gazeing This day proved verry worm and Sultery, nothing killed men complaining of their diat of fish & roots. all that is able working at the Canoes.

[Clark] *Friday (Saturday) 5 October 1805* had all our horses 38 in number Collected and branded Cut off their fore top and delivered them to the 2 brothers and one son of one of the Chiefs who intends to accompany us down the river to each of those men I gave a Knife & Some Small articles &c. they promised to be atten-tive to our horses untill we Should return.

Nothing to eate except dried fish & roots. Capt Lewis & myself eate a Supper of roots boiled, which Swelled us in Such a manner that we were Scercely able to breath for Several hours. finished and lanced (*launched*) 2 of our canoes this evening which proved to be verry good our hunters with every diligence Could kill nothing. The hills high and ruged and woods too dry to hunt the deer which is the only game in our neighbourhood. Several Squars Came with fish and roots which we purchased of them for Beeds, which they were fond of. *Capt Lewis not So well to day as yesterday.*

[Clark] *Monday, 7 October 1805* I continue verry unwell but obliged to attend every thing all the Canoes put into the water and loaded, fixed our Canoes as well as possible and Set out as we were about to Set out we missd. both of the Chiefs who promised to accompany us, I also missed my Pipe Tomahawk which could not be found.

The after part of the day cloudy proceded on passed 10 rapids which wer dangerous the Canoe in which I was Struck a rock and Sprung a leak in the 3rd rapid, we proceeded on.

Editor's Note: *After descending the Snake and Columbia rivers, the Corps of Discovery reached the Pacific on 15 November 1805. They wintered on the south bank of the Columbia, before making the return journey, reaching their jump-off point of St. Louis on 23 September 1806, having long been given up for dead by everyone except the Voyage's instigator, President Thomas Jefferson.*

A memorial to the Lewis and Clark expedition.

CHAPTER 17

THE RIVER OF DOUBT

By Theodore Roosevelt

Official portrait of Theodore Roosevelt,
courtesy of the Library of Congress.

O n the morning of 22 March we started in our six canoes. We made ten kilometres. Twenty minutes after starting we came to the first rapids. Here everyone walked except the three best paddlers, who took the canoes down in succession—an hour's job. Soon after this we struck a bees' nest in the top of a tree overhanging the river; our steersman climbed out and robbed it, but, alas! lost the honey on the way back. We came to a small steep fall, which we did not dare run in our overladen, clumsy, and cranky dugouts. Fortunately we were able to follow a deep canal which led off for a kilometre, returning just below the falls, fifty yards from where it had started. Then, having been in the boats and in motion only one hour and a half, we came to a long stretch of rapids which it took us six hours to descend, and we camped at the foot. Everything was taken out of the canoes, and they were run down in succession. At one difficult and perilous place they were let down by ropes; and even thus we almost lost one.

We went down the right bank. On the opposite bank was an Indian village, evidently inhabited only during the dry season. The marks on the stumps of trees showed that these Indians had axes and knives; and there were old fields in which maize, beans, and cotton had been grown. The forest dripped and steamed. Rubber trees were plentiful. At one point the tops of a group of tall trees were covered with yellow-white blossoms. Others bore red blossoms. Many of the big trees, of different kinds, were buttressed at the base with great thin walls of wood. Others, including both palms and ordinary trees, showed an even stranger peculiarity. The trunk, near the base, but sometimes six or eight feet from the ground, was split into a dozen or twenty branches or small trunks which sloped outwards in a tent-like shape, each becoming a root. The larger trees of this type looked as if their trunks were seated on the tops of the pole-frames of Indian tepees. At one point in the stream, to our great surprise, we saw a flying-fish. It skimmed the water like a swallow for over twenty yards.

Although we made only ten kilometres we worked hard all day. The last canoes were brought down and moored to the bank at nightfall. Our tents were pitched in the darkness.

Next day we made thirteen kilometres. We ran, all told, a little over an hour and three-quarters. Seven hours were spent in getting past a series of rapids at which the portage, over rocky and difficult ground, was a kilometre long. The canoes were run down empty—a hazardous run, in which one of them upset.

Yet while we were actually on the river, paddling and floating downstream along the reaches of swift, smooth water, it was very lovely. When we started in the morning, the day was overcast and the air was heavy with vapour. Ahead of us the shrouded river stretched between dim walls of forest, half-seen in the mist. Then the sun burned up the fog, and loomed through it in a red splendour that changed first to gold and then to molten white. In the dazzling light, under the brilliant blue of the sky, every detail of the magnificent forest was vivid to the eye: the great trees, the network of bush-ropes, the caverns of greenery, where thick-leaved vines covered all things else. Wherever there was a hidden boulder the surface of the current was broken by waves. In one place in midstream, a pyramidal rock thrust itself six feet above the surface of the river. On the banks we found fresh Indian sign.

In the morning, just before leaving this camp, a tapir swam across stream a little way above us, but unfortunately we could not get a shot at it. An ample supply of tapir beef would have meant much to us. We had started with fifty days' rations, but this by no means meant full rations, in the sense of giving every man all he wanted to eat. We had two meals a day, and were on rather short commons—both our mess and the camaradas'—except when we got plenty of palm-tops. For our mess we had the boxes chosen by Fiala, each containing a day's rations for six men, our number. But we made each box last a day and a half, or at times two days, and in addition we gave some of the food to the camaradas. It was only on the rare occasions when we had killed some monkeys or curassows, or caught some fish, that everybody had enough. We would have welcomed that tapir. So far the game, fish and fruit had been too scarce to be an element of weight in our food supply. In an exploring trip like ours, through a difficult and utterly unknown country, especially if densely forested, there is little time to halt, and game cannot be counted on. It is only in lands like our own West thirty years ago, like South Africa in the middle of the last century, like East Africa today, that game can be made the chief food supply. On this trip our only substantial food supply from the country hitherto had been that furnished by the palm-tops. Two men were detailed every day to cut down palms for food.

A kilometre and a half after leaving this camp we came on a stretch of big rapids. The river here twists in loops, and we had heard the roaring of these rapids the previous afternoon. Then we passed out of earshot of them, but Antonio Correa, our best water-man, insisted all along that the roaring meant rapids worse than any we had encountered for some days. 'I was brought up in the water, and I know it like a fish, and all its sounds,' said he. He was right. We had to carry the loads nearly a kilometre that afternoon, and the canoes were pulled out on the bank so that they might be in readiness to be dragged overland next day. Rondon, Lyra, Kermit and Antonio Correa explored both sides of the river. On the opposite or left bank they found the mouth of a considerable river, bigger than the Rio Kermit, flowing in from the west and making its entrance in the middle of the rapids. This river we christened the Taunay, in honour of a distinguished Brazilian, an explorer, a soldier, a senator, who was also a writer of note. Kermit had with him two of his novels, and I had read one of his books dealing with a disastrous retreat during the Paraguayan war.

Next morning, the 25th, the canoes were brought down. A path was chopped for them and rollers laid; and halfway down the rapids Lyra and Kermit, who were overseeing the work as well as doing their share of the pushing and hauling, got them into a canal of smooth water, which saved much severe labour. As our food supply lowered we were constantly more desirous of economizing the strength of the men. One day more would complete a month since we had embarked on the Dúvida—as we had started in February, the lunar and calendar months coincided. We had used up over half our provisions. We had come only a trifle over 160 kilometres, thanks to the character and number of the rapids. We believed we had three or four times the distance yet to go before coming to a part of the river where we might hope to meet assistance, either from rubber-gatherers or from Pyrineus, if he were really coming up the river which we were going down. If the rapids continued to be as they had been it could not be much more than three weeks before we were in straits for food, aside from the ever-present danger of accident in the rapids; and if our progress were no faster than it had been—and we were straining to do our best—we would in such event still have several hundreds of kilometres of unknown river before us. We could not even hazard a guess at what was in front . . .

Two of our men were down with fever. Another man, Julio, a fellow of powerful frame, was utterly, worthless, being an inborn, lazy shirker with the heart of a ferocious cur in the body of a bullock. The others were good men, some of them very good indeed. They were under the immediate supervision of Pedrinho Craveiro, who was *first class in every way* . . .

In mid-afternoon we were once more in the canoes; but we had paddled with the current only a few minutes, we had gone only a kilometre, when the roar of rapids in front again forced us to haul up to the bank. As usual, Rondon, Lyra and Kermit, with Antonio Correa, explored both sides while camp was being pitched. The rapids were longer and of steeper descent than the last, but on the opposite or western side there was a passage down which we thought we could get the empty dugouts at the cost of dragging them only a few yards at one spot. The loads were to be carried down the hither bank, for a kilometre, to the smooth water. The river foamed between great rounded masses of rock, and at one point there was a sheer fall of six or eight feet. We found and ate wild pineapples. Wild beans were in flower. At dinner we had a toucan and a couple of parrots, which were very good.

All next day was spent by Lyra in superintending our three best watermen as they took the canoes down the west side of the rapids, to the foot, at the spot to which the camp had meantime been shifted. In the forest some of the huge sipas, or rope vines, which were as big as cables, bore clusters of fragrant flowers. The men found several honey-trees, and fruits of various kinds, and small coconuts; they chopped down an ample number of palms for the palm-cabbage; and most important of all, they gathered a quantity of big Brazil nuts, which when roasted tasted like the best of chestnuts, and are nutritious; and they caught a number of big piranhas, which were good eating. So we all had a feast, and everybody had enough to eat and was happy . . .

Next morning we went about three kilometres before coming to some steep hills, beautiful to look upon, clad as they were in dense, tall, tropical forest, but ominous of new rapids. Sure enough, at their foot we had to haul up and prepare for a long portage. The canoes we ran down empty. Even so, we were within an ace of losing two, the lashed couple in which I ordinarily journeyed. In a sharp bend of the rapids, between two big curls, they were swept among the boulders and under the matted branches which stretched out from the bank. They filled, and the racing current pinned them where they were, one partly on the other. All of us had to help get them clear. Their fastenings were chopped asunder with axes. Kermit and half a dozen of the men, stripped to the skin, made their way to a small rock island in the little falls just above the canoes, and let down a rope which we tied to the outermost canoe. The rest of us, up to our armpits and barely able to keep our footing as we slipped and stumbled among the boulders in the swift current lifted and shoved, while Kermit and his men pulled the rope and fastened the slack to a half-submerged tree. Each canoe in succession was hauled up the little rock island, baled, and then taken down in safety by two paddlers. It was nearly four o'clock before we were again ready to start, having been delayed by a rainstorm so heavy that we could not see across the river. Ten minutes' run took us to the head of another series of rapids; the exploring party returned with the news that we had an all day's job ahead of us; and we made camp in the rain, which did not matter much, as we were already drenched through. It was impossible with the wet wood, to make a fire sufficiently hot to dry all our soggy things, for the rain was still falling. A tapir was seen from our boat, but, as at the moment we were being whisked round in a complete circle by a whirlpool, I did not myself see it in time to shoot.

Next morning we went down a kilometre, and then landed on the other side of the river. The canoes were run down, and the loads carried to the other side of a little river coming in from the west, which Colonel Rondon christened Cherrie River. Across this we went on a bridge consisting of a huge tree felled by Macario, one of our best men. Here we camped, while Rondon, Lyra, Kermit and Antonio Correa explored what was ahead. They were absent until mid-afternoon. Then they returned with the news that we were among ranges of low mountains, utterly different information from the high plateau region to which the first rapids, those we had come to on 2 March, belonged. Through the first range of these mountains the river ran in a gorge, some three kilometres long, immediately ahead of us. The ground was so rough and steep that it would be impossible to drag the canoes over it and difficult enough to carry the loads; and the rapids were so bad, containing several falls, one of at least ten metres in height, that it was doubtful how many of the canoes we could get down them. Kermit, who was the only man with much experience of rope work, was the only man who believed we could get the canoes down at all; and it was, of course, possible that we should have to build new ones at the foot to supply the place of any that were lost or left behind. In view of the length and character of the portage, and of all the unpleasant possibilities that were ahead, and of the need of keeping every pound of food, it was necessary to reduce weight in every possible way and to throw away everything except the barest necessities.

We thought we had reduced our baggage before, but now we cut to the bone. We kept the fly for all six of us to sleep under. Kermit's shoes had gone, thanks to the amount of work in the water which he had been doing; and he took the pair I had been wearing, while I put on my spare pair. In addition to the clothes I wore, I kept one set of pyjamas, a spare pair of drawers, a spare pair of socks, half a dozen handkerchiefs, my wash kit, my pocket medicine-case, and a little bag containing my spare spectacles, gun-grease, some adhesive plaster, some needles and thread, the 'fly-dope', and my purse and letter of credit, to be used at Manaos. All of these went into the bag containing my cot, blanket, and mosquito net. I also carried a cartridge bag containing my cartridges, head net, and gauntlets. Kermit cut down even closer, and the others about as close.

The last three days of March we spent in getting to the foot of the rapids in this gorge. Lyra and Kermit, with four of the best watermen, handled the empty canoes. The work was not only difficult and laborious, in the extreme, but hazardous, for the walls of the gorge were so sheer that at the worst places they had to cling to narrow shelves on the face of the rock, while letting the canoes down with ropes. Meanwhile Rondon surveyed and cut a trail for the burden-bearers, and superintended the portage of the loads. The rocky sides of the gorge were too steep for laden men to attempt to traverse them. Accordingly the trail had to go over the top of the mountain, both the ascent and the descent of the rock-strewn, forested slopes being very steep. It was hard work to carry loads over such a trail. From the top of the mountain, through an opening in the trees on the edge of a cliff, there was a beautiful view of the country ahead. All around and in front of us there were ranges of low mountains about the height of the lower ridges of the Alleghanies. Their sides were steep and they were covered with the matted growth of the tropical forest. Our next camping place at the foot of the gorge, was almost beneath us, and from thence the river ran in a straight line, flecked with white water, for about a kilometre. Then it disappeared behind and between mountain ridges, which we supposed meant further rapids. It was a view well worth seeing but, beautiful although the country ahead of us was, its character was such as to promise further hardships, difficulty, and exhausting labour, and especially further delay; and delay was a serious matter to men whose food supply was beginning to run short, whose equipment was reduced to the minimum, who for a month, with the utmost toil, had made very slow progress, and who had no idea of either the distance or the difficulties of the route in front of them . . .

During this portage the weather favoured us. We were coming towards the close of the rainy season. On the last day of the month, when we moved camp to the foot of the gorge, there was a thunderstorm but on the whole we were not bothered by rain until the last night when it rained heavily, driving under the fly so as to wet my cot and bedding. However, I slept comfortably enough, rolled in the damp blanket. Without the blanket I should have been uncomfortable; a blanket is a necessity for health. On the third day Lyra and Kermit, with their daring and hard-working water-men after wearing labour, succeeded in getting five canoes through the worst of the rapids to the chief fall. The sixth, which was frail, had its bottom beaten out on the jagged rocks of the broken water. On this night, although I thought I had put my clothes out of reach, both the termites and the carregadores ants got at them, ate holes in one boot, ate one leg of my drawers, and riddled my handkerchief; and I now had nothing to replace anything that was destroyed.

Next day Lyra, Kermit and their camaradas brought the five canoes that were left down to camp. They had in four days accomplished a work of incredible labour and of the utmost importance; for at the first glance it had seemed an absolute impossibility to avoid abandoning the canoes when we found that the river sank into a cataract-broken torrent at the bottom of a canyon-like gorge between steep mountains. On 2 April we once more started, wondering how soon we should strike other rapids in the mountains ahead, and whether in any reasonable time we should, as the aneroid indicated, be so low down that we should necessarily be in a plain where we could make a journey of at least a few days without rapids. We had been exactly a month going through an uninterrupted succession of rapids. During that month we had come only about 110 kilometres, and had descended nearly 150 metres—the figures are approximate but fairly accurate. We had lost four of the canoes with which we started, and one other, which we had built, and the life of one man; and the life of a dog which by its death had, in all probability, saved the life of Colonel Rondon. In a straight line northward, towards our supposed destination, we had not made more than a mile and a quarter a day; at the cost of bitter toil for most of the party, of much risk for some of the party, and of some risk and some hardship for all the party. Most of the camaradas were downhearted, naturally enough, and occasionally asked one of us if we really believed that we should ever get out alive, and we had to cheer them up as best we could.

There was no change in our work for the time being. We made but three kilometres that day. Most of the party walked all the time, but the dugouts carried the luggage until we struck the head of the series of rapids which were to take up the next two or three days. The river rushed through a wild gorge, a chasm or canyon, between two mountains. Its sides were very steep, mere rock walls, although in most places so covered with the luxuriant growth of the trees and bushes that clung in the crevices, and with green moss, that the naked rock was hardly seen. Rondon, Lyra and Kermit, who were in front, found a small level spot with a beach of sand, and sent back word to camp there while they spent several hours in exploring the country ahead. The canoes were run down empty, and the loads carried painfully along the face of the cliffs; so bad was the trail that I found it rather hard to follow although carrying nothing but my rifle and cartridge bag. The explorers returned with the information that the mountains stretched ahead of us, and that there were rapids as far as they had gone. We could only hope that the aneroid was not hopelessly out of kilter and that we should, therefore, fairly soon find ourselves in comparatively level country. The severe toil, on a rather limited food supply, was telling on the strength as well as on the spirits of the men; Lyra and Kermit in addition to their other work, performed as much actual physical labour as any of them.

Next day, 3 April, we began the descent of these sinister rapids of the chasm. Colonel Rondon had gone to the summit of the mountain in order to find a better trail for the burden-bearers, but it was hopeless, and they had to go along the face of the cliffs . . .

Lyra, Kermit and Cherrie, with four of the men, worked the canoes halfway down the canyon. Again and again it was touch and go whether they could get past a given point. At one spot the channel of the furious torrent

The Amazon River, Brazil.

was only fifteen yards across. One canoe was lost, so that of the seven with which we had started only two were left. Cherrie laboured with the other men at times, and also stood as guard over them, for, while actually working, of course no one could carry a rifle. Kermit's experience in bridge building was invaluable in enabling him to do the rope work by which alone it was possible to get the canoes down the canyon. He and Lyra had now been in the water for days. Their clothes were never dry. Their shoes were rotten. The bruises on their feet and legs had become sores. On their bodies some of the insect bites had become festering wounds, as indeed was the case with all of us. Poisonous ants, biting flies, ticks, wasps, bees, were a perpetual torment. However, no one had yet been bitten by a venomous serpent, a scorpion, or a centipede although we had killed all of the three within camp limits.

Under such conditions whatever is evil in men's natures comes to the front. On this day a strange and terrible tragedy occurred. One of the camaradas, a man of pure European blood, was the man named Julio of whom I have already spoken. He was a very powerful fellow and had been importunately eager to come on the expedition and he had the reputation of being a good worker. But, like so many men of higher standing, he had had no idea of what such an expedition really meant, and under the strain of toil, hardship and danger his nature showed its true depths of selfishness, cowardice and ferocity. He shirked all work. He shammed sickness. Nothing could make him do his share; and yet unlike his self-respecting fellows he was always shamelessly begging for favours. Kermit was the only one of our party who smoked, and he was continually giving a little tobacco to some of the camaradas, who worked especially well under him. The good men did not ask for it but Julio, who shirked every labour, was always, and always in vain, demanding it. Colonel Rondon, Lyra and Kermit each tried to get work out of him, and in order to do anything with him had to threaten to leave him in the wilderness. He threw all his tasks on his comrades and, moreover, he stole their food as well as ours. On such an expedition the theft of food comes next to murder as a crime, and should by rights be punished as such. We could not trust him to cut down palms or gather nuts, because he would stay out and eat what ought to have gone into the common store. Finally, the men on several occasions themselves detected him stealing their food. Alone of the whole party, and thanks to the stolen food, he had kept in full flesh and bodily vigour.

One of our best men was a huge negro named Paixão-Paishon—a corporal and acting sergeant in the engineer corps. He had, by the way, literally torn his trousers to pieces, so that he wore only the tatters of a pair of old drawers until I gave him my spare trousers when we lightened loads. He was a stern disciplinarian. One evening he detected Julio stealing food and smashed him in the mouth. Julio came crying to us, his face working with fear and malignant hatred; but after investigation he was told that he had got off uncommonly lightly. The men had three or four carbines, which were sometimes carried by those who were not their owners.

On this morning, at the outset of the portage, Pedrinho discovered Julio stealing some of the men's dried meat. Shortly afterwards Paishon rebuked him for, as usual, lagging behind. By this time we had reached the place where the canoes were tied to the bank and then taken down one at a time. We were sitting down waiting for the last loads to be brought along the trail. Pedrinho was still in the camp we had left. Paishon had just brought in a load, left it on the ground with his carbine beside it, and returned on the trail for another load. Julio came in, put down his load, picked up the carbine, and walked back on the trail, muttering to himself but showing no excitement. We thought nothing of it, for he was always muttering; and occassionally one of the men saw a monkey or big bird and tried to shoot it, so it was never surprising to see a man with a carbie.

In a minute we heard a shot; and in a short time three or four of the men came up the trail to tell us that Paishon was dead, having been shot by Julio, who had fled into the woods. Colonel Rondon and Lyra were ahead; I sent a messenger for them, directed Cherrie and Kermit to stay where they were and guard the canoes and provisions, and started down the trail with the doctor— an absolutely cool and plucky man with a revolver but no rifle—and a couple of the camaradas. We soon passed the dead body of poor Paishon. He lay in a huddle, in a pool of his own blood, where he had fallen, shot through the heart. I feared that Julio had run amuck, and intended merely to take more lives before he died, and that he would begin with Pedrinho, who was alone and unarmed in the camp we had left. Accordingly I pushed on, followed by my companions, looking sharply right and left; but when we came to the camp the doctor quietly walked by me, remarking: 'My eyes are better than yours, Colonel; if he is in sight I'll point him out to you, as you have the rifle.' However, he was not there, and the others soon joined us with the welcome news that they had found the carbine.

The murderer had stood to one side of the path and killed his victim, when a dozen paces off, with deliberate and malignant purpose. Then evidently his murderous hatred had at once given way to his innate cowardice, and, perhaps hearing someone coming along the path, he fled in panic terror into the wilderness. A tree had knocked the carbine from his hand. His footsteps showed that after going some rods he had started to return, doubtless for the carbine, but had fled again, probably because the body had then been discovered. It was questionable whether or not he would live to reach the Indian villages, which were probably his goal. He was not a man to feel remorse—never a common feeling; but surely that murderer was in a living hell, as, with fever and famine leering at him from the shadows, he made his way through the empty desolation of the wilderness. Franca, the cook, quoted out of the melancholy proverbial philosophy of the people the proverb: 'No man knows the heart of anyone,' and then expressed with deep conviction a weird ghostly belief I had never encountered before: Paishon is following Julio now, and will follow him until he dies; 'Paishon fell forward on his hands and knees, and when a murdered man falls like that his ghost will follow the slayer as long as the slayer lives' . . .

We buried him beside the place where he fell. With axes and knives the camaradas dug a shallow grave, while we stood by with bared heads. Then reverently and carefully we lifted the poor body, which but half an hour before had been so full of vigorous life. Colonel Rondon and I bore the head and shoulders.

We laid him in the grave, and heaped a mound over him, and put a rude cross at his head. We fired a volley for a brave and loyal soldier, who had died doing his duty. Then we left him for ever, under the great trees beside the lonely river.

That day we got only halfway down the rapids. There was no good place to camp. But at the foot of one steep cliff there was a narrow, boulder-covered slope, where it was possible to sling hammocks and cook; and a slanting spot was found for my cot, which had sagged until by this time it looked like a broken backed centipede. It rained a little during the night but not enough to wet us much. Next day Lyra, Kermit and Cherrie finished their job, and brought the four remaining canoes to camp, one leaking badly from the battering on the rocks. We then went downstream a few hundred yards, and camped on the opposite side; it was not a good camping place, but it was better than the one we left.

The men were growing constantly weaker under the endless strain of exhausting labour. Kermit was having an attack of fever, and Lyra and Cherrie had touches of dysentery, but all three continued to work. While in the water trying to help with an upset canoe I had, by my own clumsiness, bruised my leg against a boulder, and the resulting inflammation was somewhat bothersome. I now had a sharp attack of fever, but, thanks to the excellent care of the doctor, was over it in about forty-eight hours; but Kermit's fever grew worse, and he too was unable to work for a day or two. We could walk over the portages, however. A good doctor is an absolute necessity on an exploring expedition in such a country as that we were in, under penalty of a frightful mortality among the members; and the necessary risks and hazards are so great, the chances of disaster so large, that there is no warrant for increasing them by the failure to take all feasible precautions.

The next day we made another long portage round some rapids, and camped at night still in the hot, wet, sunless atmosphere of the gorge. The following day, 6 April, we portaged past another set of rapids, which proved to be the last of the rapids of the chasm. For some kilometres we kept passing hills, and feared lest at any moment we might again find ourselves fronting another mountain gorge, with, in such case, further days of grinding and perilous labour ahead of us, while our men were disheartened, weak and sick.

Most of them had already begun to have fever. Their condition was inevitable after over a month's uninterrupted work of the hardest kind in getting through the long series of rapids we had just passed; and a long further delay, accompanied by wearing labour, would have almost certainly meant that the weakest among our party would have begun to die. There were already two of the camaradas who were too weak to help the others, their condition being such as to cause us serious concern.

However, the hills gradually sank into a level plain and the river carried us through it at a rate that enabled us during the remainder of the day to reel off thirty-six kilometres, a record that for the first time held out promise. Twice tapirs swam the river while we passed but not near my canoe. However, the previous evening Cherrie had killed two monkeys and Kermit one, and we all had a few mouthfuls of fresh meat; we had already had a good soup made out of a turtle Kermit had caught. We had to portage by one short set of rapids, the unloaded canoes being brought down without difficulty. At last, at four in the afternoon, we came to the mouth of a big river running in from the right. We thought it was probably the Ananas, but, of course, could not be certain. It was less in volume than the one we had descended, but nearly as broad; its breadth at this point being ninety-five yards as against one hundred and twenty for the larger river. There were rapids ahead, immediately after the junction, which took place in latitude 10° 58' south. We had come 216 kilometres all told, and were nearly north of where we had started. We camped on the point of land between the two rivers. It was extraordinary to realize that here about the eleventh degree we were on such a big river, utterly unknown to the cartographers and not indicated by even a hint on any map. We named this big tributary Rio Cardozo, after a gallant officer of the Commission who had died of beriberi just as our expedition began. We spent a day at this spot determining our exact position by the sun, and afterward by the stars, and sending on two men to explore the rapids in advance. They returned with the news that there were big cataracts in them, and that they would form an obstacle to our progress. They had also caught a huge siluroid fish, which furnished an excellent meal for everybody in camp. This evening at sunset the view across the broad river, from our camp where the two rivers joined, was very lovely; and for the first time we had an open space in front of and above us, so that after nightfall the stars and the great waxing moon were glorious overhead, and against the rocks in midstream the broken water gleamed like tossing silver . . .

Next day, 8 April, we made five kilometres only, as there was a succession of rapids. We had to carry the loads past two of them, but ran the canoes without difficulty, for on the west side were long canals of swift water through the forest. The river had been higher, but was still very high, and the current raced round the many islands that, at this point, divided the channel. At four we made camp at the head of another stretch of rapids, over which the Canadian canoes would have danced without shipping a teaspoonful of water but which our dugouts could only run empty. Cherrie killed three monkeys and Lyra caught two big piranhas so that we were again all of us well provided with dinner and breakfast. When a number of men, doing hard work, are most of the time on half-rations, they grow to take a lively interest in any reasonably full meal that does arrive.

On the 10th we repeated the proceedings: a short quick run; a few hundred metres' portage, occupying, however, at least a couple of hours; again a few minutes run; again other rapids. We again made less than five kilometres; in the two days we had been descending nearly a metre for every kilometre we made in advance and it hardly seemed as if this state of things could last, for the aneroid showed that we were getting very low down. How I longed for a big Maine birch-bark, such as that in which I once went down the Mattawamkeag at high water! It would have slipped down these rapids as a girl trips through a country dance. But our loaded dugouts would have shoved their noses under every curl. The country was lovely. The wide river, now in one channel, now in several channels, wound among hills; the shower-freshened forest glistened in the sunlight; the many kinds of beautiful palm-fronds and the huge pacova-leaves stamped the peculiar look of the tropics on the whole landscape—it was like passing by water through a gigantic botanical garden. In the afternoon we got an elderly toucan, a piranha, and a reasonably edible side-necked river-turtle, so we had fresh meat again. We slept as usual in earshot of rapids. We had been out six weeks, and almost all the time we had been engaged in wearily working our way down and past rapid after rapid. Rapids are by far the most dangerous enemies of explorers and travellers who journey along these rivers.

Next day was a repetition of the same work. All the morning was spent in getting the loads to the foot of the rapids at the head of which we were encamped, down which the canoes were run empty. Then for thirty or forty minutes we ran down the swift, twisting river, the two lashed canoes almost coming to grief at one spot where a swirl of the current threw them against some trees on a small submerged island. Then we came to another set of rapids, carried the baggage down past them, and made camp long after dark in the rain—a good exercise in patience for those of us who were still suffering somewhat from fever. No one was in really buoyant health. For some weeks we had been sharing part of the contents of our boxes with the camaradas but our food was not very satisfying to them. They needed quantity, and the mainstay of each of their meals was a mass of palmitas; but on this day they had no time to cut down palms. We finally decided to run these rapids with the empty canoes, and they came down in safety. On such a trip it is highly undesirable to take any save necessary risks, for the consequences of disaster are too serious; and yet if no risks are taken the progress is so slow that disaster comes anyhow; and it is necessary perpetually to vary the terms of the perpetual working compromise between rashness and over caution. This night we had a very good fish to eat, a big silvery fellow called a pescada, of a kind we had not caught before.

One day Trigueiro failed to embark with the rest of us, and we had to camp where we were next day to find him. Easter Sunday we spent in the fashion with which we were altogether too familiar. We only ran in a dear course for ten minutes all told, and spent eight hours in portaging the loads past rapids down which the canoes were run; the balsa was almost swamped. This day we caught twenty-eight big fish, mostly piranhas, and everybody had all he could eat for dinner, and for breakfast the following morning.

The forenoon of the following day was a repetition of this wearisome work; but late in the afternoon the river began to run in long quiet reaches. We made fifteen kilometres, and for the first time in several weeks camped where we did not hear the rapids. The silence was soothing and restful. The following day, 14 April, we made a good run of some thirty-two kilometres. We passed a little river which entered on our left. We ran two or three light rapids, and portaged the loads by another. The river ran in long and usually tranquil stretches. In the morning when we started the view was lovely. There was a mist, and for a couple of miles the great river, broad and quiet, ran between the high walls of tropical forest, the tops of the giant trees showing dim through the haze. Different members of the party caught many fish and shot a monkey and a couple of jacutinga-birds akin to a turkey, but the size of a fowl—so we again had a camp of plenty. The dry season was approaching, but there were still heavy, drenching rains. On this day the men found some new nuts of which they liked the taste, but the nuts proved unwholesome and half of the men were very sick and unable to work the following day. In the balsa only two were left fit to do anything, and Kermit plied a paddle all day long.

Accordingly, it was a rather sorry crew that embarked the following morning, 15 April. But it turned out a red-letter day. The day before, we had come across cuttings, a year old, which were probably but not certainly made by pioneer rubber-men. But on this day—during which we made twenty-five kilometres—after running two hours and a half we found on the left bank a board on a post, with the initials J. A., to show the farthest-up point which a rubber-man had reached and claimed as his own. An hour farther down we came on a newly built house in a little planted clearing and we cheered heartily. No one was at home, but the house, of palm-thatch, was clean and cool. A couple of dogs were on watch, and the belongings showed that a man, a woman and a child lived there, and had only just left. Another hour brought us to a similar house where dwelt an old black man, who showed the innate courtesy of the Brazilian peasant. We came on these rubber-men and their houses in about latitude 10° 24'.

In mid-afternoon we stopped at another clean, cool, picturesque house of palm-thatch. The inhabitants all fled at our approach, fearing an Indian raid; for they were absolutely unprepared to have any one come from the un-known regions upstream. They returned and were most hospitable and com-municative, and we spent the night there. Said Antonio Correa to Kermit: 'It seems like a dream to be in a house again, and hear the voices of men and women, instead of being among those mountains and rapids.'

We had passed the period when there was a chance of peril, of disaster, to the whole expedition. There might be risk ahead to individuals, and some difficulties and annoyances for all of us; but there was no longer the least like-lihood of any disaster to the expedition as a whole. We now no longer had to face continual anxiety, the need of constant economy with food, the duty of labour with no end in sight, and bitter uncertainty as to the future.

It was time to get out.

The Amazon River.

CHAPTER 18

THE SANDS OF THE GOBI

by Nikolai Nikhailovich Przhevalsky

Nikolai Przhevalsky by
Marcus Gheerants, circa 1860.

The second week in June [1873] we left the high lands of Kan-su and crossed the threshold of the desert of Ala-shan. The sand drifts now lay before us like a boundless sea, and it was not without sundry misgivings that we entered this forbidding realm.

Without sufficient means to enable us to hire a guide, we went alone, risking all dangers and difficulties, the more imminent because the year before, while travelling with the Tangutan caravan, I could only note down by stealth, and often at haphazard, the landmarks and direction of the route. This itinerary was of course inaccurate, but now it served as our only guide.

We were fifteen days marching from Tajing to Din-yuan-ing, and safely accomplished this difficult journey, only once nearly losing ourselves in the desert. This happened on 21 June between Lake Serik-dolon and the well of Shangin-dalai. Having left Serik-dolon early in the morning, we marched through miles of loose sands, and at last came to an expanse of clay where the track divided. We had not noticed this spot on the outward journey, and had therefore to guess which of the two roads would lead to our destination. What made it worse was that the angle of bifurcation being acute, we could not decide, even with the aid of a compass, which we ought to take. The track to the right being more beaten, we determined to follow it, but after all we were mistaken, for having gone a few miles a number of other tracks crossed ours. This fairly puzzled us; however, we still pressed forward, till at length a well-beaten road joined the one we had first chosen. This we durst not follow, for it went we knew not whither, nor could we return to the place where the roads first branched off. Choosing the lesser of two evils, we resolved to persevere in our first route, hoping soon to see the group of hills at whose foot lies the well of Shangin-dalai. But it was midday, and the intense heat obliged us to halt for two or three hours. On resuming our march, with the aid of the compass we steered in the same direction as before, till at length we discerned a small group of hills to our right. These we supposed to be the landmark of the Shangin-dalai, but they were still a long way off, and the dust which pervaded the atmosphere the whole day prevented our seeing their outline distinctly even with a glass.

Evening fell and we halted for the night, fully confident that these hills were indeed those we were in search of. But on projecting our line of march on the map, I became aware how far we had diverged to the right of our proper course, and doubts arose as to whether we were really on the right road or not. In the meanwhile only five gallons of water were left for the night; our horses had had none, and were suffering such agonies of thirst that they could hardly move their legs. The question of finding the well on the morrow became one of life and death. How can I describe our feelings as we lay down to rest! Fortunately the wind fell and the dust in the air cleared off. In the morning, with the first glimmer of light, I climbed on to the top of the pile of boxes containing our collections, and carefully scanned the horizon with a glass. I could see distinctly the group of hills we had remarked the previous day, but in a direction due north of our halting-place: I could also distinguish the summit of another, which might perhaps be that of Shangin-dalai. Towards which should we direct our steps? Having taken careful bearings of the latter, and having compared its position on the map with that noted down last year, we decided to march in that direction.

In doubt and anxiety we loaded our camels and started, the hill now and then visible above the low ridges, and now and again hidden from sight. In vain we strained our eyes through the glass to see the cairn of stones ('obo') piled upon its summit; the distance was still too great to distinguish anything so small. At length, after having gone nearly seven miles from the halting-place, we descried what we sought; with strength renewed by hope we pressed onwards; and in a few more hours we stood by the side of the well, to which our animals, tortured with thirst, rushed eagerly forward.

On one of the marches through Southern Ala-shan we met a caravan of Mongol pilgrims on their way from Urga to Lhassa. The pilgrims were marching in echelons, some distance apart, having agreed to rendezvous at Koko-nor. As the foremost files met us, they exclaimed, 'See where our brave fellows have got to!' and could hardly believe at first that we four had actually penetrated into Tibet. But what must have been the appearance of the Russian molodtsi? Exhausted with fatigue, half starved, unkempt, with ragged clothes and boots worn into holes, we were regular tatterdemalions! So completely had we lost the European aspect that when we arrived at Din-yuan-ing the natives remarked that we were the very image of their own people!

In accordance with the plan we had previously sketched, we purposed marching straight to Urga from Din-yuan-ing, by way of the Central Gobi, a route which had never before been travelled by any European, and was therefore of the greatest scientific interest. Before starting, however, we determined to rest, and to take this opportunity of exploring more thoroughly than last time the mountains of Ala-shan . . . Here we stayed three weeks, and finally came to the conclusion that the mountains of Ala-shan are rich neither in flora nor in fauna.

In such arid mountains as these one would have supposed that we should not have incurred the slightest risk from water; but fate willed that we should experience every misfortune which can possibly overtake the traveller in these countries, for, without giving us the slightest warning, a deluge, such as we never remember to have seen, swept suddenly down upon us.

It was on the morning of 13 July; the summits of the mountains were enveloped in mist, a sure indication of rain. Towards midday, however, it became perfectly clear and gave every promise of a fine day, when, three hours later, all of a sudden, clouds began to settle on the mountains, and the rain poured down in buckets. Our tent was soon soaked through, and we dug small trenches to drain off the water which made its way into the interior. This

The Gobi Desert.

continued for an hour without showing any sign of abatement, although the sky did not look threatening. The rainfall was so great that it was more than could be absorbed by the soil or retained on the steep slopes of the mountains; the consequence was that streams formed in every cleft and gorge, even falling from the precipitous cliffs, and uniting in the principal ravine, where our tent happened to be pitched, descended in an impetuous torrent with terrific roar and speed. Dull echoes high up in the mountains warned us of its approach, and in a few minutes the deep bed of our ravine was inundated with a turbid, coffee-coloured stream, carrying with it rocks and heaps of smaller fragments, while it dashed with such violence against the sides that the very ground trembled as though with the shock of an earthquake. Above the roar of the waters we could hear the clash of great boulders as they met in their headlong course. From the loose banks and from the upper parts of the defile whole masses of smaller stones were detached by the force of the current and thrown up on either side of the channel, whilst trees were torn up by their roots and rent into splinters . . . Barely twenty feet from our tent rushed the torrent, destroying everything in its course. Another minute, another foot of water, and our collections, the fruit of our expedition, were irrevocably gone! . . .

Fortune, however, again befriended us. Before our tent was a small projecting ledge of rock upon which the waves threw up stones which soon formed a breakwater, and this saved us. Towards evening the rain slackened, the torrent quickly subsided, and the following morning beheld only a small stream flowing where the day before the waters of a mighty river had swept along . . .

On returning to Din-yuan-ing we equipped our caravan, bartered away our bad camels, bought new ones, and on the morning of 26 July started on our journey. Thanks to our Peking passport and still more to the presents we bestowed on the *tosal-akchi* who acted as regent during the Prince's absence,* we were able to hire two guides to escort us to the border of Ala-shan, where we were to obtain others, and for this purpose the yamen (or magistracy) of Ala-shan issued an official document: in this way we continued to obtain

---

*The Prince of Ala-shan.

guides from one banner to another; a matter of great importance, for our road lay through the wildest part of the Gobi, in a meridional direction from Ala-shan to Urga, and we could not possibly have found our way without them.

Another long series of hardships now awaited us. We suffered most from the July heat, which at midday rose to 113° Fahr. in the shade, and at night was never less than 73°. No sooner did the sun appear above the horizon than it scorched us mercilessly. In the daytime the heat enveloped us on all sides, above from the sun, below from the burning ground; the wind, instead of cooling the atmosphere, stirred the lower strata and made it even more in-tolerable. On these days the cloudless sky was of a dirty hue, the soil heated to 145° Fahr., and even higher where the sands were entirely bare, whilst at a depth of two feet from the surface it was 79°.

Our tent was no protection, for it was hotter within than without, al-though the sides were raised. We tried pouring water on it, and on the ground inside, but this was useless, in half an hour everything was as dry as before, and we knew not whither to turn for relief.

The air, too, was terribly dry; no dew fell, and rain clouds dispersed without sending more than a few drops to earth . . .

Thunderstorms rarely occurred, but the wind was incessant night and day, and sometimes blew with great violence, chiefly from the south-east and south-west. On calm days tornadoes were frequent about the middle of the day or a little later. To avoid the heat as much as possible we rose before daybreak; tea-drinking and loading the camels, however, took up so much time that we never got away before four or even five o'clock in the morning. We might have lightened the fatigue considerably by night-marching, but in that case we should have had to forgo the survey which formed so important a part of our labours . . .

The commencement of our journey was unpropitious, for on the sixth day after we left Din-yuan-ing, we lost our faithful friend Faust,* and we ourselves nearly perished in the sands.

---

*Colonel Przhevalsky's setter.

It was on 31 July; we had left Djaratai-dabas and had taken the direction of the Khan-ula mountains; our guide having informed us that a march of eighteen miles lay before us that day, but that we should pass two wells about five miles apart.

Having accomplished that distance, we arrived at the first, and after watering our animals, proceeded, in the full expectation of finding the second, where we intended to halt; for though it was only seven in the morning, the heat was overpowering. So confident were we that the Cossacks proposed to throw away the supply of water that we had taken in the casks, in order not to burden our camels needlessly, but fortunately I forbade their doing this. After nearly seven miles more, no well was to be seen, and the guide announced that we had gone out of our road. So he proceeded to the top of a hillock in the immediate neighbourhood to obtain a view over the surrounding country, and soon afterwards beckoned to us to follow. On rejoining him, he assured us that although we had missed the second well, a third, where he purposed passing the night, was scarcely four miles farther. We took the direction indicated. In the meanwhile it was near midday and the heat intolerable. A strong wind stirred the hot lower atmosphere, enveloping us in sand and saline dust. Our animals suffered frightfully; especially the dogs, obliged to walk over the burning sand. We stopped several times to give them drink, and to moisten their heads as well as our own. But the supply of water now failed! Less than a gallon remained, and this we reserved for the last extremity. 'How much farther is it?' was the question we constantly put to our guide, who invariably answered that it was near, that we should see it from the next sandhill or the one after; and so we passed on upwards of seven miles without having seen a sign of the promised well. In the meanwhile the unfortunate Faust lay down and moaned, giving us to understand that he was quite unable to walk. I then told my companion and guide to ride on, charging the latter to take Faust on his camel as he was completely exhausted. After they had ridden a mile in advance of the caravan the guide pointed out the spot where he said the well should be, apparently about three miles off. Poor Faust's doom was sealed; he was seized with fits, and Mr. Pyltseff, finding it was impossible to hurry on, and too far to ride back to the caravan for a glass of water, waited till we came up, laying Faust under a clump of *saxaul* and covering him with saddle-felt. The poor dog became less conscious every minute, gasped two or three times, and expired. Placing his body on one of the packs, we moved on again, sorely doubting whether there were really any well in the place pointed out to us by the guide, for he had already deceived us more than once. Our situation at this moment was desperate. Only a few glasses of water left, of which we took into our mouths just enough to moisten our parched tongues; our bodies seemed on fire, our heads swam, and we were close upon fainting. In this last extremity I desired a Cossack to take a small vessel and to ride as hard as he could to the well, accompanied by the guide, ordering him to fire at the latter if he attempted to run away. They were soon hidden in a cloud of dust which filled the air, and we toiled onwards in their tracks in the most anxious suspense. At length, after half an hour, the Cossack appeared. What news does he bring? And spurring our jaded horses, which could hardly move their legs to meet him, we learned with the joy of a man who has been snatched from the jaws of death that the well had been found! After a draught of fresh water from the vesselful that he brought, and, having wet our heads, we rode in the direction pointed out, and soon reached the well of Boro-Sondji. It was now two o'clock in the afternoon; we had, therefore, been exposed for nine consecutive hours to frightful heat, and had ridden upwards of twenty miles.

After unloading the camels, I sent a Cossack back with the Mongol for the pack which had been left on the road, by the side of which our other (Mongol) dog, who had been with us nearly two years, was laid. The poor brute had lain down underneath the pack but was still alive, and after getting a draught of water he was able to follow the men back to camp. Notwithstanding the complete prostration of our physical and moral energies, we felt the loss of Faust so keenly that we could eat nothing, and slept but little all night. The following morning we dug a small grave and buried in it the remains of our faithful friend. As we discharged this last duty to him my companion and I wept like children. Faust had been our friend in every sense of the word! How often in moments of trouble had we caressed and played with him, half forgetting our griefs! For nearly three years had he served us faithfully through the frost and storms of Tibet, the rain and snow of Kan-su, and the wearisome marches of many thousand miles, and at last had fallen a victim to the burning heat of the desert; this too within two months of the termination of the expedition!

The route taken by most of the caravans of pilgrims from Urga to Ala-shan on their way to Tibet turns a little to the west at the Khan-ula mountains, afterwards taking the direction of the Khalka country. We did not follow this road because the wells along it were not sufficiently numerous . . . Our course lay due north, and after crossing some spurs of the Kara-narin-ula entered the country of the Urutes, which lies wedge-shaped between Ala-shan and the Khalka country.

This country is considerably higher than Ala-shan, but soon begins to sink towards the Galpin Gobi plain, where the elevation is only 3,200 feet; north of this again it rises towards the Hurku mountains which form a distinct definition between the barren desert on the south and the more steppe-like region on the north. There is also a slope from the ranges bordering the valley of the Hoang-ho westward to the Galpin Gobi, which forms a depressed basin, no higher than Djaratai-dabas, extending as we were informed by the Mongols, for twenty-five days' march from east to west.

The soil of the Galpin Gobi, in that eastern portion of it which we crossed, consists of small pebbles or of saline clay almost devoid of vegetation; the whole expanse of country to the Hurku range being a desert as wild and barren as that of Ala-shan, but of a somewhat different character. The sand drifts, so vast in the latter country, are here of comparatively small extent, and in their stead we find bare clay, shingle, and naked crumbling rocks (chiefly gneiss) scattered in low groups. Vegetation consists of stunted, half-withered clumps of *saxaul, karmyk, budarhana*, and a few herbaceous plants, the chief amongst which is the *sulhir*; the elms are the most striking features in the Urute country, forming in places small clumps; bushes of wild peach are also occasionally met with, such as are never seen in the desert of Ala-shan. Animal life in these regions is very scant; birds and mammals are the same as in Ala-shan. You may often ride for hours together without seeing a bird, not even a stone-chat or a *kolodjoro*; nevertheless, wherever there are wells or springs, Mongols are to be found, with a few camels, and large numbers of sheep and goats.

During our progress through this country, in the latter half of August, the heat was excessive, although never so high as in Ala-shan. Winds blew ceaselessly night and day, often increasing to the violence of a gale, and filling the air with clouds of saline dust and sand, the latter choking up many of the wells; but these were more frequently destroyed by the rains, which, although rare, came down with terrific force, and for an hour or two afterwards large rivers continued to flow, silting up the wells (always dug on the lower ground) with mud and sand. It would be impossible to travel here without a guide thoroughly acquainted with the country; for destruction lies in wait for you at every step. In fact this desert, like that of Ala-shan, is so terrible that, in comparison with it, the deserts of Northern Tibet may be called fruitful. There, at all events, you may often find water and good pasture-land in the valleys; here, there is neither the one nor the other, not even a single oasis; everywhere the silence of the valley of death.

The well-known Sahara can hardly be more terrible than these deserts, which extend for many hundreds of miles in length and breadth. The Hurku hills, where we crossed, are the northern definition of the wildest and most sterile part of the Gobi, and form a distinct chain with a direction from SE to WNW; how far either way we could not say positively; but, according to the information we received from the natives, they are prolonged for a great distance towards the south-east, reaching the mountains bordering the valley of the Hoang-ho, while on the west they extend, with a few interruptions, to other far distant mountains of no great elevation. If the latter statement may be relied upon, we may conclude that they unite with the Thian Shan, and supply, as it were, a connecting link between that range and the In-shan system; an extremely interesting fact and one worthy of the attention of future explorers.

Their width where we crossed them is a little over seven miles, and their apparent height hardly above a thousand feet . . .

South of the Hurku lies the great trade route from Peking, via Kuku-kho-to and Bautu, to Hami, Urumchi and Kulja, branching off near the spring of Bortson, where we encamped for the night . . .

On crossing the frontier of the Khalka country we entered the principality of Tushetu-khan, and hastened by forced marches to Urga, which was now the goal we were so desirous of reaching. Nearly three years of wanderings, attended by every kind of privation and hardship, had so worn us out physically and morally that we felt most anxious for a speedy termination of our journey; besides which, we were now travelling through the wildest part of the Gobi, where want of water, heat, storms of wind, in short every adverse condition combined against us, and day by day undermined what little of our strength remained . . .

The mirage, that evil genius of the desert, mocked us almost daily, and conjured up such tantalising visions of tremulous water that even the rocks of the neighbouring hills appeared as though reflected in it. Severe heat and frequent storms of wind prevented our sleeping quietly at night, much as we needed rest after the arduous day's march.

But not to us alone was the desert of Mongolia an enemy. Birds which began to make their appearance in the latter half of August suffered equally from thirst and hunger. We saw flocks of geese and ducks resting at the smallest pools, and small birds flew to our tent so exhausted with starvation as to allow us to catch them in the hand. We found several of these feathered wanderers quite dead, and in all probability numbers of them perish in their flight across the desert.

The chief migration of birds was in September, and by the 13th of that month we had counted twenty-four varieties. From our observations the geese directed their flight not due south but south-east towards the northern bend of the Hoang-ho.

Eighty-seven miles north of the Hurku hills we crossed another trade route from Kuku-khoto to Uliassutai; practicable for carts although the traffic is mostly on camels . . .

Northwards the character of the Gobi again changes, and this time for the better. The sterile desert becomes a steppe, more and more fruitful as we advance to the north. The shingle and gravel are in turn succeeded by sand mixed in small quantities with clay.

The country becomes extremely undulating. The gradual slopes of low hills intersect one another in every possible direction, and earn for this region the Mongol name Kangai—i.e. hilly. This continues for upwards of a hundred miles to the north of the Uliassutai post road, when the waterless steppe touches the margin of the basin of Lake Baikal; here finally, at Hangindaban, you find yourself among groups and ridges of rocky hills, beyond which lie the well-watered districts of Northern Mongolia . . .

Our impatience to reach Urga kept ever increasing as we approached it, and we counted the time no longer by months or weeks but by days. At length after crossing the Hangin-daban range we arrived on the banks of the Tola, the first river we had made acquaintance with in Mongolia. For 870 miles, i.e. between Kan-su and this river, we had not seen a single stream or lake, only stagnant pools of brackish rainwater. Forests now appeared, darkening the steep slopes of the Mount Khan-ola. Under these grateful circumstances we at last accomplished our final march, and on 17 September entered Urga, where we received a warm welcome from our Consul. I will not undertake to describe the moment when we heard our mother-tongue, when we met again our countrymen, and experienced once more European comforts. We inquired eagerly what was going on in the civilised world; we devoured the contents of the letters awaiting us; we gave vent to our joy like children; it was only after a few days that we came to ourselves and began to realise the luxury to which our wanderings had rendered us for so long a time strangers . . . After resting a week at Urga, we proceeded to Kiakhta, which we reached on 1 October 1873.

Our journey was ended. Its success had surpassed all the hopes we entertained when we crossed for the first time the borders of Mongolia. Then an uncertain future lay before us; now, as we called to mind all the difficulties and dangers we had gone through, we could not help wondering at the good fortune which had invariably attended us everywhere. Yes! in the most adverse circumstances, Fortune had been ever constant, and ensured the success of our undertaking: many a time when it hung on a thread a happy destiny rescued us, and gave us the means of accomplishing, as far as our strength would permit, the exploration of the least known and most inaccessible countries of Inner Asia.

CHAPTER 19

ESCAPE FROM THE OUTBACK

by Ernest Giles

We were now 90 miles from the Circus water, and 110 from Fort McKellar. The horizon to the west was still obstructed by another rise three or four miles away; but to the west-north-west I could see a line of low stony ridges, 10 miles off. To the south was an isolated little hill, six or seven miles away. I determined to go to the ridges, when Gibson complained that his horse could never reach them, and suggested that the next rise to the west might reveal something better in front. The ridges were five miles away, and there were others still further preventing a view. When we reached them we had come 98 miles from the Circus. Here Gibson, who was always behind, called out and said his horse was going to die, or knock up, which are synonymous terms in this region . . . The hills to the west were 25–30 miles away, and it was with extreme regret I was compelled to relinquish a further attempt to reach them. Oh, how ardently I longed for a camel! how ardently I gazed upon this scene! At this moment I would even my jewel eternal have sold for power to span the gulf that lay between! But it could not be, situated as I was; compelled to retreat—of course with the intention of coming again with a larger supply of water—now the sooner I retreated the better. These far-off hills were named the Alfred and Marie Range, in honour of their Royal Highnesses the Duke and Duchess of Edinburgh. Gibson's horse having got so bad had placed us both in a great dilemma; indeed, ours was a most critical position. We turned back upon our tracks, when the cob refused to carry his rider any further and tried to lie down. We drove him another mile on foot, and down he fell to die. My mare, the Fair Maid of Perth, was only too willing to return; she had now to carry Gibson's saddle and things, and we went away walking and riding by turns of half an hour. The cob, no doubt, died where he fell; not a second thought could be bestowed on him.

When we got back to about thirty miles from the Kegs I was walking, and having concluded in my mind what course to pursue, I called to Gibson to halt till I walked up to him. We were both excessively thirsty, for walking had made us so, and we had scarcely a pint of water left between us. However, of what we had we each took a mouthful, which finished the supply, and I then said—for I couldn't speak before—'Look here, Gibson, you see we are in a most terrible fix with only one horse, therefore only one can ride, and one must remain behind. I shall remain; and now listen to me. If the mare does not get water soon she will die; therefore ride right on; get to the Kegs, if possible, tonight, and give her water. Now the cob is dead there'll be all the more for her; let her rest for an hour or two, and then get over a few more miles by morning, so that early tomorrow you will sight the Rawlinson, at twenty-five miles from the Kegs. Stick to the tracks, and never leave them. Leave as much water in one keg for me as you can afford after watering the mare and filling up your own bags, and, remember, I depend upon you to bring me relief. Rouse Mr Tietkens, get fresh horses and more water bags, and return as soon as you possibly can. I shall of course endeavour to get down the tracks also.'

He then said if he had a compass he thought he could go better at night. I knew he didn't understand anything about compasses, as I had often tried to explain them to him. The one I had was a Gregory's Patent; of a totally different construction from ordinary instruments of the kind, and I was very loath to part with it, as it was the only one I had. However, he was so anxious for it that I gave it him, and he departed. I sent one final shout after him to stick to the tracks, to which he replied, 'All right', and the mare carried him out of sight almost immediately. That was the last ever seen of Gibson.

I walked slowly on, and the further I walked the more thirsty I became. I had thirty miles to go to reach the Kegs, which I could not reach until late tomorrow at the rate I was travelling, and I did not feel sure that I could keep on at that . . .

24 April to 1 May: So soon as it was light I was again upon the horse tracks, and reached the Kegs about the middle of the day. Gibson had been here, and watered the mare, and gone on. He had left me a little over two gallons of water in one keg, and it may be imagined how glad I was to get a drink. I could have drunk my whole supply in half an hour, but was compelled to economy, for I could not tell how many days would elapse before assistance could come: it could not be less than five, it might be many more. After quenching my thirst a little I felt ravenously hungry, and on searching among the bags, all the food I could find was eleven sticks of dirty, sandy, smoked horse, averaging about an ounce and a half each, at the bottom of a pack bag. I was rather staggered to find that I had little more than a pound weight of meat to last me until assistance came. However, I was compelled to eat some at once, and devoured two sticks raw, as I had no water to spare to boil them in.

After this I sat in what shade the trees afforded, and reflected on the precariousness of my position. I was 60 miles from water, and 80 from food, my messenger could hardly return before six days, and I began to think it highly probable that I should be dead of hunger and thirst long before anybody could possibly arrive. I looked at the keg; it was an awkward thing to carry empty. There was nothing else to carry water in, as Gibson had taken all the

The Australian outback as Giles may have seen it.

smaller water bags, and the large ones would require several gallons of water to soak the canvas before they began to tighten enough to hold water. The keg when empty, with its rings and straps, weighed fifteen pounds, and now it had twenty pounds of water in it. I could not carry it without a blanket for a pad for my shoulder, so that with my revolver and cartridge pouch, knife, and one or two other small things on my belt, I staggered under a weight of about fifty pounds when I put the keg on my back. I only had fourteen matches.

After I had thoroughly digested all points of my situation, I concluded that if I did not help myself Providence wouldn't help me. I started, bent double by the keg, and could only travel so slowly that I thought it scarcely worthwhile to travel at all. I became so thirsty at each step I took, that I longed to drink up every drop of water I had in the keg, but it was the elixir of death I was burdened with, and to drink it was to die, so I restrained myself.

By next morning I had only got about three miles away from the Kegs, and to do that I travelled mostly in the moonlight. The next few days I can only pass over as they seemed to pass with me, for I was quite unconscious half the time, and I only got over about five miles a day.

To people who cannot comprehend such a region it may seem absurd that a man could not travel faster than that. All I can say is, there may be men who could do so, but most men in the position I was in would simply have died of hunger and thirst, for by the third or fourth day—couldn't tell which—my horsemeat was all gone. I had to remain in what scanty shade I could find during the day, and I could only travel by night.

When I lay down in the shade in the morning I lost all consciousness, and when I recovered my senses I could not tell whether one day or two or three had passed. At one place I am sure I must have remained over 48 hours. At a certain place on the road—that is to say, on the horse tracks—at about 15 miles from the Kegs—at 25 miles the Rawlinson could again be sighted—I saw that the tracks of the two loose horses we had turned back from there had left the main line of tracks, which ran east and west, and had turned about east-south-east, and the tracks of the Fair Maid of Perth, I was grieved to see, had gone on them also. I felt sure Gibson would soon find his error, and return to the main line. I was unable to investigate this any further in my present position. I followed them about a mile, and then returned to the proper line, anxiously looking at every step to see if Gibson's horse tracks returned into them.

They never did, nor did the loose horse tracks either. Generally speaking, whenever I saw a shady desert oak tree there was an enormous bull-dog ants' nest under it, and I was prevented from sitting in its shade. On what I thought was the 27th I almost gave up the thought of walking any further, for the exertion in this dreadful region, where the triodia was almost as high as myself, and as thick as it could grow, was quite overpowering, and being starved, I felt quite light-headed. After sitting down, on every occasion when I tried to get up again, my head would swim round, and I would fall down oblivious for some time. Being in a chronic state of burning thirst, my general plight was dreadful in the extreme. A bare and level sandy waste would have been Paradise to walk over compared to this. My arms, legs, thighs, both before and behind, were so punctured with spines, it was agony only to exist; the slightest movement and in went more spines, where they broke off in the clothes and flesh, causing the whole of the body that was punctured to gather into minute pustules, which were continually growing and bursting. My clothes, especially inside my trousers, were a perfect mass of prickly points.

My great hope and consolation now was that I might soon meet the relief party. But where was the relief party? Echo could only answer—where? About the 29th I had emptied the keg, and was still over 20 miles from the Circus. Ah! who can imagine what 20 miles means in such a case? But in this April's ivory moonlight I plodded on, desolate indeed, but all undaunted, on this lone, unhallowed shore. At last I reached the Circus, just at the dawn of day. Oh, how I drank! how I reeled! how hungry I was! how thankful I was that I had so far at least escaped from the jaws of that howling wilderness, for I was once more upon the range, though still 20 miles from home. There was no sign of the tracks, of anyone having been here since I left it. The water was all but gone. The solitary eagle still was there. I wondered what could have become of Gibson; he certainly had never come here, and how could he reach the fort without doing so?

I was in such a miserable state of mind and body that I refrained from more vexatious speculations as to what had delayed him: I stayed here, drinking and drinking, until about 10 a.m., when I crawled away over the stones down from the water. I was very footsore, and could only go at a snail's pace. Just as I got clear of the bank of the creek, I heard a faint squeak, and looking about I saw, and immediately caught, a small dying wallaby, whose marsupial mother had evidently thrown it from her pouch. It only weighed about two ounces, and was scarcely furnished yet with fur. The instant I saw it, like an eagle I pounced upon it and ate it, living, raw, dying—fur, skin, bones, skull, and all. The delicious taste of that creature I shall never forget. I only wished I had its mother and father to serve in the same way. I had become so weak that by late at night, I had only accomplished 11 miles, and I lay down about 5 miles from the Gorge of Tarns, again choking for water. While lying down here, I thought I heard the sound of the footfalls of a galloping horse going campwards, and vague ideas of Gibson on the Fair Maid—or she without him—entered my head. I stood up and listened, but the sound had died away upon the midnight air. On the 1st of May, as I afterwards found, at one o'clock in the morning, I was walking again, and reached the Gorge of Tarns long before daylight, and could again indulge in as much water as I desired; but it was exhaustion I suffered from, and I could hardly move.

My reader may imagine with what intense feelings of relief I stepped over the little bridge across the water, staggered into the camp at daylight, and woke Mr Tietkens, who stared at me as though I had been one new risen from the dead. I asked him had he seen Gibson, and to give me some food. I was of course prepared to hear that Gibson had never reached the camp; indeed, I could see but two people in their blankets the moment I entered the fort, and by that I knew he could not be there. None of the horses had come back, and it appeared that I was the only one of six living creatures—two men and four horses—that had returned, or were now ever likely to return, from that desert, for it was now, as I found, nine days since I last saw Gibson.

CHAPTER 20

AMAZONIA EXTREMIS

by Henry Savage Labrador

Henry Savage Labrador.

We started once more across the virgin forest, directing our steps due west. Filippe this time undertook to open the *picada*, while I, compass in hand, marched directly behind him, Benedicto following me. If I had let him go, he would have described circle after circle upon himself instead of going in a straight line.

From that point our march across the forest became tragic. Perhaps I can do nothing better than reproduce almost word by word the entries in my diary.

We ate that morning what little there remained of the *mutum* we had shot the previous evening. Little we knew then that we were not to taste fresh meat again for nearly a month from that date.

During 3 September we made fairly good progress, cutting our way through incessantly. We went that day 20 kil. We had no lunch, and it was only in the evening that we opened the last of the three small boxes of sardines, our entire dinner consisting of three and a half sardines each.

On 4 September we were confronted, soon after our departure, with a mountainous country with deep ravines and furrows, most trying for us owing to their steepness. We went over five ranges of hills from 100 to 300 ft in height, and we crossed five streamlets in the depressions between those successive ranges.

Filippe was again suffering greatly from an attack of fever, and I had to support him all the time, as he had the greatest difficulty in walking. Benedicto had that day been entrusted with the big knife for cutting the *picada*.

We went some 20 kil. that day, with nothing whatever to eat, as we had already finished the three boxes of sardines, and I was reserving the box of anchovies for the moment when we could stand hunger no longer.

On 5 September we had another very terrible march over broken country, hilly for a good portion of the distance, but quite level in some parts.

The man Benedicta, who was a great eater, now collapsed altogether, saying that he could no longer carry his load and could not go on any farther without food.

The entire day our eyes had roamed in all directions, trying to discover some wild fruit which was edible, or some animal we might shoot, but there was the silence of death all around us. Not a branch, not a leaf was moved by a living thing; no fruit of any kind was to be seen anywhere.

Our appetite was keen, and it certainly had one good effect—it stopped Filippe's fever and, in fact, cured it altogether.

The two men were tormenting me the whole day, saying they had no faith in the compass: how could a brass box—that is what they called it—tell us where we could find *feijão*? It was beyond them to understand it. They bemoaned themselves incessantly, swearing at the day they had been persuaded to come along with me and leave their happy homes in order to die of starvation in the forest with a mad Englishman! And why did we go across the forest at all, where there was no trail, when we could have gone down by the river on a trading boat?

On 6 September it was all I could do to wake up my men. When they did wake, they would not get up, for they said the only object in getting up was to eat, and as there was nothing to eat there was no use in getting up. They wanted to remain there and die.

I had to use a great deal of gentle persuasion, and even told them a big story—that my *agulha* or needle (the compass) was telling me that morning that there was plenty of *feijão* ahead of us.

We struggled on kilometre after kilometre, one or another of us collapsing under our loads every few hundred metres. We went over very hilly country, crossing eight hill ranges that day with steep ravines between. In fact, all that country must once have been a low tableland which had been fissured and then eroded by water, leaving large cracks. At the bottom of each we found brooks and streamlets of delicious water. Of the eight rivulets found that day one only was fairly large. It fell in little cascades over rock. We could see no fish in its waters.

The forest was fairly clean underneath, and we had no great difficulty in getting through, a cut every now and then with the knife being sufficient to make a passage for us. I had by that time entirely given up the idea of opening a regular *picada*, over which I could eventually take the men and baggage I had left behind.

We found that day a palm with a bunch of small nuts which Benedicto called *coco do matto*; he said they were delicious to eat, so we proceeded to cut down the tall palm tree. When we came to split open the small *cocos* our disappointment was great, for they merely contained water. There was nothing whatever to eat inside the hard shells. We spent some two hours that evening cracking the *cocos*—some two hundred of them—each nut about the size of a cherry. They were extremely hard to crack, and our expectant eyes were disappointed two hundred times in succession as we opened every one and found nothing whatever to eat in them.

We were beginning to feel extremely weak, with a continuous feeling of emptiness in our insides. Personally, I felt no actual pain. The mental strain, perhaps, was the most trying thing for me, for I had no idea when we might find food. I was beginning to feel more than ever the responsibility of taking those poor fellows there to suffer for my sake. On their side they certainly never let one moment go by during the day or night without reminding me of the fact.

On 7 September I had the greatest difficulty in getting the men out of their hammocks. They were so exhausted that I could not rouse them. We had had a terrific storm during the night, which had added misery to our other sufferings. Innumerable ants were now causing us a lot of damage. Filippe's coat, which had dropped out of his hammock, was found in the morning entirely destroyed. Those miniature demons also cut the string to which I had suspended my shoes in mid-air, and no sooner had they fallen to the ground than the ants started on their mischievous work. When I woke up in the morning all that remained of my shoes were the two leather soles, the upper part having been completely destroyed.

Going through the forest, where thorns of all sizes were innumerable, another torture was now in store for me. With pieces of string I turned the soles of the shoes into primitive sandals; but when I started on the march I found that they hurt me much more than if I walked barefooted. After marching a couple of kilometres, my renovated foot gear hurt me so much in going up and down the steep ravines that I took off the sandals altogether and flung them away.

That day we went over eleven successive hill ranges and crossed as many little streamlets between them. My men were terribly downhearted. We had with us a Mauser and two hundred cartridges, but although we did nothing all day long but look for something to kill we never heard a sound of a living animal. Only one day at the beginning of our fast did I see a big *mutum*— larger than a big turkey. The bird had never seen a human being, and sat placidly perched on the branch of a tree, looking at us with curiosity, singing gaily. I tried to fire with the Mauser at the bird, which was only about seven or eight metres away, but cartridge after cartridge missed fire. I certainly spent not less than twenty minutes constantly replenishing the magazine, and not a single cartridge went off. They had evidently absorbed so much moisture on our many accidents in the river and in the heavy rainstorms we had had of late, that they had become useless.

While I was pointing the gun the bird apparently took the greatest interest in my doings, looked at me, stooping down gracefully each time that the rifle missed fire, singing dainty notes almost as if it were laughing at me. The funny part of it all was that we eventually had to go away disappointed, leaving the bird perched on that very same branch.

As the days went by and we could find nothing to eat, my two men lost their courage entirely. They now refused to suffer any longer. They said they had not the strength to go back, so they wanted to lie down and die. Many times a day did I have to lift them up again and persuade them gently to come on another few hundred metres or so. Perhaps then we might find the great river Madeira, where we should certainly meet traders from whom we could get food.

Late in the afternoon of 7 September, as we were on a high point above the last range of hills met that day, a large panorama opened before us, which we could just see between the trees and foliage of the forest.

To obtain a full view of the scenery it was necessary to climb up a tree. I knew well that we could not yet have reached the river we were looking for, but perhaps we were not far from some large tributary of the Madeira, such as the Secundury.

Climbing up trees in the Brazilian forest was easier said than done, even when you possessed your full strength. So many were the ants of all sizes which attacked you with fury the moment you embraced the tree, that it was not easy to get up more than a few feet.

When we drew lots as to whom of us should climb the tree, Benedicto was the one selected by fate. Benedicto was certainly born under an unlucky star; when anything nasty or unpleasant happened to anybody it was always to poor Benedicto. After a lot of pressing he proceeded to go up the tree, uttering piercing yells as every moment great *sauba* ants bit his arms, legs or body. He was brave enough, and slowly continued his way up until he reached a height of some 30 ft above the ground, from which eminence he gave us the interesting news that there were some high hills standing before us to the west, while to the north-west was a great flat surface covered by dense forest.

No sooner had Benedicto supplied us with this information from his high point of vantage than we heard an agonising yell and saw him spread flat on the ground, having made a record descent.

Filippe and I, although suffering considerably, were in fits of laughter at Benedicto, who did not laugh at all, but pawed himself all over, saying he must have broken some bones. When I proceeded to examine him I found upon his body over a hundred *sauba* ants clinging to his skin with their powerful clippers.

Aching all over, poor Benedicto got up once more. I put the load upon his back and we resumed our journey, making a precipitous descent almost *à pic* down the hillside. Our knees were so weak that we fell many times and rolled down long distances on that steep incline. At last we got to the bottom, rejoicing in our hearts that we had no more hills to climb, as I had made up my mind that I would now march slightly to the north-west, so as to avoid the hilly region which Benedicto had discovered to the west.

My men had an idea that the great river we were looking for must be in that plain. For a few hours they seemed to have regained their courage. We heard some piercing shrieks, and we at once proceeded in their direction, as we knew they came from monkeys. In fact we found an enormously high tree, some 5 ft in diameter. Up on its summit some beautiful yellow fruit stared us in the face. Four tiny monkeys were busy eating the fruit. Benedicto, who had by that time become very religious, joined his hands and offered prayers to the Virgin that the monkeys might drop some fruit down, but they went on eating while we gazed at them from below. We tried to fire at them with the Mauser, but again not a single cartridge went off. Eventually the monkeys dropped down the empty shells of the fruit they had eaten. With our ravenous appetite we rushed for them and with our teeth scraped off the few grains of sweet substance which remained attached to the inside of the shells.

The canopy of the Amazonian forest.

We waited and waited under that tree for a long time, Filippe now joining also in the prayers. Each time a shell dropped our palates rejoiced for a few moments at the infinitesimal taste we got from the discarded shells. It was out of the question to climb up such a big tree or to cut it down, as we had no strength left.

We went on until sunset; my men once more having lost heart. Brazilians lose heart very easily. At the sight of small hills before them, a steep descent, or a deep river to cross, they would lie down and say they wanted to remain there and die. Filippe and Benedicto did not carry more than 20 lb each of my own baggage, but their hammocks weighed some 20 lb each, so that their loads weighed altogether about 40 lb.

We went on, crossing five more streamlets that afternoon, of which one, 2 m wide, had beautifully limpid water. We nevertheless went on, until eventually after sunset we had to camp near a stream of filthy water.

As we had now been four entire days without eating anything at all, I thought it was high time to open the valuable tin of anchovies—the only one in our possession. We had a terrible disappointment when I opened the tin. I had purchased it in S. Manoel from Mr Barretto. To our great distress we discovered that instead of food it contained merely some salt and a piece of slate. This was a great blow to us. The box was a Brazilian counterfeit of a tin of anchovies. How disheartening to discover the fraud at so inopportune a moment! I had reserved the tin until the last as I did not like the look of it from the outside. We kept the salt—which was of the coarsest description.

On 8 September we were slightly more fortunate, as the country was flatter. I was steering a course of 290° b. m. (NW). I found that farther south we would have encountered too mountainous a country.

We crossed several streamlets, the largest 3 m wide, all of which flowed south. We had no particular adventure that day, and considering all things, we marched fairly well—some 20 kil. Towards the evening we camped on a hill. When we got there we were so exhausted that we made our camp on the summit, although there was no water near.

On 9 September, after marching for half an hour we arrived at a stream 15m. wide, which I took at first to be the river Secundury, a tributary of the Madeira River. Near the banks of that stream we found indications that human beings had visited that spot—perhaps the Indians we had heard so much about. The marks we found, however, were, I estimated, about one year old. Although these signs should have given us a little courage to go on, we were so famished and exhausted that my men sat down on the riverbank and would not proceed. By that time we had got accustomed even to the fierce bites of the ants. We had no more strength to defend ourselves. In vain we strained our eyes all the time in search of wild fruit. In the river we saw plenty of fish; we had a fishing line with us, but no bait whatever that we could use. There are, of course, no worms underground where ants are so numerous. We could not make snares in the river, as it was much too deep. So we sat with covetous eyes, watching the fish go by. It was most tantalising, and made us ten times more hungry than ever to be so near food and not be able to get it.

It is curious how hunger works on your brain. I am not at all a glutton, and never think of food under ordinary circumstances. But while I was starving I could see before me from morning till night, in my imagination, all kinds of delicacies—caviare, Russian soups, macaroni au gratin, all kinds of refreshing ice creams, and plum pudding. Curiously enough, some days I had a perfect craving for one particular thing, and would have given anything I possessed in the world to obtain a morsel of it. The next day I did not care for that at all, in my imagination, but wanted something else very badly. The three things which I mostly craved for while I was starving were caviare, galantine of chicken, and ice cream—the latter particularly.

People say that with money you can do anything you like in the world. I had at that time on my person some £6,000 sterling, of which £4,000 was in actual cash. If anybody had placed before me a morsel of any food I would gladly have given the entire sum to have it. But no, indeed; no such luck! How many times during those days did I vividly dream of delightful dinner and supper parties at the Savoy, the Carlton, or the Ritz, in London, Paris, and New York! How many times did I think of the delicious meals I had had when a boy in the home of my dear father and mother! I could reconstruct in my imagination all those meals, and thought what an idiot I was to have come there out of my own free will to suffer like that. My own dreams were constantly interrupted by Benedicto and Filippe, who also had similar dreams of the wonderful meals they had had in their own houses, and the wonderful ways in which their feijãozinho—a term of endearment used by them for their beloved beans—had been cooked at home by their sweathearts or their temporary wives.

'Why did we leave our *feijãozinho*'—and here they smacked their lips-'to come and die in this rotten country?'

All day I heard them talk of *feijãozinho, feijãozinho,* until I was wearied to distraction by that word—particularly as, even when starving, I had no desire whatever to eat the beastly stuff.

The negro Filippe and Benedicto were really brave in a way. I tried to induce them all the time to march as much as we could, so as to get somewhere;

but every few moments they sat or fell down, and much valuable time was wasted.

As the days went by and our strength got less and less every hour, I decided not to cut the forest any more, but to go through without that extra exertion. As I could not trust my men with the big knife, I had to carry it myself, as occasionally it had to be used—especially near streams, where the vegetation was always more or less entangled.

That evening (9 September) we had halted at sunset—simply dead with fatigue and exhaustion. The *sauba* ants had cut nearly all the strings of Filippe's hammock; while he was resting peacefully on it the remainder of the strings broke, and he had a bad fall. He was so exhausted that he remained lying on the ground, swarming all over with ants and moaning the whole time, having no strength to repair the hammock.

When Filippe eventually fell into a sound slumber I had a curious experience in the middle of the night. I was sleeping in my improvised hammock, when I felt two paws resting on my body and something sniffing in my face. When I opened my eyes I found a jaguar, standing up on its hind paws, staring me straight in the face. The moment I moved, the astonished animal, which had evidently never seen a human being before, leapt away and disappeared.

I find that people have strange ideas about wild animals. It is far from true that wild beasts are vicious. I have always found them as gentle as possible. Although I have seen nearly every wild beast that it is possible for man to see in the world, I have never once been attacked by them, although on dozens of occasions I have come into close contact with them. I invariably found all wild animals—expect the African buffalo—quite timid and almost gentle, unless, of course, they have been worried or wounded. These remarks do not apply to wild animals in captivity.

On 10 September—that was the seventh day of our involuntary fast—we had another dreary march, again without a morsel of food. My men were so downhearted that I really thought they would not last much longer. Hunger was playing on them in a curious way. They said that they could hear

The Amazonian rainforest, in the upper Amazon basin, Peru.

voices all round them and people firing rifles. I could hear nothing at all. I well knew that their minds were beginning to go, and that it was a pure hallucination. Benedicto and Filippe, who originally were both atheists of an advanced type, had now become extremely religious, and were muttering fervent prayers all the time. They made a vow that if we escaped alive they would each give £5 sterling out of their pay to have a big mass celebrated in the first church they saw.

At this place I abandoned the few cartridges we had, as they were absolutely useless. They were Mauser cartridges which I had bought in Rio de Janeiro, and it is quite possible that they were counterfeits.

Taking things all round, my men behaved very well, but these were moments of the greatest anxiety for me, and I myself was praying fervently to God to get us out of that difficulty. My strength was failing more and more daily, and although I was suffering no actual pain, yet the weakness was simply appalling. It was all I could do to stand up on my legs. What was worse for me was that my head was still in good working order, and I fully realised our position all the time.

The country we were travelling over was fairly hilly, up and down most of the time, over no great elevations. We passed two large tributaries of the main stream we had found before, and a number of minor ones. The main stream was strewn with fallen trees, and was not navigable during the dry season. The erosion of the banks by the water had caused so many trees to fall down across it that no canoe could possibly go through.

I noticed in one or two places along the river traces of human beings having been there some years before.

In the afternoon we again wasted much energy in knocking down two palm trees on the summit of which were great bunches of *coco do matto*. Again we had a bitter disappointment. One after the other we split the nuts open, but they merely contained water inside shells that were much harder to crack than wood. My craving for food was such that in despair I took two or three *sauba* ants and proceeded to eat them. When I ground them under my teeth their taste was so acidly bitter that it made me quite ill. Not only that, but one *sauba* bit my tongue so badly that it swelled up to a great size, and remained like that for several days.

On 11 September we had another terrible march, the forest being very dense and much entangled along the stream. We had great trouble in getting through, as there were many palms and ferns, and we had no more strength to cut down our way. We came to a big tree, which was hollow inside up to a great height, and round which were millions of bees.

Benedicto, who was a great connoisseur in such matters, said that high up inside the tree there must be honey. The bees round that tree were unfortunately stinging bees. We drew lots as to who should go inside the tree to get the honey. It fell to Benedicto. We took off most of our clothes and wrapped up his head and legs so that he might proceed to the attack. The job was not an easy one, for in the first reconnaissance he made with his head inside the tree he discovered that the honey must be not less than 20 ft above the ground, and it was necessary to climb up to that height inside the tree before he could get it. In order to hasten matters—as Benedicto was reluctant in carrying out the job—I tried my hand at it, but I was stung badly by hundreds of bees behind my head, on my eyelids, on my arms and legs. When I came out of the tree I was simply covered with angry bees, which stung me all over. So I told Benedicto that, as Fate had called upon him to do the work, he had better do it.

Benedicto was certainly very plucky that day. All of a sudden he dashed inside the tree and proceeded to climb up. We heard wild screams for some minutes; evidently the bees were protecting their home well. While Filippe and I were seated outside, smiling faintly at poor Benedicto's plight, he reappeared. We hardly recognized him when he emerged from the tree, so badly stung and swollen was his face, notwithstanding the protection he had over it. All he brought back was a small piece of the honey-comb about as large as a florin. What little honey there was inside was quite putrid, but we divided it into three equal parts and devoured it ravenously, bees and all. A moment later all three of us were seized with vomiting, so that the meagre meal was worse than nothing to us.

We were then in a region of innumerable liane, which hung from the trees and caught our feet and heads, and wound themselves round us when we tried to shift them from their position. Nearly all the trees in that part had long and powerful spikes.

Then near water there were huge palms close together, the sharp-edged leaves of which cut our hands, faces and legs as we pushed our way through.

A violent storm broke out in the afternoon. The rain was torrential, making our march extremely difficult. It was just like marching under a heavy shower-bath. The rain lasted for some three hours. We crossed one large stream flowing west into the Secundury, and also two other good-sized streamlets.

We had a miserable night, drenched as we were and unable to light a fire, the box of matches having got wet and the entire forest being soaked by the torrential storm. During the night another storm arrived and poured regular buckets of water upon us.

On 12 September we drowsily got up from our hammocks in a dejected state. By that time we had lost all hope of finding food, and no longer took the trouble to look round for anything to eat. We went on a few hundred metres at a time, now Benedicto fainting from exhaustion, then Filippe, then myself. While one or another was unconscious much time was wasted. Marching under those conditions was horrible, as either one or other of us collapsed every few hundred metres.

Another violent storm broke out, and we all lay on the ground helpless, the skin of our hands and feet getting shrivelled up with the moisture.

My feet were much swollen owing to the innumerable thorns which had got into them while walking barefooted. It was most painful to march, as I was not accustomed to walk without shoes.

We went only ten kilometres on 12 September. We crossed two small rivers and one large, flowing west and south, evidently into the Secundury.

On 13 September we had another painful march, my men struggling along, stumbling and falling every little while. They were dreadfully depressed. Towards the evening we came to a big tree, at the foot of which we found some discarded shells, such as we had once seen before, of fruit eaten by monkeys. My men and I tried to scrape with our teeth some of the sweet substance which still adhered to the shells. We saw some of the fruit, which was fit to eat, at a great height upon the tree, but we had not the strength to climb up or cut down that enormous tree.

All the visions of good meals which I had had until then had now vanished altogether on that tenth day of fasting, and I experienced a sickly feeling in my inside which gave me an absolute dislike for food of any kind. My head was beginning to sway, and I had difficulty in collecting my ideas. My memory seemed to be gone all of a sudden. I could no longer remember in what country I was travelling, nor could I remember anything distinctly. Only some lucid intervals came every now and then, in which I realised our tragic position; but those did not last long, all I could remember being that I must go to the west. I could not remember why nor where I intended to come out.

Everything seemed to be against us. We were there during the height of the rainy season. Towards sunset rain came down once more in bucketfuls and lasted the entire night, the water dripping from our hammocks as it would from a small cascade. We were soaked, and shivering, although the temperature was not low. I had my maximum and minimum thermometers with me, but my exhaustion was such that I had not the strength to unpack them every night and morning and set them.

We crossed two streamlets flowing west. Benedicto and Filippe were in such a bad way that it was breaking my heart to look at them. Every time they fell down in a faint I never knew whether it was for the last time that they had closed their eyes. When I felt their hearts with my hand they beat so faintly that once or twice I really thought they were dead. That day I myself fainted, and fell with the left side of my face resting on the ground. When I recovered consciousness some time later, I touched my face, which was hurting me, and found that nearly the whole skin of my cheek had been eaten up by small ants, the lower lid of the eye having suffered particularly. A nasty sore remained on my face for some two months after that experience, the bites of those ants being very poisonous.

Bad as they were, there is no doubt that to a great extent we owed our salvation to those terrible ants. Had it not been for them and the incessant torture they inflicted on us when we fell down upon the ground, we should have perhaps lain there and never got up again.

I offered Benedicto and Filippe a large reward if they continued marching without abandoning the precious loads. Brazilians have a great greed for money, and for it they will do many things which they would not otherwise.

On 14 September we made another most painful march of 20 kil., again up and down high hills, some as much as 300 ft. above the level land of that country, and all with steep, indeed, almost vertical, sides, extremely difficult for us to climb in our exhausted condition. We saw several streamlets flowing west. When evening came we had before us a high hill, which we ascended. When we reached the top we just lay upon the ground like so many corpses, and, ants or no ants biting us, we had not the energy to get up again. Once more did the rain come down in torrents that night, and to a certain extent washed the ants from our bodies.

My surprise was really great the next morning when I woke up. I felt myself fading away fast. Every time I closed my eyes I expected never to open them again.

On 15 September we made another trying march, collapsing under our loads every few hundred metres. My men were constantly looking for something to eat in all directions, but could find nothing. Benedicto and Filippe were now all the time contemplating suicide. The mental strain of perpetually keeping an eye on them was great.

We were sitting down, too tired to get up, when Filippe amazed me considerably by the following words, which he spoke in a kind of reverie:

'It would be very easy,' he said, 'now that you have no more strength yourself, for us two to get the big knife and cut your throat. We know that you have a big, big sum of money upon you, and if we robbed you we would be rich for ever. But we do not want to do it. It would not be much use to us, as we could not get out of the forest alone. I believe we shall all die together, and all that money will go to waste.'

Filippe said this in quite a good-natured manner. The two poor fellows were so depressed that one had to forgive them for anything they said.

As the river seemed to describe a big loop, I had left it three days before, seeing plainly by the conformation of the country that we should strike it again sooner or later. We were marching once more by compass. My men, who had no faith whatever in the magnetic needle, were again almost paralysed with fear that we might not encounter the stream again. A thousand times a day they accused me of foolishness in leaving the river, as they said it would have been better to follow its tortuous course—notwithstanding the trouble we had in following it, owing to the dense vegetation near the water—rather than strike once more across country. They were beginning to lose heart altogether, when I told them I could see by the vegetation that we were once more near the water. Anybody accustomed as I am to marching through the forest could tell easily by the appearance of the vegetation some miles before actually getting to a stream.

I reassured my companions, saying that within a few hours we should certainly meet the 'big water' again. In fact, not more than half an hour afterwards we suddenly found ourselves once more on the large stream—at that point 70 metres wide.

My men were so amazed and delighted that they embraced me and sobbed over my shoulders for some time. From that moment their admiration for the compass was unbounded; they expected me to find anything with it.